20TH CENTURY REMINISCENCE SERIES

FROM THE NOLICHUCKY TO MEMPHIS

REMINISCENCES OF A TENNESSEE DOCTOR

BY DR. SAMUEL FREDERICK STRAIN

WITH A FOREWORD BY ELDON ROARK

MEMPHIS

MEMPHIS STATE UNIVERSITY PRESS

Manufactured
in the
United States of America
ISBN 0-87870-064-1

DEDICATED TO

My dear wife for her patience with me through the years and to my son, Edgar, and his wife, Libby, for their stimulation in this effort.

Table of Contents

	Preface	ix
	Foreword	xi
I	Life Along the Nolichucky	1
II	". . . follow the gleam!"	20
III	"Knoxville, 1910"	32
IV	West to Kansas	38
V	From the Marble Mill to the University of Tennessee	57
VI	"Apples of Gold, Pictures of Silver"	73
VII	Oklahoma!	89
VIII	Medical School	103
IX	Life in Memphis	119
X	Intern	140
XI	The Polyclinic	161
XII	Sanatorium, Mississippi	172
XIII	Depression and the T.V.A.	192
XIV	Silver Years	211
XV	Doctor Strain	223
	Index	229

PREFACE

From time to time I would relate to my children and, later, grandchildren, events and experiences that had occurred in my life. Because of the diverse situations through which I lived and problems I encountered, they asked me why I couldn't write a story of my life. I have attempted to do this. I must admit that to write such a story has been a rather pleasant exercise in reminiscing as I recalled my ups and downs. It has been interesting to me and I hope it will be of interest to the reader. I hope my experience in finally achieving goals I set for myself will encourage someone else to try a little harder to achieve, and will point clearly to the importance of persistence and determination to "follow the gleam."

I acknowledge with deep gratitude the encouragement I got from some of my teachers, friends, and relatives. I owe much especially to Mrs. Nellie Biddle of Limestone, Miss Josephine Hoge of Wellington, Kansas, Dr. Beard, the black doctor of Knoxville, Dr. A. H. Wittenberg, and Dr. O. W. Hyman of Memphis, my sister, Blanche, and my cousin, Walter Remine. I am grateful to Mrs. Raleigh Crawford for her work in helping prepare the manuscript.

S.F.S.

FOREWORD

Let me say right at the start of this foreword that *From the Nolichucky to Memphis* is a pleasant surprise to me. I might even say it is a rather astounding surprise.

Now, Dr. Fred Strain is an old friend, and, until his retirement several years ago, he was my family's physician. We always had complete confidence in him, and had a feeling of security because we knew he was available in case of need. He not only was a physician who kept up with the latest advances in medical science, but he also was a comforting friend who could identify with his patients. We used to laugh and say, "No matter what you have, Dr. Strain has had it, too, and knows just how you feel and what to do about it."

That was just a joke, of course, but it was almost literally true, as you will see in reading the book. He has had a variety of ills, operations, broken bones. He learned a lot—some things not in the medical books—in licking his own physical troubles. He survived them all, and today, at 83, he is enjoying an active retirement.

Some months ago I met Dr. Strain at a church dinner. I hadn't seen him in quite a while, so, just making conversation, I asked, "What are you doing these days?" I thought that perhaps his answer might make an item for my newspaper column. He is eminent in the medical profession, particularly in Tennessee and the Mid-South, and thousands of people know him.

"You'll be surprised at what I have been doing," he replied, smiling rather sheepishly. "I've been having fun writing the story of my life. My family wanted me to do it, and it's just for them. I started it rather reluctantly, but as I got going found pleasure in reliving my life."

"Well, that's interesting," I said. "When you finish it, I'd like to read it."

"All right," he replied. "I'll let you see it. But remember, I don't think I'm a writer, and I'm not writing a book for publication. As I say, this is just for the family."

Since he was an old friend, I really felt that I might enjoy browsing through his manuscript as a matter of personal interest. Might also learn something about him that I didn't know. Oh, I knew that he, a poor boy from the hills of East Tennessee, an orphan at an early age, had had a hard, rough road to travel, but had climbed to peaks in his profession despite many obstacles and problems that would have defeated a less determined man. I knew he had helped to make medical and industrial history, as health officer for the Tennessee Valley Authority in building dams across Tennessee and Alabama, as a teacher at the University of Tennessee medical school, as a physician at a tuberculosis sanitorium in Mississippi, as a clinician in Memphis and head of Memphis and Shelby County Medical Society, and the recipient of many other high professional honors.

Yes, I knew Fred Strain had had a very dramatic life—it had been a rough, zig-zaggy road from the Nolichucky to the Mississippi—but I doubted he could tell the story. He was a doctor, not a writer. So, I expected his manuscript to be heavy, dull, to read like a report to a medical seminar, or, at best, a treatise for a doctorate.

When he finally finished it, he handed it to me in an apologetic manner, still reminding me that it was just for the family. It had a lot of intimate details about his struggles, romances, triumphs, and failures that wouldn't interest others.

That night I settled in my easy chair to browse through his story. I expected it to put me to sleep in about ten minutes. And that's when I got a happy surprise. Why, I was still reading an hour later!

Dr. Strain's memory for interesting detail astounded me. His sense of human-interest and his eye for the dramas of life were delightful. His appreciation for colorful bits of local history was striking.

"Why," I said to my wife, looking up from the manuscript, "Dr. Strain's story would be good reading even if I didn't know him!"

Read it, and you'll see what I mean. *From the Nolichucky to Memphis* is a good, clean American story. And it is told with refreshing frankness. It will be enjoyed as relaxing and inspiring reading, and it will be valuable as local history.

Eldon Roark
Memphis, Tennessee

"For all our days are passed away—we spend our years as a tale that is told."—Psalm 90:9

I

Life Along the Nolichucky

The house in which I was born early one frosty December morning in 1895 was one of the oldest west of the Allegheny Mountains. My grandmother was born in it in 1828, and my father, all his brothers, and his sister were also born there. It was built of logs, in two parts, with a large rock chimney between, serving both sections with fireplaces in each section. One section was two stories, the other only one. The floors were put down with locust pegs. The two story portion was weatherboarded and both sections were covered with split shingles. Homemade nails were used throughout the construction of both sections. The smaller section had a floored attic. The only source of light in the attic was from several openings about six inches wide and twenty inches long. These openings were made by sawing out portions of the log and were used, I was told, for rifles to protect against the Indians. The house had been part of a fort. The two sections of the house were connected downstairs by a hallway built between them on one side of the chimney. A passage between the upstairs was present and connected the rooms with the attic of the smaller section of the house.

A large living room with the fireplace, and a smaller bedroom made up the ground floor of the two story section. Stairs leading to the second floor were in the living room. There were two bedrooms upstairs. I remember the large clock on the wall at the head of the stairs. It had wooden works and was run by weights that hung from it. There was also, hanging on the wall, a rather large picture of Sir Robert Peel, the British statesman. Where it came from, and how old it was, I never knew.

In the large bedroom over the living room were two beds.

1

Under one was a trundle bed. On both the larger beds and on the trundle bed were ticks stuffed with straw or corn shucks. The trundle bed had slats, no springs, and the larger bed had ropes to support the bed ticks. I remember once when the ticks were being emptied and refilled with fresh straw, which was done at periodic intervals, a dead, dried snake was found in the straw which came out of one of the ticks. I slept on the trundle bed with my brother James.

There was a back porch running the full length of the larger section of the house. It was covered with a roof. The roof was supported by posts along the edge of the porch. These posts supported, for part of the length of the porch, a shelf on which was kept the water bucket and dipper, wash pans and a soap dish. Towels, which seemed always soiled, hung from nails on one post.

At one end of the porch was the porch closet in which was kept a great variety of tools, brooms, rakes, kettles, and tubs. I remember finding a long, muzzle loading rifle in this closet. There was also a candle mold for eight candles, and a big cast iron skillet with legs and a cast iron cover for cooking in the fireplace. I never saw it used.

The dining room occupied the ground floor of the smaller section of the house. It had a large fireplace. The kitchen was built on the back of this room, two or three steps lower than the dining room. On the kitchen floor were doors that opened to steps leading into a cellar. I remember the shelves on either side of the cellar loaded with crocks of apple butter, many jars of canned beans, tomatoes, blackberries, and huckleberries. Crocks of sauerkraut were there too. Piles of Irish potatoes were always present and sometimes sweet potatoes were to be found. The kitchen was typical with its wood burning stove, box for stovewood, open shelves for dishes, and pots and pans. There was a bare wooden tabletop showing signs of knife cuts from slicing meats, bread, and other foods. The kitchen odors were pleasant and seemed to provoke the appetite of energetic youngster.

Outside in the backyard was the smoke house, and the ash hopper for making lye by pouring water through the wood ashes. A large locust tree was also in the backyard, and further back was an orchard of apple, pear, peach and cherry trees. The garden just south of the house had two fairly long grape arbors. One was of dark blue (Concord), and the other of white (slightly pink) grapes. I remember tall corn, eggplant, beans, beets, onions, potatoes, tomatoes and many other vegetables growing in the dark, sandy soil of the garden. A path, with a plank laid over it, led to the back of the garden and the primitive sanitary utility.

The front yard sloped gently down to a rock wall which seemed to keep it from sliding into the road which ran along in front of the house. Just beyond the road was the Nolichucky River. The front yard can hardly have been called a lawn. No attempt was made to keep the grass cut or trimmed, and tall weeds were constantly present. A large locust tree stood in the lower right corner of the yard. I remember when we first got a wooden mailbox. It was painted light blue with white smears and was on a post under the locust tree. Rural free delivery began for us at that time. It had officially started in 1896 as a postal service, but was delayed in getting to Chucky Valley.

A path from the northside of the backyard led up-river to the blacksmith shop and the molasses mill. In the blacksmith shop there were the usual tools and equipment: the forge, bellows, anvils and other tools, scraps of iron, horseshoes, chains, and parts of farm tools and vehicles. I recall the many hours I spent there with my father or a neighbor and watched with wide-eyed interest as the blacksmith pounded the red hot metal into the shape of horseshoes, and put them on the horses.

Our water supply came from a spring down at the foot of the hill near the Nolichucky River. The water was clear and cold. The spring branch, only 90 feet long, flowed directly into the river. Our spring was in a beautiful grove of willows and sycamores. On occasion the river would rise, cover the spring, and for several days spring water would not be available. I recall that following a flood one year, a large "red horse" fish was found trapped in the spring.

The Nolichucky was a turbulent river. It arose in North Carolina and raced through mountain passes into Tennessee past Erwin and Embreeville before it reached the Chucky Valley. Swift shoals were present every one-quarter to one-half mile. Between these shoals were stretches of beautiful, calm water. The banks of the river on the right side were steep and rocky, occasionally rising to high cliffs. Such a cliff was just across the river from our house and served to amplify the noise of the water rushing over the rocky shoals. Large river rocks were scattered through the shoals, many above the water, and frequently the rolling of rocks under the swift water was audible. The rocks, large and small, were smooth and rounded by the swift water constantly pouring over them and moving them about.

An island of several acres was in the river just in front of our house. It was covered with willows and sycamores, and piles of driftwood were present over its entire length. I recall many happy hours spent on the island playing in the sand, looking for Indian arrowheads, peculiarly shaped driftwood and rocks. We were able to wade across the shoals to the island, in our "old clothes"—swim suits were unknown to us—by holding hands and carefully clinging to large rocks to resist the pulling force of the swift water. On one occasion I lost my footing and was carried into deeper water by the swift stream. I was saved by the quick action of my sister, Blanche, who rushed to my rescue.

Our home stood on our farm about four miles down stream from the little mining village of Embreeville in Northeast Tennessee. The farm was 100 acres in size and extended back from the river for about a half mile, to the foot of the mountain. This mountain gradually rose to about 3,000 feet. A small, two bedroom house stood on the back of our farm. The Brockwell family lived in it. This little house would play an important role in our lives. The farm was about equal distance from two bridges which crossed the river. The Taylor Bridge was upstream about one mile, and the Jackson Bridge was downstream about the same distance.

A large brick house stood near the bridge where Governor A. A. Taylor lived. We called him Cousin Alf, and to us Mrs. Taylor was Cousin Jennie. My Grandmother Strain was a Taylor, and a cousin of Alf, Bob, and their sisters and brothers. The farm on which we lived was once "the Taylor place," and belonged to my grandmother's family. When she married my grandfather, James Biddle Strain, the farm was sold to him.

Other neighbors of ours lived along the river. Theodore Decker, a native of Germany, ran a pottery nearby. His son Dick, who had a big family, farmed the land adjoining ours just up the river from us. Charlie Decker, his wife Lydia, and sons Billy and Charles lived nearby. Charlie ran a country store that served as the local post office. Another son, Billy (his father called him "Pilly") lived at home and helped his father run the pottery. He was a hunchback, but was full of life and fun. Other neighbors in the valley were all widely scattered, and in those days of country roads when transportation was by horse drawn vehicles, were not frequent visitors at our house.

It was in this setting that I was born. I was the fifth child of Mary Elizabeth (she had been called Molly since her childhood Remine Strain), and Samuel Harvey Strain. I never knew where my father got his middle name. The children preceding me were, in order, Jennie Taylor (named for Mrs. Alf Taylor), Nannie Blanche, Lucy Lynn, and James Daniel. Blanche's second name was for Aunt Nanny, papa's only sister. Lucy's second name was for Aunt "Tot," mother's sister, whose real name was Sara Lynn. James was named for our two grandfathers. Kathleen was about two years younger than I.

I am amazed at the things I can remember about my life "up on the river," as we called our first home. Memory is a remarkable function. I can remember the constant roar of the river over the shoals in front of our house. Along with the unremitting chatter of the katydids and the singing of the "Wee-oo" bugs in the evening, it made a delightful bedtime lullaby. I recall how my mother at the end of a busy day would sit out in the backyard playing a guitar and singing softly. I remember one of the songs had a chorus which went "The mill wheel never turns with the water that has passed." I also can remember the fun we had playing on the river's sandy shore where we made "frog houses" by putting wet sand over our feet and gently withdrawing the foot. We hunted river rocks which were shaped like eggs. We caught crawfish and tried to catch the top minnows which were so numerous. Occasionally we would wade out into the swift water with the older children, hold on to larger rocks and enjoy the current as it pulled and challenged us to resist its power. I remember watching the making of sorghum molasses and our delight when we were allowed to eat the "skimmins" which was taken off the top of the vat as the juice from the cane was boiled to concentrate it. Watermelon feasts were frequent during the season and the taste of those delicious melons has still not been forgotten.

Later, after we had moved to Limestone, Tennessee, we frequently visited our old farm "up on the river" and stayed in the old house with the Brockwells, or with the Salts family who followed them as renters. On these visits I recall experiences like sleeping in the "watermelon shack" to guard against watermelon thieves, visiting the Decker pottery, watching the making of crocks, jugs, churns and other things, swimming in the river without swim suits, and playing ball with the Taylor boys (sons of Governor Alf). Sometimes my sister Blanche and I would stay at the Taylor home for as much as a week at a time. There, Alf, Jr. (who was nearest my age) and I were constant companions. I would help plow. Each of us, Alf, Blaine and I, took turns plowing with a walking plow around the field. The two not plowing at the time would play a card game called "Set Back." Once we looked up and saw Governor Alf coming out of the woods toward us. Since he opposed playing cards, we hastily buried the whole deck in the soft plowed ground. Once "Little Bob," as we called him, (he is presently a Federal Judge in Knoxville) was angry at me and Alf. He threw a round "river rock" which would have struck me on the neck if I hadn't thrown up my hand. It still caused a painful bruise on the back of my hand.

The Taylor boys, Dave, Blaine, Alf, and even Little Bob, chewed tobacco. They seemed to enjoy it so much that one day I took a chew. I broke out in a cold sweat, after 15 or 20 minutes and became violently nauseated. I had never been sicker and realized that tobacco chewing was not for me.

I remember when mama became ill. There had been two more babies following my birth, Kathleen in September of 1897, and finally Annie Jackson (we called her Little Annie). Mama's illness grew worse. I recall coming into her room one day, seeing her lying pale and weak in bed. I said to her, "Mama, I am afraid you're going to do like Uncle Hewt did." Uncle Hewt was an old Negro man who lived nearby and had died a few weeks earlier. Mama closed her eyes and turned her head. I have always regretted that in my innocence I made such a statement. A few days afterwards papa took us in, one at a time, to see her dying. I recall his sitting beside the bed with me on his knees when he said, "Molly, here is Fred." Mama, without moving otherwise, opened one eye for a second. I never saw her alive again. She died of tuberculosis at the age of thirty-three on April 13, 1900.

Mother's sisters, Tot and Annie were with us when she died. What a blow it must have been for Papa! He was left at the age of thirty-nine with seven children. Jennie, the oldest, was only twelve.

Mama was buried at Limestone about ten miles from our home. I recall the long ride to the cemetery in a hack with the family, with the coffin in another just ahead of us. I recall the funeral. A group of relatives and friends gathered round the grave in the little cemetery. I remember the grief they displayed as the preacher talked, and I can never forget the song they sang, "In the Sweet Bye and Bye."

I was too young to be aware of the difference in life at home, but Jennie, at the age of twelve assumed the role of mother and housekeeper with a sense of responsibility that was amazing. Aunt Tot stayed with us awhile. Little Annie was taken to Grandma Remine's at Limestone where she was cared for until she died of "brain fever" at the age of eighteen months. I am sure she must have died of tuberculous meningitis, which was the common cause of death of infants born of tuberculous mothers.

The Presidential election came in the fall of 1900. This event is firmly etched in my memory because of the celebration which accompanied it. I recall very vividly the "shooting of anvils" and the cries of "Hurray for McKinley" by my father and several neighbors. When one of our neighbors and his sons (who were evidently Democrats) cried "Hurray for Bryan," I yelled, "It ain't Bryan, it's McKinley!"

Shooting anvils was a common way of celebrating important events in those days. It was done by placing an anvil on the ground or a stump and filling a hole in the anvil with gun powder. The powder was strewn in a small amount to the edge of the anvil. A second anvil was then placed upside down on the first. A long stick with the tip on fire was then touched to the powder at the edge of the lower anvil. The powder exploded with a noise like that of a cannon being fired, and would pitch the upper anvil several feet into the air. This process was repeated as often as desired, though a sufficient amount of time was allowed between shots for the anvils to cool.

I remember that on my fifth birthday I insisted on my brother and sisters giving me a "serenade" (which we called a "charivari" or "shivaree"). I had heard a "serenade" given a young married couple a short time before. I was accommodated and stayed in the porch closet while all the kids banged pans, rang cow bells, and blew whistles until they were tired of it. I felt very important because of all the attention I received.

The next important event which took place in our lives was "The Flood." In the spring of 1901 Kathleen and I had whooping cough. We had seen the river rise on many occasions, but it did little harm and usually subsided within a day or so. But this time it was different. A heavy rain in the mountains, especially around the headwaters of the Nolichucky, resulted in a flash flood of greater than usual proportions. My father was warned (I have often wondered how) that a dangerous flood was coming. While Kathleen and I were watching the rising, swift water almost cover the shoals and the island in front of our house, and watching the driftwood, trees and timbers plunging down the stream, my father ran to the barn, opened the gates and drove the hogs, cattle and horses back toward the pasture in back of the farm. He saddled a horse and after telling the other kids to run for the hills, he put me on the horse behind him and Kathleen in front. Jennie helped him, and then holding on to the stirrup, ran along with us. Before we could get to the higher ground at the foot of the moutain, the water had entered a lower area above our house and was running down behind the orchard. We crossed a twenty-five yard wide strip of water that was nearly waist deep. Finally reaching the little cabin on the back of the farm where the Brockwells lived, we made ourselves as comfortable as possible, and lived there (fourteen of us altogether) for two weeks. The cottage had two bedrooms, a living room, dining room and kitchen. We all slept on beds, crowded pallets, or whatever can be imagined.

Papa and the Brockwell men went down to check on the flood at intervals in order to see what damage was being done. Each time they came back with sad faces. The house was in danger of being washed away. It was several days before the river had fallen sufficiently to permit a detailed inspection of the house. It was ruined. The first floor was covered with about six inches of sand, the cellar was completely filled, the large locust tree in the front yard had been washed away taking the whole front yard with it. The large stone step at our front door was found about eight feet straight down from the original location and if anyone had stepped out our front door, he would have fallen eight feet. The corner of the house sagged, as it hung over a space from which the foundation had been carried away. As a consequence there was a warp in the living room floor at that corner.

We never lived in that house after the flood. I have often thought of how our father must have felt. At the age of forty he was left with seven little children, a badly damaged, uninhabitable home, and in addition (I learned later), he was deeply in debt.

James, Blanche, and Lucy were sent to Limestone to live with our grandparents (Daniel and Phoebe Remine). Papa took Jennie, Kathleen, and me to Uncle Ed and Aunt "Vee" Strain in Johnson City. To get there we went by a hack to the site of the Taylor Bridge. The bridge had been washed away by the flood, so we had to cross the river in a row boat.

On the other side we were taken to Telford in a buggy. After waiting several hours, we boarded a train. I recall that there was a pot-bellied, coal burning stove on the car. I was seized with a paroxysm of coughing followed by vomiting (I still had whooping cough).

Fortunately, the ride from Telford to Johnson City was only about twelve miles. We were met by Uncle Ed upon arriving, and were taken to his home on Unaka Avenue. Papa left us in the care of Aunt "Vee" who was apparently not accustomed to having to contend with little children, as she had none of her own. She was rather strict with us. While Jennie helped all she could with our care and the house work, Aunt "Vee" closely supervised Kathleen and me.

Uncle Ed, an asthmatic, suffered from severe attacks at that season. Between paroxysms, however, he was cheerful and jolly, and seemed to enjoy having us.

One day Aunt "Vee" caught me picking and eating ripe raspberries from a vine in her garden. She scolded me severely and shut me up in the smoke house for punishment. While contemplating my imprisonment, I surveyed my surroundings. I discovered a miner's cap with a lamp attached over the visor. I put the cap on and seeing a pick decided to play miner. I then proceeded to excavate the dirt floor of the smoke house until I grew tired of that activity. Uncle Ed soon came out to set me free. He laughed heartily when he discovered what I had done, and teased Aunt "Vee" about it. She was pretty irritated but did not scold.

I don't know how long we stayed at Uncle Ed's in Johnson City but it must have been most of the summer. I recall that when papa came for us he was carrying a newspaper with the story that President McKinley had been shot by an anarchist in Buffalo, New York. That event was September 6, 1901. Since papa and Uncle Ed were Republicans they were especially distressed about it.

Papa then took us to Limestone, about eighteen miles from Johnson City, where he had decided to move. We found a white frame house which we later called the Mahoney House (for the family that moved in after we left a year later). Grandma Strain moved in with us. She had been staying with papa's only sister, Aunt Nannie, who lived in Limestone at that time. We were all together again at last. Jennie, with grandma's help, kept house for us. She took her responsibilities very seriously although she was only thirteen years old. She was like a mother to us younger children; her discipline and care was governed by kindness and love.

Papa, I was told in later years, had moved to Limestone with total assets of a team of horses, a cow, and thirty-five cents. The farm "up on the river" was heavily mortgaged. He left the Brockwells to farm the place for him. They cleaned up and repaired the old house so that they were able to move into it soon after we moved out.

I don't know what papa did for a living when we first moved to Limestone but I do not recall that we ever went hungry or lacked any essentials. I remember one time that papa took some cowhides to a tannery in Jockey, a little town not far away in Greene County. He allowed me to skin a cow's tail and take the hide to the tannery. The ride in the wagon with Papa was a great occasion for me; the

"Papa then took us to Limestone, about eighteen miles from Johnson City, where he had decided to move."

experience of seeing new places and people, and the thrill of being paid five cents for my cow's tail hide!

Several events and experiences of our lives in the Mahoney House still remain in my memory. There was a family named Gray that lived near us with kids about our age. We were soon playing together, romping, wrestling, and having a big time. When we complained of itching scalps, however, Jennie and papa examined our head and found that we were all infested with head lice! Papa clipped our hair close all over and applied lead precipitate which we called "Red persipity." I recall the periodic "looking" of our heads which we underwent daily, searching for nits or lice. The girls' hair was treated daily and examined carefully. We learned what a fine-tooth comb was for. Further playing with our new found friends, the Grays, was prohibited.

Our house overlooked the mill pond caused by damming Limestone Creek to supply water power to run a mill which supplied meal and flour to the community. Just back of the house ran the smaller Jockey Creek which emptied into Limestone creek just below the dam. These creeks were enjoyed by all of us for fishing, wading, swimming, and exploring. Several years later we boys would enjoy swimming in the nude in the several swimming holes in the creeks protected by trees from the public gaze.

I still recall my excitement in catching a fish for the first time — a little "sun perch" — in Jockey Creek. I was fishing with a hook and line on a small cane pole. When the fish got on the hook and the cork went under, I pulled it out with such vigor I threw it the full length of the line and pole on the grass behind me. I have had no greater thrill of success in all of my subsequent life.

We lived in the "Mahoney House" for about a year, then we moved to the "Bellas House." We called it the "Bellas House" because it was next door to the home of a family named Bellas. This house was up the creek and on the other side of town. It was also near the Southern Railroad main line. In fact, it was so close that when a wreck occurred just back of our house, an empty coal car was dumped into our garden. We gathered enough coal from the wreck in the garden to supply us with heat most of the following winter.

The house was a small, two story frame house on a lot with many large outcroppings of limestone. It had three bedrooms, a "sitting room," and a combination kitchen and dining room. There was a bench on one side of the dinner table on which three or four of the smaller children sat at meal time. A wood-burning stove was at one end of this room with shelves, kitchen cabinet, tables, and other appropriate facilities. Our water came from a cistern.

Behind the garden in the back was a small barn at the edge of the lot where we kept our cow at night. Two or three apple trees were between the house and the barn. It was in those trees that I once acquired "green apple" colic.

Papa began working in the store which was owned and run by our Uncle Charlie Jaynes, Aunt Nannie's husband. Uncle Charlie became ill and died within a few months. Papa then ran the store, and after a year or so bought it. He sold mostly groceries, but he also had some "dry goods and notions." I remember the joy of spearing a dill pickle out of the keg with a long fork, and eating it

"In fact it was so close that when a wreck occurred just back of our house, an empty coal car was dumped in our garden."

with a big cracker out of the cracker barrel on the back porch of the store.

My continuing experience with tobacco was a different story. One time the chewing tobacco which Papa kept behind the counter smelled so good I peeled off a few pieces of leaf and thought I'd try it. I seemed to have forgotten my previous encounter with the substance. It wasn't too long, however, before I broke out in a cold sweat, became violently nauseated, and had to rush to the privy behind the store. I stayed there until I was able to go home, though I was careful to let no one know I was ill. Then one day Kathleen and I had a similar experience. At the Bellas house Mrs. Barnes came regularly to do our washing and ironing. Mrs. Barnes always boiled the clothes in a huge brass kettle in the backyard near

a large rock under a mulberry tree. Mrs. Barnes was in the house
for something, when Kathleen and I found her snuff box sitting on
the rock. Mrs. Barnes seemed to have gotten such pleasure from
her snuff that we decided to try it. Each of us took a good pinch of
the stuff and placed it under our lower lip as we had observed her
doing. The results were the same as before! Two very sick children
were soon lying on our front porch, getting no sympathy at all from
Jennie and Blanche. I vowed never again to be tempted to try snuff
dipping.

It was while living at the Bellas house that James and I
conceived the idea of having a store of our own. We constructed a
shack on our front yard consisting of a slanting roof on stakes with
a shelf in front. Papa gave us some candy to sell. We sat in the
"Store" all day and called to every one who passed. Once in a while
someone would stop and buy five or ten cents worth of candy. We
had one regular customer, Mr. Bruce Yeager, who kept his horse in
the meadow between our house and the creek. He came regularly
to get his horse in the morning, and to bring him back in the
afternoon. One day he came by and when we hailed him and asked
if he wanted to buy some candy, he called out crossly, "No, and
nothing else you've got." We were pretty badly hurt. When Papa
came home we found out that he and Mr. Yeager had had an
argument. His animosity didn't last long, however, for he and papa
soon settled their differences.

We didn't have to be told about the birds, bees and flowers.
Dr. Taylor, one of the two doctors in Limestone, lived on the hill
across the creek from us on what we called Church Street. He kept
his horse, which he used for making calls, in the meadow across the
creek. His beautiful bay mare was pregnant and one day James and
I got a lot of excitement watching her deliver her colt. Dr. Taylor
ran down and ordered us away, but we retreated only a short
distance, still with a good view of the interesting proceedings. We
also were in a position to see the reproductive process carried on
around us — chickens, ducks, goats, sheep, and cows in the pasture.
We even witnessed the service of a stallion to mares in a stable only a
short distance from home.

James and I were given duties to perform at an early age. It
was our responsibility to keep the woodbox in the kitchen filled

with stovewood as all the cooking at our house was done on a wood-burning stove. Papa had old railroad ties delivered and we had to saw them up in stovewood lengths. This was done with a cross cut saw with which we struggled, arguing frequently as to who was pulling correctly. We kept the saw greased with meat rind. We were hardly strong enough to split the chunks of wood, so papa had to do that when he came home from the store.

It was also our responsibility to drive the cow to pasture in the morning and go for her at night. In addition, we had to feed the hogs. Papa always had one or two to feed. We made pets of them and enjoyed watching them lie down and grunt while we rubbed their hide with cobs. One day James decided to ride one. The hog didn't like this and he rushed along the side of the pen scraping James' bare leg against it. James suffered a rather severe laceration of his leg on that occasion.

Uncle Bob Strain, papa's brother, lived at Limestone when we moved there. He was a railway mail clerk. While we lived at the "Bellas House" he moved to Bristol. Papa bought his house and we moved into it. This was the best house we had ever lived in. The "Bellas House" was unpainted and was obviously the home of poor people, although as children, we never thought anything about it. We had this fact impressed upon us on one occasion. Uncle Dave Strain and his wife, Aunt Katie, came down from Cincinnati to visit his mother, brothers Sam and Bob, and sister Aunt Nannie. Uncle Dave was a streetcar motorman in Cincinnati. Aunt Katie refused to visit us "in that little old house!" It hurt our feelings then, but we laughed later.

Uncle Bob's house was a two story house with three bedrooms upstairs, a parlor and living room, dining room and kitchen downstairs. There were fireplaces in every room except the kitchen. There was also a cistern house just off the porch at the kitchen door, and a "store house" just behind the kitchen porch. The "store house" was a small, sturdy structure with a cellar beneath it. A front porch extended all across the front of the house with a roof which was an upstairs porch. Bannisters extended around the upstairs and downstairs porches.

The lot on which the house sat was about 100 feet wide and about 200 feet deep. Our house sat back from the sidewalk about sixty feet. The yard was enclosed in a neat, white picket fence. We had the only concrete walk in town. It extended from the front porch to the front gate. The lawn was covered with a good stand of Bermuda grass, although I remember now that dandelions, clover, and plantain were also abundant. Three beautiful maple trees stood in the lawn near the front fence. Behind the house was a garden about 100 × 60 feet in size. Behind the garden was a well-built barn with two stables, a buggy shed, crib, and loft. How proud we were of our new house! We also had new responsibilities now. The lawn had to be mowed, a garden was to be taken care of and we had to drive the cow farther to pasture.

We lived on "Church Street." It was the road on which the only churches in town were located. These were the "Yellow Church" (Southern Methodist), the "White Church" (Northern Methodist), and the African Methodist Church. The schoolhouse was next to the "Yellow Church." Our house was about midway between the Northern Methodist and the Southern Methodist churches, and less than a city block from either. We went to the "White Church" regularly. Grandpa Remine was the Superintendent of the Sunday School there, and Aunt Birdie Remine was the organist. The organ was an old-fashioned foot pedalling kind. Papa acted as substitute superintendent, and served when grandpa was absent. Preachers came and went, a practice that was then common among Methodists. They were sent to us by the Holston Conference. I recall that their preaching made as great an impression on me as the influence of my father and sisters. Although I didn't make a public confession until I was about eleven years old, I prayed earnestly and with a child's faith. I resolved that I would some day become a minister of the gospel. I told no one of my plans, however, but I was determined to announce it at the proper time.

We frequently had revivals in both churches (protracted meetings, we called them). I felt obligated to go to both morning and evening services. One day while the revival was going on I yielded to the pleadings of one of my playmates to go fishing with him. Unfortunately, the place where we were fishing was within earshot of the church. It was summertime and the church doors and windows were wide open. I didn't enjoy that fishing trip because I could hear the songs and the preaching clearly. I felt very guilty because I was not at the meeting, and never missed another service during the revival.

The parsonage for "the Yellow Church" was just two doors from our house on Church Street. Several pastors lived there during the few years we lived at the "Uncle Bob" house. Some of them had boys near my age. Carl Fogelman and Joseph Bilderback were among them. We became close friends during their stay.

When revivals were held at the Yellow Church everybody attended, regardless of which church they were members. We heard some good old fashioned "fire and brimstone" preaching by evangelists who toured that end of the state. "Goose Bill" Thompson, the "Blacksmith preacher," and others whose names I have long forgotten, regaled us with the horrible end of sinners, and the joys of accepting the Christian way of life. Emotion would be stirred to a high pitch, and yet there were the proverbial village characters who went to the mourner's bench at every revival, only to resume their old habits after the meeting was over.

It was during one of these meetings in the Yellow Church that I went to the mourner's bench and "was converted." It was a serious step for me. I was determined at that age (about ten) that not only would I live a Christian life, but I would also become a preacher.

I particularly recall how one evangelist bitterly disapproved of the reading of novels. Reading novels, he said, was a terrible sin to be ranked with dancing, playing cards, smoking, gambling, and similar vices. Until then I had been enjoying reading some of my father's books, not knowing that they were the very kind the preacher classified as novels. One day, engrossed in an interesting book, *Rassalas*, I noticed the fly-leaf statement that "this book is a novel written by Samuel Johnson." This discovery caused me great grief. Here I had been sinning without knowing it, but the story was so interesting I was anxious to find out how it turned out. I went to papa about it. He comforted me by saying the reading of novels was not sinful unless it was done to the degree that I neglected more important duties, or failed to read the Bible regularly. He also advised me to be sure the novel was the right kind of book.

Family prayers just before bedtime were a routine at our

house. Papa always read a chapter from the Bible as we gathered around the fireplace and then we'd all get down on our knees while he prayed.

I cannot remember any discipline problems in our family. Since Papa prohibited chopping wood on the Sabbath, however, James and I would be scolded occasionally for skating or playing past dark before we had cut enough stovewood to last through the week-end. We frequently had to cut wood by lantern light. I remember the only time my father whipped me. I had a sore toe—"bealing" we called it—and couldn't wear my shoe. I asked to be permitted to stay at home alone while all the others went to Sunday School and church. The family had hardly had time to get out of sight when two boys came along. Seeing me alone on the front porch, they asked me to go swimming with them. My arms didn't have to be twisted, and we were soon on our way to the Morelock swimming hole. Swimming in the creek was great fun. The swimming hole was on the edge of a wide meadow and at the foot of a wooded hill, well hidden from public view and ideally suited for swimming nude. We had such a good time that we stayed longer than we had planned.

When I got home with wet hair, muddy wet bandage on my sore toe, and shirt buttoned crooked, I found the family at home and ready for dinner. Mid-day meal was dinner to us. Papa asked simply, "Fred, have you been swimming"? I knew then how George Washington felt when his father asked who had cut down the cherry tree. I answered meekly, "Yes, sir." Papa said, "Well, I'll have to whip you, but since it is Sunday, I'll wait until tomorrow." I could think of nothing else the rest of the day, for I knew he wouldn't forget it. I was the best little boy you ever saw and I lay awake for some time that night.

I continued to be a sweet little boy the next morning, hoping against hope that papa would forget the whipping he had promised. After breakfast and before he left for the store, however, he called me out on the back porch and gave me a spanking which I have never forgotten. I have tried to remember since that time that a child's punishment should never be done in anger. Papa's example was indeed a good one.

In spite of the pain and humility I suffered as the result of my spanking I noticed that papa seemed unduly short of breath. He also seemed to cough frequently and was more tired than usual at night when he came home from the store. These symptoms grew more noticeable as time went on, and soon he developed a hoarseness that grew progressively worse. In spite of those symptoms, I slept with him regularly.

Soon papa had to give up his work and was advised by Dr. Arnold to go to bed. He had tuberculosis of the lungs—consumption we called it—and tuberculosis of the larynx. Scott's Emulsion and the tonics which he was advised to take were of no avail. He grew steadily weaker and on May 25, 1907 papa died. Just before he died he had someone read the Twenty-third Psalm, which he said expressed his philosophy. He told his doctor that he didn't fear death, but he hated to leave us children without parents. He was only forty-five years of age.

At his funeral (preached by Rev. Fogleman of the Yellow Church) six of us, ranging in age from nine to eighteen, had our grief made greater by sympathetic friends who seemed to em-phasize the pitable state in which we were left. It seemed that even Rev. Fogleman felt it his duty to stir up our emotions to such a pitch that he had us all crying audibly. In later years we all agreed that he was cruel in his failure to attempt any expressions of comfort and hope.

Papa was buried in the little cemetery next to the graves of Mama and "Little Annie." I shall never forget our ride back from the cemetery in a hack. James Whitcomb Riley's poem, "When the Hearse Trots Back," expressed our feeling very well.

II

"... follow the gleam!"

Without father or mother, Jennie, only eighteen, became the head of the family. Blanche and Lucy helped with the household duties. James and I became the men of the house. We were responsible for taking care of the lawn, the cow, the garden, supplying the kitchen with stovewood, and for performing other tasks usually taken care of by men.

Grandpa Remine was our guardian and he supervised very carefully everything we did, especially our budget. I don't know how much income we had from our farm which the Brockwells were renting, or whether papa had any insurance. I assume that our house was paid for. Grandpa, however, certainly taught us thrift. One time he came over and found me playing with a puppy I had been given. He asked me whose dog it was. I told him proudly, "It is mine." "Get rid of it," he said, "what it will eat would feed several laying hens!"

Right after papa's funeral in 1907, a Mr. Henks visited and asked if I wanted to deliver the daily "Knoxville Sentinel." I was delighted to do so. We then visited a number of people and succeeded in getting about fifteen subscribers. My paper route began next day. Every afternoon I would meet Southern train Number 42. Although it didn't stop at Limestone, the papers were pitched off at the station as it went through. I would pick them up and proceed on my delivery. At eleven years old I had a job of my own, and could even have a little spending money. It took some will power on my part, however, to stop playing ball, skating, or similar activities with my friends so that I could go for the papers and deliver them. While the number of subscribers was not great, they were distributed rather widely from one end of the village to the

20

other, east, west, north and south, and many times it was almost dark before I could get over my whole route. All the other problems of a paper carrier were encountered. Some patrons couldn't pay regularly, some stopped the paper entirely, and occasionally some moved away without paying at all. I continually canvassed for new subscribers and occasionally I'd find one.

The Knoxville Sentinel was a Democratic paper while my great uncle Cal Keezel (Grandma Remine's brother) was a staunch Republican, as were most of the people of Limestone. He asked me one day if I was ashamed to be doing business with Democrats. Before I could answer he said, "But that's all right, get all the money you can out of those rascals." Then he laughed and became a subscriber.

As I grew older other jobs were available. I helped Charles Biddle gather fodder for fifty cents a day. I swept the school house daily—two rooms—for fifty cents a week while school was in session. In addition, I would often work a few days for Grandpa at his farm when corn was being planted or hoed. On these occasions I would stay the entire night. I shall never forget Grandma's kindness to me and the wonderful food she served.

One Sunday night at church Uncle Schuyler told me he wanted me to help him on grandpa's farm Monday morning. I got up early next morning and after breakfast I hurried to grandpa's. I arrived at about 7:00 a.m. Uncle Schuyler had been out in the field for about an hour. When he saw me coming across the land toward him he called out "Hi, Fred, what did you do the forepart of the day?"

One day I was helping Uncle Schuyler haul off an old, rotting straw pile in the barn lot. He was up on the wagon spreading the load while I was down on the ground pitching it up to him. When he had about a half load on the wagon, I pitched up a fork of rotten straw when he yelled "git up" and started down through the woods with the horses in a trot. Before I could ask what was the reason for his driving away so hastily, I was surrounded by angry yellow jackets and was stung in nine places about my face, hands, and arms. I had pitched up a yellowjacket's nest. My face and hands swelled considerably, and the lobe on my left ear grew to about the size of a golf ball. It was some time before we got the angry wasps settled so we could proceed with our work. Fortunately, neither the horses nor Uncle Schuyler were stung. I felt slightly ill for a while. Grandma was sympathetic, while all the others laughed at my swollen and distorted face. She prepared especially for me rice cooked and sweetened in milk. She knew it was one of my favorite dishes.

An old man named Scott Collett, at least he seemed old to me, often worked on the farm too. We planted corn in those days by dropping a few grains in each mound. Mr. Collett always asked me whether I wanted to "drap" or "kivver." One of us would "drap" (usually with two or three pumpkin seeds in every other hill in every other row) while the other came behind with a hoe "kivvering" the seed.

In spite of the fact that I made a few dollars occasionally, I was never able to save enough to buy things I wanted, which most of the other boys had. I always had to borrow someone's skates, baseball glove, or bat. I usually had to spend my money on clothes, school books, or things I needed.

I trapped muskrats in the wintertime. They were rather plentiful along Limestone Creek. I could get twenty cents for the hide of the animals dried on a board, and cut to the proper size and shape. I would find a slick place on the creek bank where the muskrats slid down into the water, then I would very carefully set a steel trap, and cover it with thin mud just under the water. A stake driven in the ground anchored the chain to hold the trap. Early in the morning before school I would go down to "run the traps." When I found a muskrat caught with his leg gnawed nearly off, I felt so sorry for him I could hardly persuade myself to kill him. To avoid damaging the hide, I had to kill him with a club, usually a homemade baseball bat. I caught an average of eight or ten muskrats each winter.

My elementary schooling played an important role in my life. I had several teachers that inspired me with the determination to live a good life, and to set a goal for myself that would be worth achieving. I recall a baccalaureate sermon delivered by an elderly Southern Methodist Presiding Elder, Rev. Ketron (grandpa called him an "old, moss-backed Rebel"). The sermon ended with the words of Tennyson's poem "Merlin and the Gleam," "After it, follow it, follow the gleam!" These words were in my mind continually for years and kept me constant in my determination to succeed.

Grandma Strain, who lived with us, taught me my "A B C's" before I started to school. I had started school in the fall of 1901 (I would be six in December). Miss Davis was my first teacher. Since I had already been given a start, I had no difficulty in keeping up with the class, and learning became a very pleasant experience. By my third year I had learned to read better than the average. One day I asked my teacher, Mrs. Biddle, since on that day I was the only one in my class, if I could recite with the fourth grade reader class. She said I could. I did well reading with the fourth graders.

Mrs. Biddle was teaching six grades in one school room at that time. There was a long "recitation bench" at the front of the room where the classes were called for having the lesson. I was surprised when she called me as the fourth grade class came up for recitation of their arithmetic lesson. "Come on, Fred, you wanted to go into the fourth grade, didn't you?" she said. Arithmetic was difficult at first, but I studied hard, and within a few days I could hold my own with the rest of the class in the various subjects they were studying.

One year, while I was in the fourth grade, the school board was unable to support a school in the usual way. A "subscription" school was created and Mrs. Biddle was employed to teach all grades from first through twelfth. The parents of the pupils paid a small amount to meet the expenses of each child. I often look back on that year and wonder at how much we learned, and how well Mrs. Biddle managed to teach so many subjects. She was one of the many teachers I encountered through the years who made me feel more conscious of my capabilities and helped me overcome an inferiority complex.

An addition to the school house was soon made, and instead of two rooms we had five. Five new teachers who were generally good, dedicated, and conscientious, were hired. It seems to me that we were taught reading, writing and arithmetic better than school kids are being taught now. We had to read out loud with some expression, and had reading classes through the fifth grade.

Moreover, penmanship was stressed. We had copybooks and were graded carefully on our ability to write. "The very fact that you write means that you intend what you write is to be read by someone, if only yourself," said one teacher, "and therefore it must be legible." I have never forgotten and my pet peeve has been with medical students, interns and doctors whose handwriting was illegible.

We also memorized our multiplication tables. I shall never forget how proud I was when I could say my "nines" without a hitch. Adding, subtracting and division were drilled into us so that square root, and cube root (which came later,) was not difficult. Because of my good foundation in mathematics, algebra was not difficult.

Another discipline we were given a good grounding in was history—American, English and Tennessee history. Years later when my granddaughter was complaining that she was having trouble with history, I said to her, "Susan, when I studied history I liked it, and made good grades in it." "Yes, granddaddy," she replied, "but you must remember there has been a lot of history written since you studied it!"

We also studied Geography, Civics, Biology, and the Geology of Tennessee. It was a common practice to teach spelling also. Our little spelling book which we used, had numerous verses, mottos and proverbs in it which we memorized. We were taught not only the spelling of words, but the diacritical marks, and to give them as we spelled the words.

We had a spelling match every Friday the period after "evening recess" (we accented the first syllable). We lined up along the wall and words were given by the teacher. When the word was misspelled, the student to the left—the next in line—was given the word. If he spelled it, he went ahead of the student missing the word. He "turned him down." If the student at the head of the line didn't miss a word he got a "head mark" and went to the foot of the line to work himself up for a head mark later. At the end of a month or other designated period, the student who had the most head-marks got a prize. I recall how proud I was when I got one—a fountain pen.

Our teacher, Mrs. Biddle, was a Virginian and had that typ-ical Virginia brogue in her speech. She had a daughter named Virgie who was about my age and was in my class at school. On one occasion when we were in a "spelling match" I was next to Virgie but nearer the head of the class. Mrs. Biddle, giving out the words, came to me and said "room." However, she pronounced it as Virginians do, "rum." I spelled the word, "r-u-m, rum." She said "next." Virgie spelled it "r-o-o-m—rum." I protested, "that spells "rum!" Mrs. Biddle became obviously irritated, allowed Virgie to "turn me down" in spite of my protest, and scolded me for talking back to her. I felt that I had been treated unfairly, but soon forgot the matter. I have never ceased to love and admire that wonderful teacher.

And grammar. We were drilled in syntax, and were taught to diagram sentences. We were made to know parts of speech and were taught how to use them. Our teacher instilled in us the idea that poor grammar in conversation or writing was a sign of lack of education. This idea was drilled into us to such an extent that since then I have been acutely aware of any grammatical error I have heard a speaker make, or have found in a newspaper.

Rhetoric was an important subject too. We were taught figures of speech, the meaning of a paragraph and other important rules of composition. I had two years of Latin at Limestone in which I did well, for language was most interesting to me. The learning of declentions, conjugation, and other rules of grammar in Latin, made the same rules in English have much greater meaning for me. I regret that Latin is no longer a requirement in the preparation of high school students for college.

At the close of school it was customary to put on a "play." These attempts at dramatics were always fairly well done. The actors were chosen carefully, from the student body, and there was always at least one teacher who was a fairly good director. I was chosen for the leading role in one play, at the end of my last year in the Limestone High School, 1912. The title of the play was "The Masonic Ring." It was a story about a family quarrel caused by a misunderstanding about the owner of a ring. I was the husband. My "wife," played by a classmate, found in my coat pocket (without my knowing it) a ring on which was engraved "Ruth Hall." Thinking it was a ring belonging to a young lady, my "wife" became very much incensed. Without my knowing why, she was cross, and threatened to leave me. Our happy marriage was virtually on the rocks when in the nick of time, a friend came by and asked if I was ready to go down to Ruth Hall with him. Only then did my wife learn that Ruth Hall was the name of the building in which the Masonic Lodge met. The play ended with the wife apologizing, and a happy reunion of the couple.

Preceding the staging of the play I experienced some anxiety. I was always acutely aware that my clothes were not the best. I often wore hand-me-downs from my brother or some cousins. At the time we were planning the play and practicing for it, my clothes consisted of a pair of peg trousers (they were in style at that time) which were somewhat worn, and a coat that didn't match. I wore these to school every day, and Sunday too. I wore overalls most of the time at home.

One afternoon after school I went over to see my grandfather in order to get permission to buy a new suit so I could look well in the play. I walked the mile and a half to his house. My grandmother told me he was working in the watermelon patch, but would be in soon. I waited for about an hour. When "grandpa" came at last he was hot and tired and somewhat cross. His first words when he saw me were, "What do you want now?" "Grandpa," I said, "I came to ask if you'd let me get a suit of clothes." "What's the matter with the clothes you've got on?" he asked in a cross voice.

"They are the only clothes I have," I told him, "and since I'm to be in a play at school, I wanted some better clothes to wear."

"That's no excuse," he said, and stamping his foot on the ground he yelled, "Git. Go home!" and went into the house.

Grandma followed me to the gate and consoling me the best she could said, "Fred, you come back in the morning when he isn't hot and tired." I dried my tears and hurried home.

The next morning I got up early so I could go to grandpa's again and get back before school began. I found him in a better humor. I am sure grandma had talked to him. He reluctantly told me to go to Ben Brabson, the storekeeper, and get a suit, "If nothing else will do you." I did, and found one that cost $12.00. On the night I wore it to the "close of school play," all the boys and girls asked from whom had I borrowed it. I was proud to tell them it was my own. When grandpa saw me in the suit at church the next

Sunday he asked me what it cost. When I told him twelve dollars, he said, "I knew you'd get the most expensive one you could find!"

In a little town like Limestone we had no need for organized and supervised recreation. There were plenty of activities we devised which kept us busy. The school grounds were large enough for baseball and any other outdoor sports we cared for. At recess and at the noon interval we played various games. We rarely had enough boys at one time to play baseball with nine players on each team. Instead we played "scrubb" or "one-eyed cat."

Each player was on his own in these games. Scrubb was played with a minimum of six or eight players. There were the pitcher, the catcher, a first baseman and several others who were both infielders and outfielders. The number of bases we used depended on the number of players. Usually two players were "at bat" at one time. When the batter was put out he went to outfield and everybody moved up. The catcher became a batter, the pitcher became the catcher, the first baseman became the pitcher, and the second baseman became the first baseman. The batter who could get a hit and finally come in for a run stayed "in bat" until he was put out.

"One-eyed cat" could be played with only four players. The batter had to hit and run to first base and back home before the ball could be fielded and thrown home to the catcher. When he was put out he went to the field and the catcher became the batter, the pitcher the catcher and so on.

One day while we were playing ball on the school grounds, "Uncle" Johnnie Klepper, a highly respected and much loved old Civil War veteran, watched us for a little while, and said, "When I was a boy we didn't play ball like that."

"How did you play, Uncle Johnnie?" I asked. "We played Bull Pen with Irish potatoes," he said.

Bull Pen was a game we sometimes played. In this game the players all formed a ring about twenty feet in diameter. One player was "It." He was alone in the center of the ring. A baseball, usually home-made, was tossed from one player in the ring to another. If he caught it, he tried to hit the man in the center with it, usually throwing as hard as he could. If he missed, he had to swap places with the man in the center so he became "It." We could imagine the fun Uncle Johnnie and his boy friends had playing with Irish potatoes!

Crack-the-Whip was another popular game. In this game we all lined up holding hands and started running around with one end of the line standing still. The player on the end of the line had to run so fast that almost invariably he was thrown tumbling to the ground.

"Dare base," "Baa-Hoo" were also popular. The latter was played by simply lining up at one base and running through to another about sixty or ninety feet away, trying to avoid being caught by the boy who started as "It" in the middle. When he caught one, that one had to stay with him to help catch the others as they came running through again. This kept up until the catchers increased and the runners diminished. The object was to see who could avoid being caught the longest. This game resulted in torn shirts, broken suspenders, and sometimes in almost disrobing the runner who was determined to avoid being caught. The game got its name from the fact that we would holler just before we started running "Baa-Hoo, I'm coming through."

On Saturdays and holidays we played Hare and Hounds, Hide-and-Seek (we called it "whoopie hide") or "anti over" (a game played by throwing a ball over the house). If the ball was caught by the team on the other side, they would slip around and try to hit one of the other team. If they succeeded, the player who was hit had to join the team that hit him.

As we grew to be teenagers we frequently had parties. These parties were for boys and girls. We played such games as "spin-the-plate," "musical chairs," "clap-in-and-clap-out," "winkum," and "Who's got the thimble."

One time at a party given by Hazel McCallum, the dentist's daughter, we were playing "Winkum." This game was played by having a circle of chairs with a girl behind each one. A boy sat in each chair except one. The girl behind the empty chair would look all around and then wink at a boy. When he was winked at he would attempt to jump up and make a dash for the empty chair before the girl behind him grabbed him by the shoulders and held him.

Pauline Arnold, a pretty little red haired girl was one of my favorites. I was always hoping she would pay some attention to me. There she was behind an empty chair. I gazed at her, hoping she would wink at me. She did! I jumped before the girl behind me could touch me. I rushed over to Pauline's chair in high glee, but as I attempted to sit in the chair, she jerked it out from under me and I sat hard on a bare floor. I suffered agonizing physical pain, and I think I have never been more humiliated in my life. The result was uproarious laughter on the part of everyone, but it took all the will power I had to keep from crying from pain and humiliation. I never felt so kindly toward Pauline after that.

One time after a similar party I approached Lucy Gaby and timidly asked her, "Can I see you home tonight?" "I don't care," she said, and I felt great. We walked down to the front gate together, and when we got out in the road (we didn't call them streets) she said, "Let's run." With that she started running as fast as she could, and ran all the way home, about a half mile. Sixty-five years before the jogging phenomenon swept over America I jogged along behind her hoping she would slow down, but she continued without a let-up. When she got to her house she ran up on the porch and yelled, "Good night" and darted in the house. I slowly walked home feeling very dejected, and ready to conclude that romance was not for me.

In the winter skating was a great sport. We had good skating ice on the ponds and millponds nearly every winter. There was nothing I enjoyed more, but I always had to use borrowed skates. I would have given anything for skates, and felt humiliated when I had to watch all the others skate while I sat by a fire or slid on the ice without skates.

One time when a crowd of young people were skating, the town photographer came out and took a picture of the gay skaters. I saw him and to avoid being in the picture with no skates on, I sat down on the ice with my feet behind me until he got all the pictures he wanted.

Limestone was a great place for all sorts of outdoor fun. Chestnut hunting in the fall, exploring caves, fishing, swimming, playing in the woods, riding saplings, climbing trees, and exploring

"I saw him and to avoid being in the picture with no skates on, I sat down on the ice with my feet behind me until he got all the pictures he wanted."

new territories. A few miles from Limestone was the Nolichucky River. At this point there were high cliffs overlooking the river. It was great fun to go to the top of the cliff and try to throw rocks to the other side.

Limestone Creek emptied into the Nolichucky River about two miles below town. I had learned to swim by the age of six as we had several swimming holes on the creek. There was the "Turtlehole," "Morelock's," "Cedar Branch," and a good place to swim where Jockey Creek emptied into Limestone Creek. Only in the latter did we have to wear something in the way of swimming clothes. Near the mouth of the creek was a large rock on which was written, "Davy Crockett was born on this spot in 1786." That spot was one of our favorite swimming holes and this rock was an admirable place on which we could place our clothes as we stripped for swimming.

In those days picture shows were found only in larger towns. Radios and television were unheard of. Phonographs were rare. I remember when papa brought home a Graphaphone, which was, as far as I know, the first one in Limestone. Then one day Mr. Kansas Henley came to Limestone with a "Magic Lantern" and gave shows at the schoolhouse, admission ten cents. At first he only showed still pictures, illustrating the songs he sang. Since we had no electricity in Limestone, his projector was run by a battery. I recall one song that he sang and illustrated. It was a very sad song and invariably brought tears to the eyes of the audience.

> "Papa, I'm so sad and lonely" sobbed a tearful little child,
> Since dear mamma's gone to heaven,
> Papa, dear, you have not smiled."

The picture showed a little girl looking wistfully into her sorrowing father's face. Then after another verse the little child goes to the telephone and Mr. Henley sang as he showed the picture.

> "Hello Central, give me heaven, for my mother's there.
> You will find her with the angels on the golden stair.
> (Picture of angels on an ornate stair.)
> When the girls received the message coming o'er the telephone,
> All their hearts were torn with sadness,
> And the wires seemed to moan."
> (Picture of telephone girls drying their eyes) and so on.

Other similarly illustrated songs were shown. Mr. Henley's voice wasn't the best, but its quality was overshadowed by the emotion in the songs.

Mr. Henley later bought a moving picture projector. What a marvelous invention! He showed jerky but exciting films, "The Great Train Robbery," and "The Crucifixion." What did it matter if the lights went out or the film broke? The audience didn't mind waiting until someone lit a lamp or the film was repaired.

Then there was "Blind Smith." He went around giving violin concerts, and when he came to Limestone, he pretty well filled the schoolroom at 10¢ admission. His program consisted of familiar tunes sawed out on his squeekie violin (we called it a fiddle). I was so envious of my brother James! He got a job leading "Blind Smith" around, even going by train to little towns nearby like Chucky or Telford!

III

"Knoxville, 1910"

One of the great thrills of my life was my first trip to Knoxville. The Appalachian Exposition of October, 1910, was taking place. Aunt Tot (mother's sister) had been there and was so impressed that she sent word that I must see it. I went to Chucky where she lived, and she gave me five dollars for the trip. The railroad was running a special round trip excursion to Knoxville with the fare being only $2.00. The train left Limestone at midnight.

I bought the ticket and planned to catch the train. Bedtime came early in Limestone, and few people were out at midnight. Consequently, I went to the depot where John Nelson was on duty as telegraph operator. He let me take a nap in the freight room until the train arrived. I lay down on a coffin box with a sack of sugar for a pillow and slept soundly until John called me.

I was the only passenger waiting at Limestone. I found the train so crowded that there were no seats available. I sat on the conductor's stool which he used to help the passengers climb on and off the car. As the train rattled and swayed while it sped the eighty-eight miles to Knoxville, I tried to sleep sitting on that stool with my head on my hands and elbows on my knees; all on a platform between cars! When the train stopped, I'd jerk to my feet and let the conductor take the stool to help a passenger embark.

The train arrived in Knoxville at about 5:00 a.m. I was all eyes for that was the first time I had seen a city larger than Johnson City. Automobiles were there! I remember examining one that had parked by the sidewalk. I pressed on the tire with my finger and remarked to myself that it was solid, when I had thought the tires were hollow.

Even though it was still early in the morning Knoxville was

already beginning to stir. I saw a Greek restaurant just across Depot Street from the station and remembered it was time for breakfast. I didn't want to waste my money on food (I had three dollars left) so I read the menu on the window of the restaurant before I went in. The cheapest article was "Soup 5¢." I had never been in a restaurant before, so I entered timidly and sat on a stool at the counter. A large Greek waiter asked, rather gruffly, "What you want, boy?" "Soup," I said. He seemed surprised. I am sure he thought, "Soup for breakfast?" Nevertheless, he brought it with croutons and gave me a little round tag with a five on it. I put the tag in my pocket wondering what it was for.

After eating my soup I went to the cashier and said meekly to the still larger Greek who had a sharply pointed mustache, "I had a bowl of soup." With that he pounded on a bell and yelled at the Greek who waited on me, "Why didn't you give this boy a check?" The waiter yelled back, "I gave that boy a check! Boy, where's that check?" It then dawned on me what the little round card with a big five meant. I meekly pulled it out of my pocket and handed it with a nickel to the scowling Greek at the cash register and hastily left the place.

Out on the sidewalk I watched people come and go. Occasionally an automobile would go by, but most of the traffic was horse drawn vehicles. Street cars rattled by occasionally. Since the fair grounds didn't open until 9:00 a.m., I had time to explore the streets. I asked someone which way was the Tennessee River. There was a picture of the bridge over the river at Knoxville in my geography book, and I wanted to see it. I started walking south on Gay Street, wide-eyed at all the wonders of a big city. When I crossed the viaduct over the railroad at Jackson Street, I encountered an Italian man who was opening his fruit store. He saw me and called, "Here, boy, come and help me." I didn't know what to do and he soon had me carrying boxes of fruit, apples, oranges, grapes, and bananas from a room in the back of his store to arrange them on the sidewalk for display.

I didn't want to work, I wanted to see the Tennessee River. I didn't know how to tell my new employer, however, so I arranged my trips with a load of fruit so that I'd get to the sidewalk when he had gone back in the storeroom for more fruit. Thinking I had earned it, I snitched a banana and hurried down Gay Street. The banana complemented my soup and furnished more nourishment for a busy day.

Continuing down Gay Street, I was thrilled to find a monument in the courthouse yard which marked the burying place of John Sevier and his wife, Dolly. The famous frontiersman had made history around my birthplace and was the first governor of Tennessee.

The bridge and the river were all I could hope for. For me it was a magnificent sight. There were some steamboats and a few small fishing craft out early. The mountains could be seen in the distance. A railroad bridge crossed the river a short distance below the bridge I was on. The buildings of the University of Tennessee could be seen on the hill down river to the right.

My sightseeing came to an end when the clock on the courthouse indicated it was time for opening the Appalachian Exposition. It was a cool, cloudy, October morning. It had rained the night before, but there was no indication of further rain. I saw a street car marked "To the Chilhowee park." I asked a man standing nearby if that was the car to the Appalachian Exposition. I got my nickel ready and got on. The ride to the Chilhowee Park was up Gay Street, across the viaduct near the railroad station and out Magnolia Avenue.

I soon arrived and following the crowd, paid twenty-five cents admission and immediately began seeing wonders of wonders. There were rows of tents with men outside of each declaiming the spectacles within. I saw The Fat Lady ("seven hundred pounds of loveliness"), The Alligator Girl, Eskimos from Alaska, The Wild Man from Borneo, and on and on. Admission to each side show was five cents. I saw one after another of these "amazing," "marvelous," "spectacular," and "the greatest" phenomena.

While taking in these side shows I heard a loud cheering down toward the park entrance. I ran down to see what the excitement was all about. There was a big automobile driving slowly, while standing up in the back waving his hat and grinning was none other than Teddy Roosevelt! I ran to the car and trotted all around the lake beside it watching this great man who had been my hero.

Without knowing it, I had come to the Appalachian Exposition on Roosevelt Day! — October 10, 1910.

I followed the car as far as I could. The driveway around the lake was lined with crowds of people. When Teddy was no longer to be seen, I again began to explore my surroundings. I saw a house built entirely of coal, the exhibit of a coal company. I then went into a building where I was fascinated by the navy exhibit. Uniformed naval officers and personnel were demonstrating the marvel of the age — wireless telegraphy. They had a replica of the radio room on a battleship where they were receiving and sending messages to a distant station. The sailors were eager to explain things and I spent some time asking questions and learning something about this great invention.

Outside the building, I counted my money. I didn't want to spend any more than necessary for food, but I was growing hungry. The soup and banana had been pretty well used up by this time. I passed a tent-like arrangement that was open on all sides. A large man stood there (why are cooks always large?) with a tall, white chef's cap on, and wearing a large white apron. He was frying hamburgers on a big grill. He turned them, pressed them, and put them on a platter. Another man, similarly clad, put them on buns, sprinkled chopped onions on them, and then sold them as fast as possible. It was a cool, cloudy day, and a slight breeze was blowing. The smoke from the wood fire, and the odor of frying hamburgers and onions was more than I could resist. I got in line and bought one for five cents.

I had never eaten a hamburger before, but if I could ever find one that tasted as good, I would gladly pay five dollars for it. It was delicious! I couldn't resist the temptation, as much as I wanted to save my money for more shows, to buy another. Those two hamburgers constituted my mid-day meal. I hurried away before I was tempted to buy a third.

The rest of the day was spent seeing the wonderful sights. I watched men throwing at a circular target with a baseball. If the target was hit, a poor, shivering, wet Negro fell into a tank of water, much to the amusement of the crowd. There was also a tight rope walker and a high diver. Both produced "oohs and ahs" from the fascinated witnesses. I saw the Ferris wheel, merry–go–rounds, and other rides give patrons a thrill, but couldn't see much fun in that sort of entertainment. You paid your nickel, rode round and round, but didn't get anywhere. To this day I have never ridden a merry–go–round or a Ferris wheel.

The day ended all too soon. I finally had to leave with only a few cents left, but I did have my return ticket home. At the railroad station I bought a five cent Hershey bar and drank a lot of water—my supper. I was tired. I had slept very little the night before and had not slowed down all day. Furthermore, for a growing, vigorous, fourteen year old boy, I had not had very much food. The train trip home was not so bad. I got on the train in time to get a seat this time. Although the train was crowded I did manage to get some sleep. We reached Limestone at about 11:00 p.m. I have never had such an exciting day.

In the days that followed, I was full of tales about my experience. I made hamburgers and told Lucy how to make them. I also made a contraption like I saw the Eskimo use to start a fire. I remained fascinated by the wireless telegraph and was eager to learn more about it.I felt somewhat surprised and disappointed, however, when Aunt Tot, whose husband was the wealthiest of all my relatives, asked me the next time I saw her, when I was going to return the five dollars she had loaned me. I eventually paid, but I remained thankful she had given me the five dollars to spend as I did.

Shortly after my trip a circus came to Limestone. It was a small circus as circuses go, but Limestone with its 250 inhabitants was hardly large enough to attract a larger one. It had one elephant, a cage with a few monkeys, and an old, mangy, flea-bitten lion. There were trapeze actors, tight wire walkers, and clowns—all in one ring! The circus traveled by road in wagons pulled by horses. There was one tent for horses only, where they were kept and fed.

My friends and I spent the entire day watching the tents being erected and all the surrounding activities. A youngster my age who was in a trapeze act joined us wading in the creek and searching for mud turtles. The only water available for the horses was in the creek, for Limestone had no public water supply. Two or three other boys and I were promised tickets admitting us to the circus if we would water the horses. We were each put up on a horse bareback, and riding him, led two others to the ford in the creek where we watered them. I made two such trips, each time riding a boney, old horse (one of them was blind) with the result that I literally wore the skin off my tail bone. Sitting for several days afterwards was an uncomfortable experience. Still, the show was exciting. However, early next morning it moved on.

The circus was far more interesting than the occasional visit of a man leading a trained bear, or an Italian organ grinder with a monkey on a chain. Limestone was so quiet it didn't take much to create excitement.

Grandpa and grandma Remine had family reunions every year or so. They usually occurred at the end of November near Thanksgiving. They had raised twelve children so that with all the wives, husbands, and children there was usually quite a crowd. I had lots of uncles, aunts, and cousins.

"Uncle Cephe" always came to these reunions. He was a dear old Negro man who had been with my grandparents since the age of nineteen when he had been given to them as a slave for a wedding present. He was considered part of the family, for he had helped raise all my uncles and aunts. He also had a family of his own, and was highly respected in Limestone. When he died he had one of the biggest funerals Limestone had ever seen. More whites than blacks attended.

At the reunion all the women folks helped grandma, and the dinner was sumptuous. The grown-ups ate at a long table in the dining room while all the cousins ate at a long table in the kitchen. The adults sat around and talked, reminiscing and telling tales, while we younger ones played hide and seek ("Whoopee Hide") out by the barn.

IV

West to Kansas

Things went fairly smoothly with six of us keeping house together. Jennie was the head of the house. Blanche got a job in the Post Office. Lucy took everything seriously and was given to periods of depression. She was very anxious to go to college, but realized there was no possible way it could be arranged. She sent for several college catalogues, and as she studied them she would weep bitterly because she couldn't attend one of them.

In 1909, James, who was fifteen, quit school and got a job with an "extra gang" on the railroad. He lived in a "shanty car" with a labor force which was moved to work at various places. I tried to persuade him to remain in school but he preferred to work. He said he didn't want to ask grandpa for anything. Kathleen and Blanche seemed to take life without a worry. They were never despondent and seemed to be cheerful always. Jennie finished high school, but never expressed a desire to go to college. She went with Clarence Walker occasionally, but never cared much for him. Clarence was a professional baseball player. He played with the Boston Red Sox, and later the Philadelphia Phillies.

On a trip Jennie made one time to Morristown to visit Uncle Fred Remine and Aunt Mattie, she met Aunt Mattie's cousin, Henry Greene. Henry had come back to Tennessee from Kansas to visit relatives and friends. He had formerly lived in Hancock County, but a few years previously his family had moved to Kansas where his father had bought a farm. Jennie and Henry seemed to like each other very much, and they corresponded regularly after their first visit. This relationship resulted in Henry's returning to visit Jennie. Their courtship led to marriage in 1909.

Jennie's leaving was a rather sad occasion for us, but Blanche and Lucy assumed her place in our family. Henry took Jennie to Kansas where he rented a quarter section of land and started farming. They had been there only shortly when they sent for James. Henry needed help on the farm, and James was delighted to go.

Blanche, who was "going with" Russell Good, a telegraph operator, was next to leave us. She and Russell got married and she moved to live temporarily in the Lone Oak Inn, an old hotel in Limestone. This building was the only three story structure in town. It served as a hotel for transients—mostly "Drummers"— and furnished accommodations for a few couples who lived there.

Lucy, Kathleen, and I were the only ones left. The three of us continued keeping house for two years with Lucy directing the housekeeping. I did those things the man of the house was supposed to do. I chopped the wood, took care of the cow, made the garden, kept the lawn, and was proud to do the best I could. Even grandpa complimented us for keeping things going so well.

I don't know why, but a decision was finally made that Lucy and I should go to Kansas to live with Jennie, and Kathleen would go to live on a farm near Limestone with Aunt Annie Keebler, mama's sister. I was excited about the move. I did not know what it meant for us, but I was anxious for the adventure. To travel such a long way, to see new sights, and to live in a different state appealed to me somehow.

With no more preparation than packing our bags, a trunk, and some of my favorite books, we were ready to go. We left our house completely furnished, everything as if we were going for a few days' visit. Our departure was arranged by grandpa and others. I remember winding and setting the alarm clock just before I left, wondering if anyone would hear it ring. Our old cow was taken to grandpa's pasture where she was to be taken care of. At sixteen I didn't seem to worry or even think about what we were leaving.

Uncle Maynard, mama's brother, was the station agent at Cleveland, Tennessee. He got passes for us on the Southern and the Rock Island railroads. We left Limestone May 5, 1912 and went by train to Whitesburg, to spend the night with Blanche and Russell. The next day we caught a train to Cleveland, where we spent the night at the home of Uncle Maynard. On the following day we learned that Blanche's baby (Mary Evelyn) had been born that night. It has always been easy for me to remember her birthday.

Uncle Maynard and Aunt Bess decided they would go with us as far as Memphis. We left Cleveland on the afternoon of May 7th. Lucy and I rode in the day coach. Uncle Maynard and Aunt Bess rode with us until bedtime and then they went back to the Pullman. I slept very little that night. I was afraid I might miss something. The people on the train, the things I could dimly see through the windows as the train sped along through the country, the sights in the little towns when we stopped along our journey—all these were too interesting to miss. Sleep came only in short naps as I tried to curl up on the day coach seat.

Finally, daylight came. The countryside along the railroad was different from that to which I was accustomed. There were no mountains to be seen. There were fewer curves on the railroad. Few hills of any significance were noted. Then we were informed that we were approaching Memphis.

I was too excited to be sleepy. The noise and bustle of the big city and the depot were too interesting to let me think of sleep. Uncle Maynard and Aunt Bess joined us on the platform as we arrived at Union Station. We got our baggage and then walked over to the Central Station about a block away. We found that it would be several hours before the Rock Island train left for the West. This would give us a chance to see some of the city.

We all walked up Main Street wondering at the busy traffic (most of it horse–drawn) and the hurrying people on the sidewalks. At the Chisca Hotel we saw what looked like a good restaurant: The Black Cat Cafe. We had breakfast there. I felt more at ease in the restaurant with Uncle Maynard to guide us.

After breakfast we decided we'd like to see the Mississippi River. We walked up to Beale Street (the street was not yet famous as Handy's "Beale Street Blues" still had to be composed) and then turned down toward the river. Our vantage point was partially blocked so we walked out until we could see it. There it was! The river was at flood stage—one of the biggest floods on record—when we saw it. It was a sight to behold. The water seemed only a few feet below the bridge while the river was so wide that we couldn't see the West bank. This was the flood of May 1912. We were told that the level of the flood had fallen during the previous days. The railroad had been opened only the day before we were to travel on it.

After sight–seeing awhile along South Main Street, Lucy and I said good bye to Uncle Maynard and Aunt Bess, and resumed our journey aboard a Rock Island train. We found that the train crept along slowly, stopping frequently so that it took two hours for us to travel forty–one miles. The water was over the track most of that distance and a hand car was traveling along ahead of the train.

All along the track, sometimes standing in water, were hundreds of poor negro "rivergees" (a corruption of refugee) holding their hats up and begging for the train passengers to drop coins into them. We finally came to the Western edge of the flooded river at Madison, Arkansas, forty–one miles from Memphis. As we stopped at Forrest City I heard of the newspaper "Commercial Appeal," for the first time as a paper boy shouted to sell it.

We continued across Arkansas. I got off the train in Little Rock for enough time to get fresh air, exercise, and some sandwiches for our lunch. As we continued westward, I took my shoes off and curled up on the seat, at last succumbing to the desire for sleep. At Shawnee, Oklahoma, I decided to get out again. When I tried to put my shoes on, however, I found that my feet had become so swollen that I had considerable difficulty. A man across the aisle saw my struggling and said, "What's the matter son?"

"I'm trying to put my shoes on, but my feet are swollen and I am having a hard time," I replied.

"Now, ain't that too bad," he said, "I ain't never knowed a man to live more than two year atter his feet started swelling."

I laughed, for I knew that thirty or more hours on a train, with my feet hanging down, was a good reason for the swelling. I got my shoes on just as we pulled into Shawnee. It was getting dark by then and so we each had another sandwich for our supper. We traveled all night again as we went through Oklahoma. We arrived at El Reno in the morning, but had to wait until afternoon to catch a train going north to Wellington, Kansas. We were amazed at the level country around El Reno—no hills as far as we could see in any direction. We were fascinated also by the sight of Indians, the first we had ever seen. Some of the Indian men had long braids of hair, and wore wide brim hats.

The last leg of our journey was a few hours ride north to Wellington, Kansas. This trip was through monotonously level country, and we were tired of sightseeing. We also traveled through a hard rain which continued into the night. When we finally arrived in Wellington during the downpour, no one met us at the station. We waited awhile, the only passengers there, and then asked if we could use the phone. I finally got Henry on the line, and remember his exclamation, "Good God!" when I told him we were at the station. He told us he'd be in for us as soon as he could. Meanwhile the downpour continued. It was about 9:00p.m. when we called and it was more than an hour later when we heard a buggy pull up outside. Henry and Jennie lived four miles from the station, and he had to go to the pasture to catch the horses to hitch up the buggy. I could never understand why he failed to have the buggy ready when he knew we were coming. Still, it was good to see Jennie and her two children, Lawrence, age two, and Martha, two weeks old. Jennie prepared a light supper for us—about 10:30p.m.—and showed us to bed.

I soon found that living with Henry and Jennie in Kansas meant a radical change in my sixteen year old way of life. All the tales I had heard about the amount of work on a Kansas farm were true.

Getting out of bed at 4:00 a.m. became a regular habit. Henry and I would then hurry to the barn with milk buckets and cans to milk thirteen cows — by hand. The milk was then brought in and separated with the skimmed milk being fed to the calves, and the cream saved to be sold in town. In addition, we fed and harnessed the horses. Finally, we would have an early breakfast, which usually consisted of steak or fried chicken, gravy, biscuits or homemade lightbread and syrup, and then we would go to the field.

I soon learned to harness horses, and to drive four horses abreast hitched to gang plows, cultivators, drills, harrows and various types of farm machinery. The day's work ended just before sundown, and then early morning chores would be repeated. The cows would be milked again, the horses unharnessed and fed, and then after supper, turned out to pasture. If the windmill didn't run enough to pump adequate water in the water tank at the barn, pumping by hand was required. When rainy weather came and work in the field was not possible, the stables were cleaned, or the harness would be greased. With the chores finished and supper over, an early bedtime was welcomed.

During my stay in Kansas there was no more playing, no more parties, and no more swimming or fishing. The work never ended, although it varied with the seasons. The year consisted of planting corn, oats, and Kaffir corn, cultivating the corn and Kaffir corn in the spring, cutting and baling hay in the summer, harvesting wheat and oats in June, and gathering corn and sowing wheat in the fall.

Wheat was the principal crop in that part of Kansas. Harvest time was a busy period. When wheat ripened it had to be cut at once for if it stood too long after ripening it would shatter, with much grain being lost. Then there was always the possibility of rain or hail storms which would beat the ripened wheat into the ground.

In those days we didn't have combines. The wheat was cut by "binders," machines that cut and tied the wheat in bundles. The binder would be followed by field hands who shocked the wheat. They would stand a number of bundles up together in a "shock." The wheat stood for one or two weeks, if necessary, until thrashing could be done.

The thrashing period was a busy one. The owner of the thrashing machine (called a "separator" in Kansas) would arrange to take care of a number of farmers in a community. These farmers would swap labor, helping one another as the separator went from one to the other. The farm women would follow to help feed the thrashing men.

The thrasher was driven by a big steam tractor with a belt from the tractor to the separator. "Bundle wagons" would go into the fields where a "bundle pitcher" would pitch the bundles of wheat up on the wagon. The driver of the wagon would then arrange the bundles so that a maximum amount could be carried back to the separator. There the man on the bundle wagon would pitch the wheat, bundle at a time, as fast as he could, into the thrashing machine. The straw was blown out on a straw pile while the wheat poured into the tight bed of a wagon. When the wagon was filled with grain it was then hauled off to the grain elevator in Wellington about four miles away. The farmer whose wheat was being thrashed furnished drivers for the bundle wagons, pitchers in the field, and drivers of the grain wagons. Usually four or five of each were required to keep the process going without delay. During the season I served in every position.

Operations were shut down at noon, and all hands would go the farmhouse for dinner. They would find buckets of water, wash pans, and soap on benches in the yard where they could "wash up," and then go into a dining room. The table groaned with real food. Each farm wife vied with the other in preparing the best. The men applied themselves to the business of eating the bountiful meal. It was a gay time. Laughter, joking, teasing, and banter went on among the men and ladies. Just as soon as the meal was over, however, all the men hurried back to their tasks. In the meantime, the horses had been taken care of and fed.

Sometimes the farmer's wheat could be finished in one day, although many had enough wheat to require two or three days to thrash. During the harvest time insufficient labor was available locally so that it was necessary to hire transient labor. This transient labor was a varied group of men such as hobos, vacationing college boys, and city boys trying to make an extra dollar. They were all mixed up, dressed alike, often unshaven, and all looked alike — with no way of telling one from the other. They were called by "nick-names," rarely by their real names. There were "Slim," "Tubby," "Arkansas," "Texas," "Indiana," "Red," "Bad Eye," and "Shorty." We all slept in the barns of our employers. Some stayed on after wheat harvest. Others caught freight trains and went farther north where harvesting was a little later than in Sumner County. Railroads tolerated hoboes during harvest time.

One character who stayed with Henry to help cultivate corn was an interesting professional hobo. We called him "Arkansas." He and I slept on the hay in the barn loft where he told marvelous tales of his experiences. "Arkansas" had a number of rings which were good imitations of diamond engagement rings. He said that when he was broke he would take one of these rings to a grocer or some merchant in town who, he felt sure, knew nothing about diamonds. He would tell a pitiful tale about how his money had been stolen by a fellow traveler, and that he had to have something to use in order to get home to his wife and children. His only possession was his mother's engagement ring, he would continue, and he couldn't part with that for anything. He would then beg the merchant to let him borrow twenty–five dollars in return for the ring as security. The only condition was that the merchant mail it to him when he returned the twenty–five dollars. My friend would take the merchant's name and address so that he could send him the money or he could return to get the ring if it wasn't mailed to him promptly. The story was so convincing that "Arkansas" rarely had trouble getting twenty–five dollars or more for the ring. He was careful to drop only one or two in each town. Of course he never sent the money to the merchant. His net profit was twenty–three dollars or more, for the rings had cost him only two dollars apiece.

One day while we were out in the fields near the railroad, we stopped to watch a freight train go by. A hobo waved at us from one of the coal "gondolas." "Arkansas" got up, standing on his cultivator seat and waved back. That night he told Henry and me that the rails were calling him, and he had to go. Henry paid him off and "Arkansas" walked into town. We never heard of him again.

After the wheat harvest came the job of cultivating the corn, and then plowing so that wheat could be sowed in the fall. Tractors were very unusual in those days, so the plowing was done with horses and riding plows. Gang plows had two "moleboards" and were pulled by four horses abreast. Once plowing started, it did not stop until all the wheat acreage was plowed. Harrowing and drilling followed the plowing. Henry, who farmed a half section of land (320 acres) which he rented, usually planted about 120 acres of wheat, and at least forty acres of oats.

Then came time to harvest corn. This was done in two ways. Sometimes it was cut with a corn binder, and shocked for hauling to the barn later. The ears of corn were removed after hauling it in and the rest of the stalk and blades were used as fodder for the cattle. The corn was also gathered by husking in the field. A wagon with a deep bed on it and a baffle board built up on one side was slowly pulled down along the corn rows while the farmer deftly shucked the ears and threw them into the wagon. We became very skillful in this maneuver and could usually husk (shuck) two rows of corn as the wagon moved along without stopping.

Kaffir corn was harvested, sorghum cane was cut, stacked and cared for. Sorghum was excellent feed for cattle and horses. Hay was then cut and baled. All of these activities were done with a feeling of urgency, and leisure time on a Kansas farm rarely came. And with all of these activities the "chores" (milking, feeding calves, hogs, horses, etc.) had to be carried on twice daily.

During winter we hauled fodder out to the pasture to feed the livestock. We cleaned out the stables, and frequently had to pump water for the stock because the pasture pond and water tank were frozen solid. Hedges of Osage Orange, or Hedge stood along the borders of the fields and broke the wind. They also furnished shade in the hot summer weather. These had to be cut or trimmed occasionally, and winter was the best time for that work. The wood was hard and the trunk of the hedge was frequently four inches or more in diameter. Chopping and sawing on this hedge was hard work but not unpleasant in cold weather. We would cut up the hedge along the edge of a forty acre field in one winter. In this way we obtained plenty of wood for our cook stove and heater. Hedge also made good fence posts.

Late in the first summer that I spent in Kansas I told Henry that I wanted to go to school. The high school in Wellington was four miles from where we lived. Henry tried to discourage me, saying that he needed help on the farm. But I let him know I intended to go to school anyhow. I thought I could earn my keep by doing the chores, and working on Saturday. Consequently, I went to the Sumner County High School to register.

The little lady to whom I was sent to register, Miss Josephine Hoge (who was to be my English teacher), was somewhat sarcastic at first. She asked me the usual questions and looked at the Limestone High School grade cards which I had brought. Noting that I had done well academically, she said, "You should have made good grades, as old as you are." Then she asked, "What course do you want to take?" According to the catalogue a "General Course" was offered for those students who did not plan to go to college. "I suppose the General Course, I replied. "Well," she asked sarcastically, "don't you ever intend to go to college?" "I'd like very much to, but I see no way I could possibly do it," I said. "Well, I'm going to register you for a collegiate course anyway, I believe you will go to college someday," she said.

I have always been grateful for her decision. The course she suggested was just what its name indicated, preparation for college. The subjects required were four years of English, four years of Math, at least three years of Latin, Chemistry or Physics, General Science, and Biology. After two years at Sumner County High School I would be well–equipped to enter the University of Tennessee.

In 1922, ten years after my interview with Miss Hoge, I went to Kansas on a visit. I had already received my M.D. degree and was on vacation. At Wellington I looked her up and found that she was working in the editorial office of the Wellington Daily News. I went to tell her how grateful I was for her advice and inspiration. While I was talking I noticed she was making notes, and the next day there was a six inch column in the paper telling of my visit and what I had accomplished.

But a long time before that return to see Miss Hoge, I had to register for her Collegiate Course. Even though I would have finished the school at Limestone in one more year, she registered me as a sophomore. Still, each teacher I had at Wellington, was a superior and dedicated teacher. They stand out as amongst the best I had in my school career.

In my first year I took English, Latin, Mathematics, Ancient History, and "Elocution and Music Appreciation." This latter course was required of all students. It was conducted by a Mrs. Petite. She gave us an introduction to some of the more prominent composers and their works. We learned the stories of major operas and listened to records of them played on a Victrola. She taught us to read music and organized the class as a mixed glee club. Even though I never had a good voice, I developed into one of the bass singers in the boys glee club. Clear speaking was emphasized in Elocution. We were also required to give either impromptu, or assigned talks to the class. In addition, the Literary Club was organized, and we studied a *Robert's Rules of Order*

My school work was made interesting and pleasant by excellent teachers. Attending school, however, was not easy. I rode my bicycle part of the time, but during winter the generally poor condition of the roads made bicycle riding almost impossible. I found that by walking diagonally across the prairie to the railroad I could reduce the distance appreciably. Consequently, I walked most of the time—taking the route across the fields. It generally took forty-five minutes to one hour for me to walk the proverbial "four miles to school through rain, sleet, or snow." In the early part of the school year the days might still be rather warm but, in the winter frigid weather was common. I recall walking one morning when the temperature was twenty degrees below zero. I was dressed appropriately, of course, with heavy underwear, woolen shirt and heavy suit, wool sox and "Arctic" overshoes fur lined mittens, overcoat, a cap with flaps to cover my ears, and a muffler to wrap around my neck and face. When the wind didn't blow too much I might even sweat. If the north wind was strong and blowing snow horizontally, however, no amount of clothes could protect against the cold.

I recall times when the weather was mild and I'd go to school without being too warmly clad. By the time the day was over the wind would have switched to the north, and a "Blue Norther" would be blowing. The temperature would drop as much as fifty degrees and I'd nearly freeze before I got home. But I never missed a day because of bad weather. The snow was usually dry and would drift with the wind. It was not a rare occurrence for the roads to be blocked completely with drifts four to six feet deep. Occasionally I'd walk to school on snow that was so frozen that I wouldn't even make tracks.

My route across the prairie was interrupted temporarily one year when the owner got a drove of longhorn cattle to fatten. He put them in the very ranch I had been crossing. As I climbed the fence one morning on my way to school, thinking I could go through safely as usual, all the longhorn cattle ran from me except one. A large steer with exceptionally long horns stood looking at me. I didn't want to get too far away from the fence until I saw what he intended. The steer shook his head, lowered it, and charged. I ran toward the barbed wire fence, fell on the ground, and scrambled under it. I don't believe I could have climbed it before he reached me. I was glad the lower wire was high enough for me to roll under. Needless to say, I took a different route to school until the cattle were moved.

Wellington High School had an active athletic program in sports such as football, basketball, track, and baseball. I was urged to participate, and believe I could have made the team in some of these sports, but I had to hurry home to do the chores. Unfortunately, I never had the chance to take part in athletics. I didn't even get to see the games. I would sometimes run all the way home pretending to myself that I was a long distance runner on the track team. I know I could have done well in such an event.

At the beginning of my second year in school I decided I'd try living in town awhile. I was able to secure a room in the private home of a family at a price I could pay. The room was furnished with a bed, dresser, table, and two chairs. It was heated by a coal burning heater, but there was no bathroom in the house. An outside privy was all that was available.

I could not get meals in the home so I decided to cook for myself. Jennie let me have a few cooking utensils and dishes, and she supplied me occasionally with eggs and other food. I would usually cook an egg, or a little oatmeal, and have a cup of coffee with my meager breakfast. I bought my groceries in town, though I had little money. Consequently my diet was poorly balanced. It was only on weekends when I went out to Jennie's that I could get a real meal. I read of the nutritional value of foods in a magazine and decided it was foolish to buy things like turnips, cabbage and leafy vegetables with so little food value. For a while I would buy only the most highly nutritious and concentrated foods such as cheese, meat, bread, and starches. Unfortunately, this diet left me so obstinately constipated that I developed acute appendicitis—at least that is my present diagnosis of the symptoms I had. Fortunately, I recovered without benefit of medical attention.

I soon decided that maybe it was better to walk to school than to live in such a way. Consequently, I went back to the farm and returned to the old walking routine. Then one day Henry told me that if I let him trade my bicycle in on a motorcycle, he would take me in to school. He bought an Indian motorcycle, took me to school a few times, but soon decided the trip was too inconvenient. Back to the long walk again, twice a day.

Jennie would fix a lunch for me; usually boiled eggs or a sandwich, an apple, or banana and cake, or cookies. If it wasn't convenient to do so, she would give me a dime for a sandwich and ice cream cone. I recall one time when I was riding the bicycle to school a flock of chickens ran across the road in front of me. I was riding downhill rather fast, and before I could stop, I not only ran over an old hen, but was thrown into the ditch by the side of the road. My lunch box was broken open and my lunch was scattered on the ground. Not having time to go back for another lunch, I salvaged a hard boiled egg and an apple, ate them at once, and went on to school. I didn't have any lunch at noon that day.

While I was satisfied with my school work, and was happy I had such good teachers, I had no social life at all. I enjoyed being with my classmates in school and at brief periods at times but I very seldom saw any of them off the school grounds. I had a deep sense of inferiority mainly because I dressed in the same clothes constantly. Even though I made good grades, and was often asked by other students to help them read their Latin, or to solve a math problem, I was very shy. I noted, however, that Bill Murphy didn't dress any better than I did, and his shoes were as worn and poorly shined as mine, yet he was one of the most popular boys in our class. He was an extrovert, I was an introvert. He had an outgoing personality and always seemed to be at the center of some social activity. He became one of my closest friends in our class and did much to boost my morale.

Living as far from town as we did, I almost never got to go to church. While I was living in Wellington, however, I attended the Congregational Church regularly. Jennie was very religious and was active in a movement called "The Way." This was a group which didn't have churches. They worshipped with one another in "the church in their house" (I Cor. 16:19). Itinerant preachers (usually women) came in pairs and occasionally stayed as much as several weeks at a time. They would hold meetings in a schoolhouse or some other building in the region. They worked hard on the farm doing any tasks the women did, and were a great help with the washing, cooking, cleaning, and caring for the children.

I had a high regard for them, and admired their sincere dedication to their belief. They were truly Christians in every sense of the word. I couldn't accept their absolutely literal interpretation of the Scripture, however, for they felt that only people who thought and lived as they did could be saved. They opposed the practices of more formally organized churches. They also thought I was doing wrong in getting an education, instead of joining them and becoming an itinerant preacher.

I worried about my spiritual life and longed to attend church regularly. One Sunday I persuaded Henry to let me have a horse and buggy to go into town for church service. It was in the summertime and I was asked to stop at the ice plant on my way home to get some ice to make ice cream.

After church service I stopped at the ice plant. I got out of the buggy to put the ice in the back. When I stepped to the rear of the buggy, the horse started up. When I yelled "Whoa," she knew that when I didn't pull the rein she was free. She ran and turning a right angle nearby, overturned the buggy across a guy wire to a utility pole. Loose from the buggy, the horse ran as hard as she could go in the direction of Henry's farm. I knew she would go home for she had a young colt there. Hurrying home, I caught up with a man I knew who said he had seen "Old Bess" (that was the mare's name), and knew that she would go home because he could see by her distended udder that she had a colt. He had stopped her, tied up the harness so it wouldn't drag, and let her go. When I finally got home she was there. Henry was very angry, however, and assured me that I had taken my last trip to church with his horse and buggy. I didn't get to attend church much following this incident, since I didn't feel like walking four miles to town after doing the Sunday morning chores.

One of my subjects in school was Ancient History. As we studied about the nations that had risen, flourished, and fallen we learned about their governments, economy, culture, and religion. I grew to appreciate how Egypt, Persia, Greece, Rome and others all had a religion of their own. We also studied about the Hebrews, and in the same way, studied about their religion. I then began to wonder whether this Hebrew religion (upon which our own is so largely based) was just another religion. Doubts began to occur to me which I could not quite resolve.

I knew that the principles of Christianity were grand, and that no philosophy was so satisfying as that exemplified by the teaching of Jesus. Without discussing the matter with anyone, I determined to go on trying to live by the Christian doctrine whether it was true or not. I knew absolutely nobody with whom I could discuss the matter. I didn't want to tell anyone of my doubts because I was afraid I would cause them to doubt too (Psalm 73:15,16). It was only years later that I would have my doubts dispelled (Psalm 73:17). Meanwhile my plans to study for the ministry began to change. I decided that someday I would like to enter the teaching profession.

In the second decade of the twentieth century, Wellington was a typical western American town with a population of about seven thousand. The principal streets were paved with asphalt and were unusually wide. Washington Avenue crossed Harvey Avenue in the middle of the town. The other streets were designated by letters or figures. Those running east and west had numbers, while those running north and south, had letters. Only a few streets had names. The principal business houses were on Washington and Harvey.

At the intersection of these principal streets every Monday evening in the summer a band concert was given. On one occasion in 1912, however, national politics came to Wellington in the form of William Jennings Bryan who gave a rousing speech after the band concert. He extolled the virtues of Wilson, and pointed to the deficiencies of William Howard Taft, the Republican nominee for reelection as President, and Theodore Roosevelt who was running on the Bull Moose ticket. Bryan was a great orator and I was thrilled to hear him. The one sentence I can remember was, "You must remember, Roosevelt was the old Santa Claus that put Taft in our stocking!" Kansas was predominantly Republican and Roosevelt carried the state that year, but in November Wilson was elected President of the United States.

That fall grandpa and grandma Remine came out to Kansas

for a visit. I was in school and was supposed to meet the train when they arrived. The train came in after school was out. On that same day, however, a man and his wife brought an airplane to Wellington. Airplanes were just beginning to be developed and being a teenager, I was more anxious to see the airplane, than to meet my grandparents. The plane was to be flown from a pasture a short distance from the school. Twenty-five cents was charged for admission, but I could get within two hundred yards of it and watch it fly from a choice spot. As I watched, it seemed that either the plane took a long time to get started, or they were waiting for a more favorable wind. I heard the aviator's wife say later, "It's as gusty as the deuce."

At last the engine started, the plane taxied a short distance, and was airborne. To my delight it was coming directly toward me. The aviator was sitting behind the engine in plain view from the ground and hardly protected from the wind or "propeller wash." He sailed just about 200 feet over my head and about the time he reached me the motor died. He attempted to turn slightly to glide to a landing in the pasture, but he didn't have enough altitude to make it. Instead, he came down in a field that had grown thick with tall sunflowers. The sunflowers had been killed by the frost but the tough stalks were still standing. When the wheels of the plane reached the tops of the sunflower stalks, the plane took a nose dive, falling to the ground. I jumped on my bicycle and rushed to the field. I was about the first person to get to the fallen plane. I found it standing on its nose with the propeller broken. The aviator was limping toward the plane from a position he reached, when he jumped just before the plane hit the ground. He had only a sprained ankle fortunately, but he was pretty shaken.

The fallen plane was soon surrounded by a crowd of people who hurried to the scene. I then remembered grandpa and grandma, and realized that the train had already arrived by this time. I sped away from the scene as fast as I could go. It was at least two miles to the railway station. By the time I was in sight of the station I saw the poor old couple walking up Harvey Avenue from the station, grandpa carrying a big suitcase. I got to them as soon as I could. I found them very angry because they had come all this distance and found no one to meet them. They had waited about an hour, and were going to the Antlers Hotel, where they would stay until they could catch a train back home!

I apologized profusely, and urged them to let me call Henry to come for them. I finally persuaded them to let me carry the suitcase and go back to the station to wait for a ride home. I called Jennie and after another half hour's wait, Henry came for them. I could never imagine why Henry didn't meet the train when he knew they would arrive. I could hardly blame the dear souls for being put out. But I, too, should have been there when the train came in. My conscience hurt me but I was glad I got to see an airplane.

Henry and a group of farmers had a baseball team. Henry was a pretty good pitcher. I would catch for him while he warmed-up at home, but I wasn't on the team. One Friday afternoon his team of farmers challenged the high school team for a game. When school was out that afternoon the town banker brought his car to the high school to take the team to the game. I saw the boys all dressed in their uniforms getting in the car, and knew they were going within a short distance from my home. Thinking of the long, four mile walk before me, I got up enough courage to ask if I could ride with them. The owner of the car told me he'd be delighted to have me. I got aboard, sitting on the floor in the front with my feet on the running board (the car had no front doors). The car was cranked up and the motor started. Away we went, (nearly thirty miles an hour!) out the Chisholm Trail all the way to the site of the baseball game. It was a thrill for me that young people today may find difficult to imagine. It was the first automobile ride I had ever taken. Within a few days I had seen an airplane fly and had rode in an automobile!

Grandpa and Grandma got over their irritation caused by their rather indifferent reception, and seemed to enjoy their visit. They had never been to Kansas before and many things were strange to them. We all did everything we could to entertain them. They stayed four days before returning to Tennessee. When they left I wished I could have gone with them! I didn't express that feeling to anyone, however.

School work and walking to school continued for a second year. I was still unhappy with my lot. I was two credits away from graduating from high school. The thought occurred to me that I might then get a job teaching in a rural school, save my money, and eventually go to college. Kansas University appealed to me.

A "Normal Course" was given by the Department of Education in the high school building during the summer. I applied for admission and was accepted. This course lasted three weeks. It consisted of an intensive review of about fourteen subjects being taught in elementary schools. I found a room near the schoolhouse which I shared with a young man taking the same course. We studied together and I enjoyed his fellowship. I had taken all the subjects they taught except Kansas history. I found this subject very interesting and was glad to study it.

The final examinations came at the end of the course. They were held in the study hall of the high school on a hot June day when the temperature hit 110 degrees. Air conditioning was still unheard of, and there were no electric fans in the building. With the windows wide open, our coats off, shirt collar open and a handkerchief to mop the sweat, we spent most of the day taking examinations on fourteen subjects.

There were thirty or forty "students," most of them teachers already, the majority being women. I went back to the farm after the exams, and within a few days, I received notice that I had passed and was given a certificate entitling me to teach elementary grades. The man in charge of the course congratulated me on my grades. I applied for the job of teaching at several rural schools, but the members of the school boards to whom I applied were probably wise in looking me over and telling me that there was no vacancy. With my career as a public school teacher abortive, it seemed I was doomed to remain a farmhand. I still did not give up hope completely.

In the meantime, however, the summer of 1914 was an eventful one. War had started in Europe, and the Kaiser's army seemed to be invincible. Work went on as usual on the farm. In addition, I helped build a silo and assisted in erecting a windmill. I also worked for Henry's father on a farm near Belle Plain, Kansas for several weeks. His name was Joab Greene. Mr. Greene was an eccentric old gentleman, somewhat conceited, and at times rather profane. One day I was helping him stack oats. I was pitching the bundles up from the shocks in the field to him on the wagon and he would arrange them so that they would "ride" without falling off over the bumpy ground in the field. We had about a half load when one bundle I pitched up fell back. When the bundle fell back the third time I looked up to see what the trouble was. There Mr. Greene stood leaning on his pitchfork gazing motionless toward the road. After awhile he said, "Lord God, look at that elephant. Ain't he a S.O.B.?"! An elephant was the last thing I expected to see in rural Kansas, but I walked around the wagon where I could see the road. There on a country road in Kansas about 100 yards away was the biggest elephant I have ever seen. He was walking along behind a small cart pulled by a shetland pony. A small circus was moving through the country. We did not continue with our oats until the elephant was out of sight. For years afterward my brother and I would speak of something unusually large as being like Joab's elephant.

In August of that year my sister Blanche, her husband, Russell Good, and Mary Evelyn came to Kansas for a visit. They stayed a few days and when they spoke of returning, I was like old "Arkansas." The rails began calling me and I had to go. I thought of the prospects of another hard winter, walking to school and made up my mind that I would go back to Tennessee. I thought I could stay at Grandma's and finish my high school education at the "Wesleyan Academy" at Chucky, and surely, I thought, I could get some kind of work.

Jennie said she hated to see me leave and questioned my going without more definite plans. Blanche and Russell, however, encouraged me. I had enough money from the summer's work to pay my fare, and a little left over for other expenses for awhile. So when Blanche and Russell left for Tennessee, I went with them.

V

From the Marble Mill to the University of Tennessee

Russell had train passes through Kansas City, so I bought a ticket to Tennessee that would take me back the same way. I was glad as I had never seen Missouri, Illinois, Indiana, or Kentucky. The trip home was uneventful. When we arrived in Kansas City and waited to change trains, Russell and I walked around on the streets near the station. Blanche stayed in the station with Mary Evelyn. Meanwhile, out of curiosity, Russell and I went into a saloon. Neither of us had ever seen one before. We ordered lemonade and were surprised to find that they cost twenty-five cents apiece, but they were unusually good. Except for lots of bottles on the shelves, the saloon wasn't very different from a restaurant or an ice cream parlor.

We continued our trip across Missouri toward St. Louis. Blanche and Russell went back to the Pullman while I spent another restless night in the day coach. From St. Louis we traveled on the Queen and Cresent Railway, through Illinois, Indiana to Evansville, into Kentucky, and then down to Nashville. We then boarded a Tennessee Central train for Knoxville. I remember how good it felt to see trees, hills, and mountains again after living on the plains of Kansas.

Blanche was then living at Bulls Gap in Northeastern Tennessee and that was our destination. Russell was a dispatcher there. The very air seemed better to breathe. The wooded hills around that little town were beautiful. At last I was back in Tennessee. I remembered an example of a rhetorical figure of speech, the apostrophe, William Tell's statement, "Ye crags and peaks, I am with you once again!" It was a grand and glorious time for me.

After a few days visit at Bulls Gap I went to Limestone where I visited Uncle Schuyler, Aunt Lena Remine, and Daryl, their son, who was a few years younger than I. I then went over to see grandma and asked her about the possibility of staying with them while I went to the Wesleyan Academy at Chucky to finish High School. Grandma said it just wouldn't do. Grandpa had died recently, and she said she didn't feel like taking me on. I was very disappointed as it now seemed I had not planned well. ·

I decided my best plan was to go to Knoxville to see if I could get a job. Aunt Nannie (papa's sister) lived there. She had married Charlie Campbell a few years after Uncle Charlie Jaynes had died. They had moved to Knoxville where Mr. Campbell was working for an insurance company. I was determined not to ask Mother's brother, Uncle Maynard, who was then our guardian, for any help because he had told me originally that he didn't think it was a good idea to leave Kansas. I decided to go to Knoxville, try to find work, and if I couldn't, I would ask Uncle Maynard for enough money to pay my way back to Kansas. I knew Henry could use me.

At Knoxville Aunt Nannie was glad to see me. She said I could stay at her house without charge until I could find work. Her son, Herbert, Rhea Anderson, Charlie Laws, and I all stayed in one large room. Rhea and Charlie were both from Limestone. In fact, Rhea and I had been classmates there. He was a stenographer for the Wright Hardware Company while Charlie was a salesman in the Newcomer Department store. Herbert worked in the Fulton Machine Shop. We were a congenial group.

I began looking for a job at once. I spent day after day searching for work. Everywhere I got the same answers: "No experience? We are looking for men with experience." Or, "Son, we're laying off men now." I was getting discouraged when I saw a Mr. Stone at church. Aunt Nannie had talked to him about me. "Son," he said to me, "Are you Sam Strain's son?" When I told him I was, he said that Sam Strain had helped him out of a very tight place once and if he could ever do anything for Sam Strain's son he would be glad to do it. Mr. Stone was the head of the Empire Marble Works. He pulled a card out of his pocket and wrote on the back of it, "Bob, give this boy a job." He then told me to take it to Bob Jones at the Empire Marble Works.

Early next morning I found out how to get to the Marble mill. I presented the card with its message to the foreman. He took me to the personnel office where I was put on the payroll and was shown how to punch the clock. I then started on the hardest labor I have ever done. I was put in the "coping shed" where the principal work at that time was making marble tile. My job consisted of helping carry huge marble slabs in from the yard, and then placing them on a large table where the marble cutter, by means of an air–driven chisel, marked them off so that they could be broken into the desired tile size.

The marble slabs were from one to two inches thick, and varied in length from six to eight feet, and from four to six feet in width. These slabs were stacked in the yard on eight inch by eight inch timbers. They had been sawn originally from huge blocks of marble. The slabs would be straightened up on the edge and "walked" out so that three or four men could get between the slab and the stack. The same number of men would stand on the other side. A large rope, five or six feet long, would be held by each man on one side. One end of the rope was thrown under the slab and picked up by the man on the other side. We would all catch the rope tightly, put our shoulder to the marble slab, and when the leader would call out, "Humph," we would all pick up and walk in step into the coping shed. I, another white boy, and four burly black men made up the team. Then with the help of an overhead crane we would place the slab on the coping table. The coping man would mark the stone, and then cut it according to the size of tiles needed.

It was also my duty to carry marble scraps in a wheelbarrow to the scrap pile. It didn't take long for me to learn that marble is heavy. A wheelbarrow full of marble scraps is quite a load. On occasion the work was done on thicker slabs of marble, very much in the same way.

Once cut, the rough cut tiles were stacked and fastened together with plaster of paris to be handled as one block for hauling to the polisher. The polisher would then grind and polish them to the proper size. Then the tiles were separated and one surface was polished.

Every step in the process involved hard work. We worked ten hours a day, six days a week—sixty hours for fifteen cents an hour. Fortunately, I had been hardened by hard work in Kansas, so that while I was tired at the end of the day, I was not completely exhausted. This type of work went on day after day. I had to walk about two–and–a–half miles to work in the morning, and the same distance back in the evening. This went on all winter with only two days off for Christmas.

I recall that it was bitterly cold on my nineteenth birthday, December 8, 1914. It had snowed the day before and there was about two inches of snow left on the ground. The coping shed was merely a shed with the wind blowing through without anything blocking it. The only source of heat was a coke fire kept going in a perforated oil drum. At intervals we could stop and warm our hands.

On that particular day I was sent to the yard where I was put in a line of six or eight black laborers to load tile into a box car. The tile had been stacked in layers and had to be handled in pairs, so that the finished sides would not be scratched. The snow on the piles had melted a little the day before and the water running down between the tiles had frozen. The frozen tiles were separated, but they were cold, wet, and covered with sand. They were swung in pairs from one man to another, and passed on to the men in the car who stacked them evenly.

The process took most of the day. Standing in snow with wet feet, I caught two tiles, passed them on to the next in line, over and over hour after hour. The rough tile with wet sand ate at my cloth gloves and in only a short while the skin on the tips of my fingers was so worn that every finger bled. As I stood there, mechanically swinging from side to side, grabbing tiles and passing them on, my hands sore and cold, my feet numb from the cold wet snow, aching all over, I thought, "What a way to celebrate my birthday!" I gritted my teeth and determined I'd stay with it, consoling myself with the thought that this can't last forever, and that someday the experience would be something to talk about.

I then began to discover why people who labor day in and day out, never get away from that kind of life. It got to the point that my chief ambition was to hurry home after a day's work so that I could get supper, and then go to bed early so that I could hurry to work next day. Before I realized it I had lost all ambition one day in March of 1915 to do anything else.

Then deliverance came in the form of misfortune. The threat of the United States becoming involved in the European war had brought building requiring marble to a virtual halt. The foreman of the marble mill called employees together and made a speech. He explained the situation and stated sympathetically that the time had come when the operation would have to be curtailed.

It was necessary to lay off a number of employees and those without families to support would be the first to go. That meant me. What would I do without my nine dollars weekly pay?

I walked slowly home after work that day, worried and puzzled. When I told Aunt Nannie she was sympathetic and tried to console me. I had been paying her three dollars a week for my board, but she told me not to pay a thing until I found another job. I thought seriously of writing Henry to send me enough to return to Kansas. I would work it out on his farm. But before I did that I decided I would see if I could find other work.

I immediately set out looking for a job. I went everywhere I thought there was a possibility. As before, the answer to my appeal was: "Have you had any experience?" or "We're turning off employees now. No vacancies." I tramped the streets of Knoxville day after day. I finally replied to a want ad in the paper and called on a man who was looking for somebody to sell "Toilet requisites." I paid him a dollar and he gave me a sample package containing about a dozen articles such as soap, toilet water, tooth paste, and talcum powder which I was to sell house to house. I was given some instructions on how to sell by order and told to memorize a spiel: "Strain is my name. I represent the E. M. Davis Soap Manufacturing Company of Chicago, Illinois. No doubt you have heard of our firm. It is the largest manufacturer of toilet requisites in the nation, etc.; I am introducing their products by presenting these samples to the public. This valuable package is being given to you for only one dollar to cover the cost of delivering it."

Taking my little sample box, I began attempting house to house selling. My commission was thirty-five cents for each box I sold. To my surprise I sold four boxes on the first day. I would take the order one day, and deliver it the next. I was told that selling directly would be considered peddling, and I would therefore need to have a license. After a few days, however, it became evident that I couldn't sell enough toilet articles to make a living. I sold only one or two a day and was becoming increasingly discouraged. My meager savings were disappearing fast. I then began applying for other work.

One morning I happened to be walking down a back street fingering two quarters I had in my pocket, the last money I had, when I met a pitiful old man who stopped me. "Young man," he said, "could you help me out? I haven't had anything to eat for twenty-four hours. I have been on a job laying brick," he continued, "and was on my way home when a man in a flop–house where I spent the night stole everything I had while I was asleep. I want to get to my wife and children in Virginia and now I can't do it." He showed me the callouses in his hands to prove he was a working man.

I felt sorry for him. At least I didn't have a wife and children who were waiting for me. The two quarters couldn't help me much. I couldn't turn him down, so I gave him one of my quarters. I had a feeling of satisfaction, for his smile made me feel that I had helped to make someone happy. Happiness, I had read somewhere, is a biproduct. To be happy, make someone else happy.

The next day it was raining. I had looked for a job in vain for four weeks. I was walking down Gay Street trying to decide what to do. I made up my mind I would go to my room, write Henry, and try to go back to Kansas. I passed a soda fountain and decided I might as well have a little pleasure, so I turned, went in, and bought a coca cola, the first I had had in years. As I came out I saw a movie theater next door advertising a comedy. In desperation I turned and bought a ticket to the show. Why not? I asked myself. Even if it took the last nickel I had, I could borrow a two cent postage stamp.

I saw one of the funniest comedies I ever saw, and temporarily forgot that I was broke, without a job, and without means to pay my room and board. It was getting dark when I got out. A light rain was falling. I hurried on to Aunt Nannie's. I had gone up to my room and was getting ready to write Henry when I heard a knock on the door upstairs. Aunt Nannie answered it and called, "Fred, there's someone here to see you."

I rushed down and there was Charles Biddle. Charles had been one of my friends in Limestone, the stepson of my old school teacher, Mrs. Biddle. He had been in Knoxville for two or three years and at that time was a teller in a bank. "Fred," he said, "can you jerk soda?" "I never did," I said, "but I can learn mighty fast." He replied, "I think I've got you a job."

I got my rain coat and went with him. We hurried to a little drug store on the corner of Vine and Central. There Charles introduced me to the owner, Joe Carty. I explained my situation to Mr. Carty and he asked me a few questions. Charles put in a good word for me and I was told to report for duty next morning. He would teach me how to "jerk soda" and start me at four dollars a week. He promised a raise if I made good. I jumped at the chance to get the job, and was determined to make good. I reported to work the next morning. I was given a white coat to wear behind the fountain. I had never made any fountain drinks before, but I knew I could learn with a little instruction.

Anyone familiar with Knoxville knows that the corner of Vine and Central was a section of town where the majority of the population was black. The neighborhood, however, proved to be an amalgam of many cultures. The Economy Drug Store in which I was to work was on one corner, a Jewish grocery store on another, a Greek movie theater for negroes on another, and an Italian fruit market on another. Next door to the drug store was a Greek restaurant. The second story of the building in which the drug store was located housed the offices of black doctors and lawyers. Moreover, most of our customers were blacks.

On my second day, the poor, hard working, hungry man on his way to his wife and children, who had had his money stolen, and to whom I had given my next to last quarter, came in with a prescription for morphine. I found that he was a regular customer for the narcotic. He was a morphine addict. The quarter I gave him was the last coin I have given to a street beggar since that day. I was to see much of the seamy side of life on the corner of Vine and Central.

I soon learned to "jerk soda" like a professional, and also began waiting on customers for cigars, tobacco, cosmetics, and patent medicines. I kept the soda fountain and all the dishes, glasses, and spoons clean and shining, making every effort to please Mr. Carty, my employer, and to satisfy my own pride in doing a job well. It was the first time I had been employed in work that wasn't hard labor. I also got a book on pharmacy thinking that maybe it would be a good profession to get into.

It was only a few weeks until my pay was increased. I was given more responsibility when another boy was hired, and under my supervision ran the soda fountain while I took care of customers for everything but prescriptions.

By the middle of the summer my pay had risen to twenty dollars a week and I was asked to take over the night shift. The store was kept open twenty–four hours a day. I was assigned the 11:00 p.m. to 7:00 a.m. shift. I was alone in the store during this time. One day Mr. Carty said he would loan me the money to go to The Southern School of Pharmacy for a three month crash course. The student, upon completion of the course, was guaranteed to be able to pass the state examination to become a registered pharmacist. He offered the loan on the condition that I would come back and work for him. The long hours and confinement a pharmacist had to endure, in addition to working on Sundays and holidays, didn't appeal to me. But I told him I would think it over.

Work continued. I became acquainted with all the people who had to be out at night in that part of town. Policemen came in regularly at night to call headquarters and stop for a free coke or ice cream; taxi drivers would stop for a soft drink and occasionally a sheriff or his deputy would drop in also. Our store was one of the few places open all night in that area. Gus, who was the all night man in the Greek restaurant next door would come over for an ice cream soda and I'd go to the restaurant for a fried egg sandwich. We simply swapped. I enjoyed his company.

One night a large, somewhat agitated Negro man, whom I knew to be a drug addict, came in and wanted morphine. I told him I couldn't let him have it without a prescription. He said he didn't have a prescription but was going to get it anyway. When he started behind the counter I grabbed a 38 pistol which we kept in a drawer and pointing it at him, I told him I would shoot if he took another step. I ordered him to get out of the store at once, or I would shoot him anyway. I was afraid of him. He began to laugh, saying that he was just fooling, but I told him I wasn't and that he had better leave at once. He did.

At another time in the wee hours of the night a negro man came running into the store followed by the Sheriff in hot pursuit. Just as he was in the center of the store, the Sheriff tackled him and both fell on the floor wrestling. By that time the black man's wife came running in. She grabbed the heavy glass lid of a chewing gum jar on the show case, and raised it to hit the Sheriff on the head. I grabbed her arm as her hand came down. The jar lid flew out of her hand and went through the top of a show case into the candies. With the help of two other men, handcuffs were put on the man being chased, and he was taken off to jail.

My drug store was in a shambles. The top of the show case was broken. Items placed on top of it along with large chunks of cut glass had fallen into the candy case, breaking glass shelves, mixing with candy, and scattering the loose candies all over the bottom of the show case. An uninstalled ceramic drinking fountain standing in the center of the floor was knocked over, broken, and completely ruined. I spent the rest of the night trying to straighten things up the best I could.

One night I saw two negro men fighting just outside the drug store. One knocked the other down and ran. The man on the ground got up and threw a pint whiskey bottle at the one that was running. The bottle struck the fleeing one on the back of the arm just above the elbow, broke and caused a deep flesh wound. When he noticed the intense bleeding he rushed into the drug store for help. This was the first time I had been called on to treat a severe wound. I took him into the drug room, cleaned the blood away as best I could, and applied a thick pad of gauze and a fairly tight bandage. I advised him to see a physician as soon as he could after daylight.

I also met a number of Negro doctors who were good customers for medical supplies, and learned to respect their ability. Late one night a Dr. Beard came and stopped for a coke. We talked of many things. He asked, "Doc," (people called us working in the drug store doctor) "Why don't you study medicine?" I told him I had no way of financing it. Dr. Beard then told me that he felt sure "Dr." Carty would let me work part-time while I took a pre–med course at the University of Tennessee.

In the days that followed I began to give the idea serious

consideration. I had often wished I could be a doctor, but the opportunity to study medicine seemed too unlikely to contemplate. But the more I thought about it, the more plausible the idea became. The next day I went to the university to talk to the registrar about whether I could be admitted. He arranged to have my credentials sent from the Kansas high school. From the information he obtained I found that I was eligible for admission, but on two conditions. I would have to complete two high school subjects, before I could earn a college degree. One of these was American history, while the other was to be anything which I had not yet taken.

My next step was to see Mr. Carty about the possibility of working part-time. Mr. Carty initially tried to discourage me, but I apparently got his sympathy. He told me he would let me work every other night from six to eleven p.m., and on Saturday afternoon and Sunday for five dollars a week. I knew I could live on that for I had lived on four dollars a week earlier in the year. I was elated by the prospects. It appeared that I would get to go to college at last!

Just before school began I applied for a room in the dormitory (Reese Hall) where I could live for one dollar a week. I could continue eating at Aunt Nannie's for two dollars and fifty cents a week for three meals a day. The custodian of Reese Hall bought the furniture from students leaving the dormitory and sold it next year to students entering school. I was able to buy enough second hand furniture from him to meet my purposes: a bed with mattress, dresser, table, two straight chairs, and a wardrobe—all for twenty dollars.

I had to pay a fifty dollar "matriculation fee" which I didn't have. I hurried over to the Southern Railway Depot to see the telegraph operator. I told him who I was and asked to get in touch with my guardian Uncle Maynard who was the depot agent at Newport. I asked him to tell Uncle Maynard to send fifty dollars immediately in order to pay my matriculation fee at the University of Tennessee. Uncle Maynard responded by saying a check would be put in the mail at once.

The check arrived next day and I matriculated at once. I was so proud to finally be a college student. The subjects I took that year were Zoology, German, English, Mathematics, General Chemistry and Free Hand drawing. These subjects were required for a one year Pre-med student. The German medical literature was said to be the best in the world at that time and therefore a reading knowledge of the language was advisable.

I found that without exception my professors were excellent. Their teaching methods were good, their personalities pleasant, and I was eager to succeed in their courses. I also found that I had obtained good preparation in the Kansas High School. None of the courses seemed hard for me.

My only problem was finding sufficient time for study. Working every other night until eleven and on Saturday afternoons and Sundays, left barely enough time for studying. Participation in other school activities was out of the question. Moreover, electricity in the dormitory was cut off at eleven p.m. On the nights I worked I didn't get in until 11:30 p.m. or later, so that when I got to my room I literally had to study by candle light. I had three candles on my table which when burning furnished enough light for me to read or write. It was common for me to have to study by candle until 2:00 a.m. or later to prepare my lessons for the following day, or to write a composition for English.

Working at night and studying kept me busy. On the nights I didn't have to work, I sometimes found myself getting very sleepy as I tried to study. I found that a good way to stay awake was to study standing up under the light hanging from the middle of the ceiling. I would often stand for as long as an hour so that I could stay awake and concentrate while reading. To save money on pressing my trousers, I placed them on newspaper under the mattress and slept on them. The next morning I would find them nicely pressed.

My first class came at 8:00 a.m. so that I had to awaken early to get breakfast in order to get to class on time. I would often set my alarm clock to go off at fifteen minutes before eight, feeling I needed the sleep more than breakfast. When during especially cold weather I found my bed cover was not sufficient to keep me warm, (the heat in the dormitory was also cut off) I would spread a large piece of heavy paper between the blanket and the bed spread, and use it for a blanket. Paper is a good insulator, and it was very effective in keeping me warm. I thought seriously of suggesting to some manufacturer of paper products that they make a "paper blanket" which could be sold at a small price to people who couldn't afford a woolen blanket. I still think it is a good idea.

One night toward the first of the school year as I got home from work about midnight, I saw the lights still burning in the front hall of the dormitory and heard a commotion. I hid behind a tree until I could see what was going on. There were expletives hurled back and forth, and loud laughter. Things finally quieted down as a group slipped out of the dormitory with their lanterns. I then entered the dormitory and found several freshmen huddled together discussing the situation. Swaths of hair had been closely clipped from their heads and led from the forehead all the way back to the neck. They told me I had just missed getting the same treatment as upper classmen had been hazing freshmen. Although my door had been broken open, I had managed to barely escape.

During the Christmas vacation at University of Tennessee, I worked full time in the drug store. We worked on rather peculiar shifts which Mr. Carty arranged. One day I would work from 6:00 a.m. to 11:00 p.m., a half hour off for lunch, and the next day from 11:00 a.m. to 6:00 p.m.

All the boys in the dormitory went home for Christmas except Graydon Sanders and me. Graydon got a job at Newcomers Department store. He didn't tell me what he was doing there, but one evening I was passing down Gay Street on my way to the drug store when I met a Santa Claus. As I attempted to pass him, he grabbed me by the arm and said, "Slow down, there, boy!" He made me angry and, jerking away from him, I said, "Keep your hands off me." That night at the dormitory Graydon laughed and told me he was the Santa Claus for the store. Graydon, like me, was willing to take any kind of a job to make a few dollars.

On one of my long days, I had gone to work Saturday at 6:00 a.m. and had worked all day until 11:00 p.m. I was dog tired and my feet were aching after being on a tile floor all day. It was about seventeen blocks from the drug store at Vine and Central to the university. I didn't have to go to work next day until 11:00 a.m. so I wasn't in a hurry to get home. I stopped at Thompson's Restaurant and, as was my custom, ate a bowl of shredded wheat with "half and half."

I then proceeded toward the university in a leisurely manner. I went down Cumberland Avenue and had almost reached the K.S.&E.* railroad station at the foot of the hill on which the university is located. I had come to within a block of my dormitory when I saw a policeman walking toward Cumberland on another street. Thinking he might be one of the many policemen with whom I became acquainted as they came into the drug store to check in to the station when I was on the all night shift, I thought I'd have a little fun with him. I began to stagger and pretend I was drunk. To my surprise, when I came closer to the policeman who was waiting for me, I realized I had never seen him before. He walked up to me and, grabbing my overcoat sleeve, said, "Where you going, boy?" "I've had a long day and I'm turning in," I said. "Do you think you can make it by yourself?" he asked. "I've done pretty well so far," I replied. "Well, I guess I'll have to take you in, you've had too much to drink," he said, gripping my coat sleeve more tightly, and swinging his "billy."

I then realized that he was serious, and that the joke was on me. In spite of my explanation about the long day I had worked, and that I was a student at U.T., trying to get to the dormitory, he took me to the K.S.&E. railroad station nearby. He then asked the telegraph operator to call the police station for "the wagon." While we were waiting in the cold on the platform of the station, he was absolutely deaf to my pleading.

I soon heard the police wagon coming—"The Black Moriah" as it was called in Knoxville. A policeman jumped off the front seat, ran around, unlocked the rear door, and told me to climb in. He then got in the wagon with me. Although I hadn't met him, he was an intelligent young man who believed my story. There we went clanging down Gay Street all the way to the jail at Vine and State Streets, just a block from the drug store. The driver of the wagon came back to unlock the door and let us out. When he saw me he

*Knoxville, Sevierville and Eastern Railroad (it was commonly referred to as the K.S.&E.—or "Kills 'em Slow and Easy!"

exclaimed, "For the Lord's sake, Doc, what are you being arrested for?" He had been one of my policeman friends.

A captain of the police was there who knew me, as well as a newspaper reporter, and a deputy sheriff, all of whom were night prowlers who frequently came into the store when I was on duty at night. Fortunately, they recognized me. I called Mr. Carty who was at the store that night. He ran up to the jail and with all my friends laughed at my plight.

I didn't think it was funny. Captain Lee told me he would let me go but I should report to police headquarters Monday. I asked the police to take me home, but they refused. Consequently, I had to walk that long, tiring journey on foot. By this time it was about 2:00 a.m.—and quite cold.

When I reported to the Chief of Police on Monday, the officer who arrested me was present. I explained the whole affair to the Chief. I emphasized that I would have had to stay in jail until Monday if my friends hadn't been there to let me go. The policeman who arrested me apologized, but he was suspended a week without pay for making a false arrest.

I was given a week off after Christmas. Since school didn't start again until after New Year's Day, I decided to go up to Bulls Gap to visit Blanche. Freshmen at U.T. were supposed to wear a little green cap (a student regulation) with a *19* on it to indicate that I was in the class that would graduate in 1919. I didn't mind wearing the cap, since I was so proud I was a college student that I wanted the world to know it. I therefore wore this cap to Blanche's. Naturally, I got some attention from my fellow passengers on the train and I had to explain what the cap meant. I could understand years later why a little lady of very poor circumstances wore her probation nurse uniform when she went by bus to Mississippi to visit her home.

At Blanche's I spent a quiet and profitable week. I got a high school textbook on United States history. Blanche and I then took turns reading it aloud to one another, and discussed it as we read. Before I left for Knoxville we had read the whole book, and she had quizzed me on it. When I got back to the university, I told Dean Hoskins ("Jimmy D", we called him) that I was ready to take my exam on American history to erase one of my conditional High School credits.

He set a time and in a few days I went to his office for the examination. He had made out a number of questions and gave me some paper on which I was to write the answers. I looked them over and found them to be on the very things Blanche and I had studied. I was quite satisfied when I handed the paper to him.

Dr. Hoskins leaned back in his swivel chair and read the paper. He straightened up, took up a pen ready to sign a statement giving me credit for American history. Then he paused and said, "How much time did you spend on this, young man?" Feeling proud of myself for doing so well in such a short time I told him "about two weeks." With that Dr. Hoskins leaned back in his chair, put his pen down and said as if astonished, "Do you mean to tell me that you expect to get credit for two weeks work on a subject in which high school students are required to study nine months?"

I did some fast thinking. I felt that I knew as much American history as the average high school student and I didn't want to spend more time studying it. I told Dr. Hoskins that while high school students took history for nine months, they generally spent less than five hours a week studying it. I had studied it exclusively, however, for at least five hours a day for two weeks. Besides, United States history had always been interesting to me and I had read historical stories for a number of years. I also told him (hoping he wouldn't) that I would be glad to have him give me another examination, written or oral. I felt sure, I said, that I know as much about the history of America as the average high school graduate.

Dr. Hoskins sat back and looked at me for several minutes without saying a word. Then he leaned forward, picked up his pen again and said: "Well, young man, I am not sure I am right but I'll let you have credit for the subject." With that he signed the paper. With this, I had one of my conditions removed. I thanked him and left his office happy. The other condition was removed after I entered medical school.

I became congenial friends with many of the fellows who lived in the dormitory where I roomed. Occasionally, when time permitted, several of us would get together for "Bull Sessions." We sat around on chairs, beds or tables, and just "chewed the rag." All sorts of topics were discussed, yarns were told, experiences were related and arguments were carried on. We would often discuss philosophy, and then branch off into religion. Darwin's theory of the origin of species and evolution were popular subjects.

It was in these discussions that I again found my faith slipping in my boyhood Christian teaching. I had gone to church regularly while I was working in the marble mill, since I began working in the drug store every Sunday, I could no longer attend church. I had enjoyed the religious experience in the church, and felt my faith returning. Our "Bull Sessions" and lack of opportunity to get the spiritual encouragement and stimulation in church resulted in my becoming an agnostic. I didn't know. Yet I felt that the philosophy of Christianity and the joy one gets from faith in Jesus and His teaching were superior to anything else. I hoped and prayed I would somehow regain my faith.

Jason Harbert, a boy from Savannah, Tennessee, was one of the boys who was a part of our "Bull Sessions." His arguments were always slanted toward the support of Christian teaching. I enjoyed his arguments and tried to believe he was right. I encountered Jason years later and he had become a fine Presbyterian minister.

I had no social life at all while I was a student in the university. I had neither time nor money for dating. The only suggestion of dating for me was the two or three occasions when I would arrange to study German with Virginia Priestly at Barbara Blount Hall. She was in my German class and I thought she was a very attractive lady. I corresponded with her at her home in Henderson, Tennessee, after school was out during the summer of 1916.

VI

"Apples of Gold, Pictures of Silver"

In the spring of 1916 an upper classman, Henry Snell, called on me in my dormitory room and told how he had made $3,000 selling books the summer before. His story was so convincing that I became interested in trying my hand at that sort of work. Several other boys asked him to tell us more about it. The result was that he got us to sign up with the Southwestern Publishing Company of Nashville, Tennessee, to sell books the following summer. We got together with Henry on several evenings before school was out, became familiar with the catalogues, and memorized sales talks about each book we had for sale: Bibles, *The White House Cook Book, The Business Man's Guide,* a dictionary, and several religious books. I remember that one of the latter was titled *Apples of Gold, Pictures of Silver.*

Paul Johnson and John Hart from Chattanooga and Franklin, Tennessee, and Paul Smith from Scottsboro, Alabama, were the other boys in the group. Smith and I were assigned to Wythe County, Virginia, while Johnson and Hart were to go to Bradford, Virginia. I talked it over with Mr. Carty who told me he would let me go back to work in the drugstore when I returned to school in the fall. We were anxious for school to end so we could start selling books and making lots of money.

School finally was out and we prepared to set off on our adventure. We had the caretaker of the dormitory store our furniture after we had made application for a room for the following year. Then I went to Wytheville, Virginia, with Smith. After arriving, we asked the telegraph operator if he could suggest where we might rent a room for the summer. It turned out that he was the one to ask since he and his wife lived across the railroad tracks from the depot in a large three story building which had once been a hotel. They were the only occupants, and were glad to have us. They prepared a room for us on the second floor. The location was ideal, and we found our host and hostess to be lovely friends.

Ready for work, we spent the rest of the afternoon becoming acquainted with our surroundings. The "hotel" in which we had a room and the railroad station were about a half mile from Main Street. We found a little restaurant where we could get our meals at a moderate price. We then explored Main Street and located stores, shops, and other features of the little town. We saw a plaque on the front of a building occupied on the ground floor by a barber shop. It informed us that Edith Galt, the second wife of Woodrow Wilson, had been born on the second floor of the building.

The two of us went to work the next morning. We found on a map that the railroad divided the county fairly equally into two sections. Smith agreed to take the southern section, and I was to take the northern one. We then set out on foot with our sample cases and no baggage, except a comb, safety razor, tooth brush, and tooth paste. Following our instructions, we planned to call on rural homes only.

After I was well out of town I stopped at a country home. I introduced myself and told the lady the purpose of my visit. I gave her the sales pitch I had memorized for each book. She was hospitable and pleasant but said she could not buy anything. I asked her the name of the people who lived in the house about a half mile up the road, thanked her, and moved on.

This experience was repeated time after time with little success. When noon came I was approaching a prosperous looking farm home. I told the lady my business and asked if I could have lunch there. I was received cordially and showed where to wash my hands — on the back porch in a wash pan. The water was obtained from a large bucket with a dipper in it. I was then given the morning paper and told to wait a few minutes. I had hardly sat down before a lovely teenage daughter came out to talk to me. She brought a guitar and after a few words, she volunteered to play for me. She strummed a few chords and sang several little songs. Her voice was only fairly good but I enjoyed her attempt to entertain me. I must admit it was effective in helping to overcome a slight feeling of depression due to my lack of success.

Soon the father and his grown son came in from the field for "dinner." I found them to be very hospitable people. Mrs. Lindamood soon called us to eat. I could not think of when I had enjoyed a more delightful meal. Not only was the food delicious and ample, but everyone seemed to be happy and in a good mood. I was grateful for this experience. I sold no books, however, at the Lindamoods.

I continued my quest after lunch. I made a few sales during the afternoon, stopping at every house along the road. Some of the homes were very poor. I could tell that purchasing a book of any kind would be more than they could afford. I just could not press them to buy. Moreover, I found out that a high pressure salesman was preceding me. I was told at many homes that a man had called on them the day before and had sold them a book, *Daniel and the Revelation.* Consequently, they could not afford to buy another book. I was amazed at the number of books this man had sold. He was apparently very convincing; he had made it appear that the end of this era was approaching as prophesied by Daniel and John in Revelation). I did not have the heart to press poor people into buying something that they did not need, or could not afford.

One afternoon after a hard day, with a few sales to make me feel a little better, I approached a beautiful country home. It had a white picket fence around a large yard, a well-built, painted barn, a tool shed and other buildings. Here, I thought, would be a good place to spend the night. I walked up the long walk from the road toward the house. I heard laughter and voices of young people as I drew closer. I knocked on the door. A boy about my age and his little teenage sister came to the door. I asked them if their mother was home as I was going to ask her if I could spend the night. They said she wasn't home, but "Come in. You can spend the night with us. We'd be glad to have you." They told me that "Mama and papa have gone to Wytheville to meet Elsie who is coming home from school—Elizabeth College at Roanoke."

I have never been more hospitably received. I was treated as if I was one of the family. It wasn't long before I heard a buggy drive up. All the family were in high glee and Elsie was greeted affectionately by all. They seemed surprised to see me but they made me feel welcome. Two other boys had gone with their parents to meet Elsie, who was a charming young lady.

After a bountiful supper we all gathered in the living room to hear Elsie tell of her experiences at school. She got out her school annual and showed me all the pictures and other features in it. She appeared to have been a popular girl there, for she was in many of the school activities. Elizabeth College was for girls only, but it was near Roanoke College for boys. Virginia had no coeducational colleges in those days.

Next morning I said goodbye to the Huffards and again set out in my efforts to sell books, but feeling very good from the pleasant experience. Unfortunately such hospitality wasn't always encountered in my attempt to find a place to eat a meal or to spend the night. We had been instructed to offer to pay for meals or lodging by a discount on a book we might sell our host. Very seldom, however, would we be charged for our food or lodging. We were also instructed to live on what we could collect in advance on any books we sold. Some weeks I would do pretty well and would have enough cash to buy food and necessities over the weekend. Often, however, I didn't do so well.

One weekend I came in with only one dollar. Smith had been unable to collect any more. Between us we had two dollars and thirty cents. It began to rain on Sunday night and the rain kept up practically all week. We couldn't work during rainy weather. Consequently, we had to be very careful about what we spent that week. I would get a loaf of bread for five cents, a quart of milk for a nickel, and then we would go to our room and divide the milk and bread equally. That would be our meal. Sometimes, however, it would only be a five cent Hershey's chocolate bar and two or three glasses of water. Apples falling across the fence into the road at a nearby orchard were a free addition to our food supply, but too many apples resulted in a gastro-intestinal upset.

During this week at home we met two young ladies who lived near the railroad depot, Winifred BeCraft and her sister, Joanna. We walked up and down the tracks with them between showers and found them delightful company. On Wednesday evening they told us that a moving picture was shown once a week in Wytheville. It was approaching Thursday evening, and "let's all go see it." Smith, without thinking that if we took them to the show we couldn't eat any more until we started working again, immediately replied, "Yes, let's do!"

What to do? Neither of us had more than sixty cents. The price of admission was a quarter. That would leave about twenty cents between us to buy food for three or four days. Thursday came, still rainy. Nothing to do but take the girls to the picture show. Then about the hour that the show was scheduled to begin, one of the hardest thunder storms I have known struck the little town. The lightning was frightening during the storm. One unusually loud clap of thunder and a blinding flash of lightning occurred and — praises be! It blew out the electrical supply of the whole town. The picture show could not take place. Total darkness all night! Result: we didn't have to take the girls to a show and we still had money for food. I have felt kindly toward thunder storms most of the time since then.

Another interesting experience I had that summer occurred as I waited for a train one Friday afternoon at Crockett, Virginia, a little town just west of Wytheville. As I stood on the platform watching the activities of the small country town, I noticed a Model–T Ford drive up behind the depot. I was struck by the fact that two men got out of it and walked across the tracks toward the town bank, although they had left the motor of the car running. In about ten minutes the men came out of the bank walking rapidly. They hurried to their car and left at high speed, leaving a cloud of dust as they rounded a corner, and disappeared from sight.

About ten minutes later, a man came running out of the bank yelling "Which way did those men go? They have just robbed the bank." Soon the town was alive with men carrying guns, jumping in cars, and rushing off in the direction the robbers had taken. Two little boys twelve or fourteen years of age riding a horse bareback and carrying a twenty–two caliber rifle joined the pack. I waited for my train long enough to learn that the men had gone into the bank, forced the bank employees and one customer into the vault, closed the door without locking it, and gotten away with $2,500. Shortly afterwards, a young man came into town with twine tied around his arms and ankles. He told me the robbers had engaged him to bring them from Rural Retreat in his taxi. Just outside town they had him stop in the woods. They then took him away from the road and tied him to a tree. However, they inadvertently left an open knife near his feet which he was eventually able to use to cut the twine that bound him. His taxi was found about two miles out of town where the robbers had evidently changed cars. The taxi driver found a ten dollar bill on the front seat. I learned a few days later that the sheriff came to Wytheville and asked about Smith and me. Could we be the guilty ones? So far as I have been able to learn, the bank robbers were never caught.

Our sales in Wythe County were not too good and after we had covered the rural sections pretty well, we decided to move to Smyth County, Virginia. Accordingly, we said goodbye to our landlords and the BeCraft girls and moved to Marion, the county seat of Smyth County a few miles west. In Marion we found a good room at the home of a Mrs. Wolfe.

There was a small restaurant nearby where we ate when we were in town. We also became acquainted with the two young men who ran it. I recall how one of them refused to give me a glass of milk to drink after I had ordered catfish. He insisted that milk and fish taken together was poisonous. I promised that I would not hold him accountable if it made me ill. He reluctantly gave me the milk.

I took the southern half of Smyth County while Smith took the northern half. I found Smyth County to be very interesting and initially had a little more success in selling books. Sales soon slumped, however. A short railroad line led from Marion to Sugar Grove in Rye Valley. I called on many homes along this railroad, and had little success. I then tried a little village called Ataway a few miles from Marion. This community was a "company town" built around a mill engaged in making barrel staves. Nearly all the houses in Ataway were owned by the mill and occupied by its employees. In addition, the only store in town was owned and operated by the mill. The mill's employees were paid in "script" which was accepted in the store, but was not accepted for goods and services provided by other businesses. The prices in the company store were also higher than those elsewhere.

I found the people living in Ataway to be very poor and

"This community was a 'company town' built around a mill engaged in making barrel staves."

practically slaves of the company for which they worked. I was therefore unable to sell any books in that unhappy village. I followed the road paralleling the railroad and moved toward a mountainous region. One day I stopped at a farm house around noon and asked the lady of the house if she could let me have lunch. She invited me in telling me that lunch would be ready in a short time. I washed my hands — on the back porch as usual — and sat on the front porch reading an old paper. Soon I heard the man of the house and the son, about my age, come in from the field. After washing up they came out on the porch to join me.

We were having a friendly discussion about politics and general topics when it occurred to me it was a good time to make a pitch for selling a book. I had hardly mentioned the subject when the man stood up. "Do you mean to tell me you are one of these guys going around trying to make a living without working?" he said. I tried to explain that I was trying to make enough to pay my expenses in school.

"Well," he said, "if you want a job, they are looking for men in a lumber camp in the mountain nearby. Now you pick up your little case and get off down the road — right now!" I did just that for both the man and his son were standing, and a large unfriendly dog was looking at me threateningly. Therefore, I went down the road hungry after smelling the good food being prepared in the kitchen, and depressed by the reaction of the man to the type of work I was doing. I was beginning to agree with him about it.

After going about a mile I came upon a large, beautiful brick home surrounded by lovely shade trees in well cared for grounds. I knocked at the door. A pleasant motherly looking lady invited me in. I asked her if she would be kind enough to give me a slice of bread and a glass of milk. She laughed and said, "The very idea! I'll fix you a real lunch." It was nearly 2:00 p.m. and she had already made lunch for the men, who had gone back to work. Not only did she give me a good lunch, but she brightened my spirits considerably. She told me she had a son about my age off at college, and could understand my situation. Her kindness was just what I needed. I bade her goodbye and with new energy pushed on toward Sugar Grove.

Sugar Grove was a little community in beautiful Rye Valley. It was almost completely surrounded by mountains and a sparkling little stream ran through the center of the valley. There must have been a lack of iodine in the water and vegetables grown there, as I found that in a number of homes many of the women had large, nodular goiters. I also saw several mentally defective children. In two of the homes there were children with hydrocephalus. One child, in particular, had the largest head I have ever seen. In addition, I was told that the families in the valley were all related and that intermarriage was common.

I secured lodging for the night in a home in the vicinity. After supper that night the lady of the house took me upstairs to show me my room. She carried two lamps, one for me and the other to light her way back down the stairs. She left my room, closed the door, but stood just outside for a minute or so. She then rapped on the door, opened it, and said, "If anything unusual happens tonight I hope you'll understand." Without further explanation she closed the door and went downstairs leaving me to wonder what she could have meant. What might happen? I went to bed thinking of nothing else, but being a tired, healthy American boy, I was soon fast asleep.

After a good night's rest, I got up, dressed, and went down. On my way to the back porch to "wash up" in the tin pan on the porch shelf, I passed an open door. I looked in and saw a middle aged woman sitting in a rocking chair, mumbling incoherently, and rapidly rocking back and forth. Her hair was cut short over her head and it was easy to assume that she was insane. Some form of erratic behavior was what was likely to happen last night, I thought. She probably caused disturbances sometimes. I was glad I didn't see her the night before. I said nothing to my hostess, however, and she said nothing to explain her remarks of the previous night.

After I left Sugar Grove I took a road out of the valley and went over the mountain. Thinking there might be no houses for a number of miles, I decided I had better find lodging for the night. The next house I came to was little more than a cabin beside the road. I stopped and asked if I could have supper and spend the night.

A young mountain couple lived there. He was mining manganese by himself; digging it from the mountain and hauling it away in a wagon. Both husband and wife were cordial and said they were glad to have me. They were very serious and quite religious. The supper consisted of fried side meat, gravy, corn pone (without milk or eggs) sorghum molasses, and black coffee. That was all! There was no sugar, no butter, no milk or cream. I was told if I wanted to sweeten my coffee I could use molasses.

The young man said the blessing. I have often thought that if God ever hears anyone saying thanks, I am sure he heard that humble young man's prayer. After he was through he said to me, "There it is, my friend. If you love the Lord that is good enough for you. If you don't it's too good!" I have often thought of that statement.

After supper I was shown my bed. To my surprise it was one of two in the only bedroom. I went to bed early and before I fell asleep, I heard them going to the other in the dark. Again my youth, the mountain air and exercise caused me to sleep soundly that night. At breakfast the next norming I was asked to return the thanks. I prayed earnestly for God to bless that home, and thanked Him for leading me to them.

I also heard that I could catch the train back to Marion from Sugar Grove. Consequently, I returned to Sugar Grove in order to take advantage of the opportunity to ride the remaining ten or twelve miles.

The train was interesting. It was pulled by a small, wood-burning engine which had a smoke stack that flared wildly at the top, and was covered with a screen. There were two boxcars and a combination passenger and baggage car. I was one of about a half dozen passengers. The train puffed slowly up the mountain. At one place it stopped in the woods. I got off with most of the other passengers to see what the trouble was. I was told that the engineer had seen a big snake. He and the fireman had stopped the train to kill it. Their mission accomplished, we reboarded the train and continued our journey.

Back at Marion I found Smith at our room. We were both discouraged. Neither of us had done well with our book selling and we were ready to give up. I had an aunt living at Konnarock, Virginia, about thirty miles south of Marion. She was Aunt Kate (Remine) Stonecifer. Her husband was Dr. "Ab" Stonecifer. He was the doctor for a big lumber company. I called Aunt Kate and asked her if we could visit her. She would be glad to have us, she said, so we decided to take a few days off for a visit to Konnarock.

Having no means of transportation, we decided to walk. We started early next day carrying a minimum of baggage in one of our sample cases. There were no settlements along our route, only widely scattered farm homes. The terrain was rolling and the closer to Konnarock we came the more mountainous it became.

We both began to feel hungry and thirsty about noon. We passed a large brick house in beautiful surroundings on a hill. A path led down to an idyllic scene that reminded me of James Whitcomb Riley's "under the cool green gloom of the willow tree. . .." We decided this would be a perfect place to get a good drink. Climbing a fence we hurried to the springhouse and found the cool clear water. I lay down to drink directly from the spring when Smith said "Wait, don't drink that." I turned to see what he had in mind. He was standing nearby with a half gallon crock of buttermilk in his hand. He had taken it from a trough through which water was running to keep milk, butter, and such foods cool. He turned the crock up and drank about half of it contents. He handed it to me and I finished it. Hunger, thirst, and the vigor of my youth made me think it was the best buttermilk I had ever tasted. Feeling guilty, we scrambled back over the fence and hurried down the road.

After we had gone about a mile farther we saw a potato patch near the road. There was house in sight. Smith said, "Why not get some potatoes for lunch?" We then climbed through the fence, and each dug two large potatoes. We took them up the side of the mountain away from the road to build a fire to roast our potatoes. On the way we encountered a flock of chickens in the woods. Smith said, "Let's get a chicken too." With that he picked up a stick, slipped up to the chickens, and threw the stick hitting a young rooster. The crippled chicken began squalling loudly and all the others started cackling. I yelled at him to catch the chicken quickly and choke it. He did, and with our prize in hand, we ran deeper into the woods.

We found a barren spot on the side of the mountain where we had a good view, and thinking we were safe, built a fire. We put the potatoes in the fire, and then began to prepare the chicken for barbecue. We had pocket knives but no water. Consequently, we each took a drumstick and thigh, and threw the rest of the chicken away. We then tried to cook our pieces over the fire without waiting for hot coals to form. We were a little impatient as we felt we should get on the road as soon as possible. The result of our cooking was a half cooked chicken leg that was flavored with pine tar from the smoke, and big potatoes cooked about one fourth of an inch deep, and raw in the middle. What a meal! Half cooked chicken and partly raw potatoes—without salt! Suffice it to say we didn't eat much. We extinguished our fire and struck out for Konnarock.

During this march my shoes became badly worn. The sole of my right shoe somehow broke loose from the upper and doubled back with each step. I could walk more comfortably by goose stepping along and flipping the shoe sole forward and slapping my foot on the ground.

We were soon in Konnarock and had no difficulty finding

Aunt Kate's house. She was glad to see us. She then told us that some girls living nearby had been told of our coming, and wanted us to come to their house for a party that night. I told Aunt Kate of my shoe problem. She said, "Maybe you could wear a pair of Ab's. If you can, I'm sure he would be glad to sell them to you." Sure enough the shoes fit perfectly. They were button shoes, but looked much better than mine.

That night we went to the party and found a congenial bunch of girls who were about our age. They were mostly daughters of officials in the local lumber company. They were primarily of Swedish descent with names such as Johnson, Magnuson, and Fargason. One girl (a student at Randolph Macon) was of Italian origin—Helena Fopiana. All went to college in Virginia. The hostess was a young married woman. She and her husband were charming people.

We had a great time at the party. Playing "500" was the principal activity. Fortunately, I had learned the game while living with Aunt Nannie in Knoxville. The girls were excited about their camping trip on top of White Top Mountain. They were leaving early the following morning. Our hostess for the evening and her husband, Mr. and Mrs. Bill Johnson, were to be the chaperones. There were very few young men in town who could go, and Mr. Johnson could stay only two days. All the girls insisted that Smith and I should go and spend the week with them. Why not? We had nothing else to do. Aunt Kate also urged us to go.

So next morning we headed for the 5,500 foot summit of old White Top. A wagon carried the provisions and the girls. Smith and I, however, were told how to go a more direct way on foot. Consequently, the wagon with the supplies and girls left early, while the two of us started a little later. We followed our directions and climbed the gentle slope, while we admired the wonderful scenery. We had no trouble until about noon in noting the land-marks we had been told about. A cloud then seemed to descend over the mountain and we soon found ourselves in a situation where the visibility was less than 100 yards. Our only guide to the cabin on top of the mountain was the knowledge that we must continue upward. Unfortunately, the cloud grew denser, the wind blew harder, and finally rain was added to the picture. We came upon a large treeless area. No land marks were to be seen anywhere in the dense cloud. Occasionally we'd stop for shelter under a large overhanging rock and discuss our situation. We knew the sun would be going down in a few hours and the prospect of spending the night lost on a mountain top in a cold rain, was beginning to occur to us. That prospect prompted us to push on, always upward.

As we came closer to the top of the mountain the wind seemed to blow harder and colder but the cloud was more dense. Just when we began to get concerned, we heard the laughter of girls. We yelled and to our great joy our cry was answered. With the visibility in the cloud only a few hundred feet we hurried toward the source of the reply. There, dimly outlined in the fog, was a cottage. Running toward it, we found the crowd waiting for us. I have never been happier to see friendly faces.

The girls took us to a big fire in the hearth where we got warm and dried our clothes. As Mr. Johnson had just left, driving the wagon back to town, Smith and I were the only men in the group. Mrs. Johnson was the chaperone. We were soon put to work by the girls, cutting wood for the stove and the fireplace, disposing of any garbage which might accumulate, and other odd jobs about the place.

The cottage, belonging to the lumber company in Konnarock, had been built several years earlier for recreational purposes. It had a large room on each side of a hallway that ran down the center of the structure. A chimney and fireplace were at one end of the hallway while the kitchen was situated in the back of the building. Arrangements were made for us to sleep on one side of the hall and the women on the other.

The weather after that first day was ideal. The girls were extraordinarily congenial and about as fine a bunch as I have ever known. We played games they had brought, laughed and sang, and just loafed. I could not imagine a more pleasant experience than lying on a big rock in the sun on top of a mountain surrounded by indescribably beautiful scenery. We enjoyed this bliss for five days. I have often wished I could find a place like the summit of White Top Mountain for my vacations. The fact that there was no traffic, no commercial development, no noise of commerce, no crowds of people, no dust, no fumes of automobile exhaust, made such a

"Smith and Mr. Johnson rode the horses down, while the rest of us walked, each carrying small bags or packages."

situation ideal. I felt like Peter must have felt when he wanted to stay on the Mount of Transfiguration.

But all good things come to an end. When the time came to go, Mr. Johnson brought horses up and began packing. Smith and Mr. Johnson rode the horses down, while the rest of us walked, each carrying small bags or packages. Even the walk down the mountain was fun, but at the same time, it was tinged with sadness when we realized the friendships we had enjoyed were soon to end.

When we got back to Aunt Kate's, Uncle Ab was at home. When Aunt Kate asked him if he would sell me the shoes I had been wearing he seemed indignant. "Sell them, nothing," he said, "I'll give them to him."

Uncle Ab (Dr. Stonecifer) was interested in the fact that Smith and I were planning to study medicine. He talked to us and told of some of his experiences as a student and as a practicing physician. Our conversation with him made me all the more interested in pursuing my plan to study medicine.

As was the custom in many small towns a picture show came once a week to Konnarock. It happened that a movie was being shown the night we came down from the mountain. Aunt Kate asked me if I wanted to go and take one of the girls. I told her yes, but I had no money. She said she would let me have a dollar. I then called Effie Magnuson, and made a date with her. She was the first girl I had ever taken to a movie. We enjoyed a good show. I took her home (a short walk up the hill), told her goodbye, and got her promise to write me.

Next morning Smith and I headed back to Marion, refreshed by the best vacation either of us had ever had. Our return trip was uneventful. In Marion we decided that since summer was drawing to a close it would soon be time to deliver the books for which we had taken orders. We therefore ordered them and prepared for delivery.

We then went back to Wytheville where we each hired a horse and buggy and proceeded to deliver the books. It didn't take us long to go over the area we had canvassed, for we stopped only at the houses where we had sold books. I was disappointed in a good many places, for the people who had ordered books were unable to take them when they were delivered. To make matters worse, we had to pay express both ways on books we ordered but could not deliver. After three or four days in Wytheville we moved on to Marion and delivered the books in Smythe County. We encountered the same problem there. Several families which had ordered books refused to take them when they were delivered.

Smith went on to Knoxville but I decided to visit Limestome on my way back. Altogether the summer, while filled with both pleasant and unpleasant experiences, was not a very profitable one for me. When I reached Knoxville I reckoned my summer's earnings amounted to paying my expenses, the cost of a new suit of clothes, a pair of shoes, and seven dollars left over. I was fortunate to have my job at the drug store waiting on me.

Stopping off at Limestone I visited Aunt Annie, Aunt Birdie (mama's sisters), Grandma Remine and Uncle Schuyler Remine. Aunt Kate from Konnarock was visiting Aunt Annie when I got there. When she saw me she asked me when I was going to pay her the dollar she had loaned me. If I hadn't had a cent more I would have paid her. I paid her the dollar and thanked her for loaning it to me.

I saw a number of my old childhood friends in Limestone and enjoyed my visit there very much. I also stopped off at Bulls Gap for a short visit with Blanche and Russell. In Knoxville I stayed with Aunt Nannie for a week or so until I could move into the dormitory again.

VII

Oklahoma!

When I moved into Reese Hall my room was on the third floor. My roommate was John Hart of Franklin, Tennessee. John was also a premed student, and he and I had much in common. I liked him very much, however, our schedules conflicted. He had a job delivering the morning paper, the Knoxville Journal, and got up at 4:00 a.m. to make his route. On the other hand, I came in from the drug store at eleven thirty at night or later, and frequently had to study after I got back. These schedules resulted in our disturbing one another's sleep. We each tried to be as considerate of the other as possible and managed to have few quarrels.

Reese Hall was divided by partitions into a north and south section. The only way to get from one to the other was by going outside and walking around to the door at the other end of the building. There was only one bathroom on each end and that was on the ground floor. When we took a shower we had to go down to the first floor. Neither Hart nor I had bath robes or house slippers, so that when we took a shower we would strip in our room, put on a raincoat and shoes, run down to the first floor for our shower and take our soap and towel with us. After the shower we would come clomping back in our raincoats to our room on the third floor. We didn't feel bad about using them for bath robes, as there were several others who had the same problem.

During my second year as a premed student I took the following subjects: Zoology III and IV, German II, Psychology, Organic Chemistry, and Physics. All of my professors were superb. Zoology was taught by Professor Schaeffer, of German extraction. He had such a pleasant method of teaching that zoology was easy to learn. His lectures were well-organized and he had a way of making

89

the laboratory work very interesting. Professor Darnell taught German. He had a great sense of humor and frequently told German jokes. It was said that when war broke out in 1914 that he had a hard time getting out of Germany to come back to America, for he spoke the language so perfectly that the Germans couldn't believe he was an American.

Dr. Frost taught Psychology. He had a most effective plan for getting us to learn his subject. On entering the class every session the student found on his desk a yellow, blank sheet of paper. Dr. Frost would write a question on the board and give us five minutes to answer it. This question might be on the lesson of the day, on the lesson of the last period, or on anything previously covered. That meant that we had not only to study the lesson for the day, but we had to review quickly anything we had had previously. This system resulted in my being ready for the final examination. Psychology was one course for which I didn't have to "cram" before the examination.

Physics was easy for me. We used the same textbook I had used in my Kansas high school. One morning in chapel (which we had every day), Dean Hoskins warned that he had heard some students were repeating courses they had taken in other schools. He announced that they would not get credit for that subject at the University of Tennessee. This worried me since I was taking the same physics I had in high school. I went to the Dean's office and told him I had heard his statement. I told him I was using the same text. He told me he was sure I was getting better laboratory work. When I told him I thought my high school laboratory work was about as good as I was getting at U.T. he smiled and said, "Well, young man, that was high school physics. You are now taking college physics." My final grade in physics in the spring was ninety-eight.

Professor Hill made Organic Chemistry interesting and I had no trouble at all. He was an excellent teacher. I have been fortunate. With very few exceptions the teachers I had in high school and college were unusually good.

My second year at the university was particularly pleasant. I made many friends even though I had no time for social affairs. John Hart was a good roommate. We had lots in common, socially, economically and philosophically. He was a Presbyterian, but neither of us had a chance to go to church. Moreover, 1916 was a great year for the University of Tennessee in football in spite of the fact that only twenty-two men came out for football that fall, U.T. won the Southeastern conference championship. "Chief" Bender, the coach, made repeated appeals in the chapel for men to come out for football. One boy, "Slob" Shofner, who had never seen a football game, became tackle. He was a big, husky, country boy who had the strength, weight, and agility necessary to become a star. Chief Bender even grabbed me by the arm one day and said, "You big Swede, why don't you come out for football?" I would have liked to but I had to work. In those days there was no such things as athletic scholarships.

During the two years I was at the university I got to see only two games. Both were on Thanksgiving Day. I didn't have to work on Thursdays. Football was then played on Wait field off of Cumberland Avenue on the old west side of the campus. A high iron fence which ran along Cumberland Avenue was draped with a long tarpaulin during games so non-paying fans would be unable to see from the sidewalk. The bleachers on each side of the field were wooden with no more than twenty rows of seats running considerably less than the full length of the field. Only two or three hundred fans could be accommodated. Each time I saw a game, I was able to get a job ushering, so I didn't have to pay for admission.

When football season was over, the tarpaulin was kept in a large empty room in Reese Hall. We spread it out so that it covered the whole floor. It was still folded over several times, however, so that it made a good mat for wrestling and gymnastics. We boxed, wrestled, and did gymnastics in this room. The college Y.M.C.A. building had a swimming pool and gymnasium which we could use.

The university had teams in basketball, track, and baseball but none was as popular as football. College yells and songs were practiced, and rallies were held before each game. The entire enrollment of the University at the time was only 700, but these rallies developed considerable enthusiasm.

After school had started in September of 1916, I received a telegram telling me of the death of my sister, Lucy. She was only twenty-two years old. She died in Topeka, Kansas, where she had been a patient in the Kansas State Psychiatric Hospital. She had been sent there because of severe and prolonged depression. Lucy had always been depressed because of her frustrated ambitions. She never had the opportunity to accomplish her aims. She finally developed tuberculosis of the lungs in the hospital, and died within a few months. I was greatly saddened by her death, and because I could not go to Kansas to her funeral. I especially felt bad because I had not been able to help this lovely, talented girl achieve her goals.

At this time my brother James was working in Iowa, and Kathleen had married Fred Judd. They were living in Miami, Oklahoma, where Fred and his brother, Floyd, were running the Judd Brothers Motor Company, dealers for Maxwell automobiles.

In the spring of 1917 the war in Europe began to take a serious turn for the United States as German U-boats continued sinking American ships, and Wilson's attempt to keep us out of war appeared to become more hopeless. War was finally declared against Germany and her allies. Much excitement was engendered among the students. Military training was required at U.T. for all male students except those in pre-med and law. I am not sure why they were exempt. Many volunteered, and those that had commissions in the cadets were given special consideration by the army. The university gave full credit to those enlisting for the courses cut short by their leaving to enter military service in late April and beyond. The president of U.T., the Dean of the Medical School and the Army and Navy medical authorities wrote pre-meds urging us to continue our studies. Doctors, we were told, were badly needed in the military and we would be worth more if we continued our study. All of us, however, had to register for the draft.

A few weeks before school was out one of my friends in the dormitory, George Paulk, from Savannah, Tennessee, came to my room one evening. He was very depressed, almost to the point of tears. He told me that his father had a farm and a cotton gin in Hardin County. He had sent George to the university for four years at considerable sacrifice. George's father had never been to college and therefore didn't know how to advise George as to what courses he should take. George didn't know either, so he took a straight liberal arts course, with a major in Greek.

George told me, "Here I am about to graduate. My father will expect me to help him on the farm when I get back, but I know less about farming than I did when I left. I should have studied agriculture instead of Greek. You knew what you were preparing yourself for—I didn't." Years later, after I had received my M.D. degree and was practicing medicine in Memphis, I saw George. He told me he was raising hogs on his father's farm, and was doing well. I did not ask him what he had done with his Greek. I think George's story is a good lesson in the importance of having a goal and driving toward it with a purposeful plan.

I became twenty–one years old in December of 1916, and Kathleen was eighteen. Our birthdays meant we were of age and therefore our farm could be sold. Accordingly, Uncle Maynard, our guardian, sold it to settle our father's estate. My one fifth share of the estate came to $1,000. This money was sent to me in the spring of 1917. I deposited it in a bank and was careful to spend as little of it as possible, for I knew I would need more than that to get through school. A short time later I received an additional $300 from the sale of our home in Limestone.

About that time Fred Judd, Kathleen's husband, wrote and asked me to come to Oklahoma and work with the Judd Brothers Motor Company. He told me I could sell Maxwells. I had never even driven a car but somehow his offer was challenging, and I decided to accept it.

When school was out I went to Bulls Gap for a short visit with Blanche and then boarded the train for Miami, Oklahoma. This time I went first class and rode in a Pullman. I had to lay over several hours in Memphis, and so I got in touch with Bill Whitehead. Bill, a classmate of mine at the university, also planned to attend the University of Tennessee College of Medicine. He and I went over to look at the Medical School. We visited the anatomy laboratory where we saw "Gillis," the black technician, embalming "stiffs." It was an eye-opener for us to see several human corpses hanging by ice tong-like clamps in their ears, and being infused by a formaldehyde embalming solution. He opened a large vat and we were shown a number of already embalmed bodies lying like so much cordwood in a solution containing formaldehyde. In those days bodies were easily obtained for dissection. Instead of being repulsive to me the whole affair made me more eager to get in medical school.

After the visit with Whitehead, I returned to the station and caught the "Frisco" train toward Oklahoma. The trip was interesting since I was traveling over territory I had not seen before. I changed cars at Fort Scott, Kansas, and then caught a train going south to Miami in the northeast corner of the state. Miami was the county seat of Ottoway County, Oklahoma, the greater part of which was Indian land that could be leased but not sold. The terrain was flat, with no hills. Kathleen and Fred met me at the station and I was taken to their home where Fred's father and mother lived with them and their son, Billy, who was two years of age.

The first activity on my program was to learn to drive a car. Fred took me out to the edge of town where there was very little traffic and in a short time I was driving with no difficulty. He had me drive back home. We got Kathleen, and with her and Fred in the back seat, I drove to Commerce, a little town about five miles north. I had a thrill driving the automobile, and made the trip to Commerce and back with no trouble at all.

To sell cars, as with anything else, the salesman must know the product. I can still recall that the Maxwell automobile had a Sims–Huff generator and starter, Atwater–Kent ignition system, demountable rims (an innovation in 1917) and Mason tires with a 3,000 mile guarantee against blowout. Maxwells were mostly touring cars, or roadsters. Both had tops which could be put down and canvas curtains which could be rolled down in rainy weather. The touring cars were priced at only $715.00. Coupes and Sedans, however, were just being put on the market and were more expensive. I got thirty–five dollars commission for every new touring car I sold, or five percent of the price we got for used cars.

Just north of Miami was a large lead and zinc field with many mines in operation. Commerce, Pitcher, Tarwater, and Quawpaw were sizeable communities built around mining. The miners, getting good wages, were prospects for buying cars. I made it a practice to be around one of the mines at quitting time. I would offer miners rides to their homes and during the trip try to convince them that they could afford a Maxwell. I sold four cars the first week I worked. That was the most money I had ever made in one week.

Then came a one month period when I didn't make a sale. Although I was living with Kathleen, who would not let me pay for my room and board, I could not help being depressed. I was told such periods of inactivity were not uncommon and should be expected. I finally sold a sedan on the condition that I would drive it to Webb City, Missouri, to take the buyer and his family to visit relatives. Since the sedan sold for $1,200 and my commission was five percent, I made a good deal. Besides, the trip to Webb City was only about forty miles.

I sold a car once and took in a cow and a calf on the deal. I delivered the car to Quawpaw and led the cow back on foot ten miles to Miami. I was able to sell the cow for a slight profit a few days later.

There are many Indians in that part of Oklahoma. We often visited and enjoyed their dances and festivities. They owned the land and received royalties on the lead and zinc obtained from the mines. This resulted in many of the Indians becoming very wealthy. I met a young Indian on the street of Miami one day and after I told him about the advantages of owning a Maxwell, he told me to come to his house the following day and he might buy one. He then gave me specific directions to his home.

The following day I went and found it on the prairie fully a mile from any other house. It was a plain, unpainted, frame house. There were no screens on windows or doors. An old Indian woman came to the door when I knocked. I noticed the living room floor was bare and somewhat rough. The furniture was of the cheapest kind, and there was apparently no attempt on the part of the occupants of the house to furnish it with any but bare necessities. The old lady told me her son had gone to Joplin, about 30 miles from there, but he was expected to return within the hour.

Anxious to make the sale, I decided to wait. I drove my car about fifty yards from the house and parked it in the shade of a little cottonwood tree, the only tree within a half mile of the house. There I sat in the boiling sun, moving my car as the shade moved. After about an hour I saw a cloud of dust about a mile away which

was made by a rapidly approaching car. As it approached I could
see it was a wire-wheeled sports model "Pathfinder," which I knew
cost $3,500. My Indian friend got out of it, smiling proudly, telling
me that he had seen it in Joplin and decided to buy it. I asked him if
he could pay $3,500 for a car why he even considered a Maxwell
which sold for $715. He told me that the price didn't matter as he
liked the looks of the Pathfinder.

One day I was visiting with the Buick dealer a few blocks down
the street. We were discussing the automobile business in general,
and nothing in particular, when an old Indian man with a braid of
hair hanging down on his chest from each side of his head and
wearing a broad brimmed hat, came in. My friend approached him
and said, "Could I do anything for you?" The old Indian said,
"Want to buy automobile." The salesman asked, "What kind do you
want?" The Indian walked slowly around looking at each car in the
salesroom. He soon stopped in front of a gray, wire wheeled sedan.
He stood there a few minutes and said, "I'll take this one." When
the salesman asked him when he wanted it he said, "Now. How
much it cost?" When the salesman told him $2,000 the old Indian
pulled out a roll of bills from his pocket, and slowly counted out the
exact amount. Then telling the salesman his son would be by to pick
it up soon, he left. I watched as he walked about a block down the
street and sat down on the sidewalk with feet in the gutter by the
side of an old Indian woman who had been waiting for him there.

The salesman said he never made a sale so easily. He got the
car serviced quickly to take out. In about thirty minutes, a sportily
dressed, good looking, young Indian came in, got in the car, and
drove off. The young man then stopped by the old couple sitting
on the sidewalk, let them get in, and took off at high speed toward
the country.

Judd Brothers had a service garage on Main Street, but our
salesroom was on A street N.E., several blocks away. One day while
my demonstrator was being greased and serviced, the shop manager asked if I would be kind enough to drive a "Model T" Ford
they had just finished repairing around to the salesroom. I had
never driven a Ford before, and in those days the clutch, brakes,
and reverse pedals were entirely different from Maxwells and
other cars. I was shown how to manage it, the motor was cranked,

and I was off. I did fairly well until I got to Main and Central, where there was a traffic jam. Being unaccustomed to driving a Ford, I put on the brake too soon and killed the engine. There I was in the middle of a busy street with a car that wouldn't run. I got out to crank it, hoping I could get it going again, when a large, burly Oklahoma highway patrolman seized me by the arm and said, "Consider yourself under arrest!" I said, "What for? I couldn't keep the engine from dying." "For driving a motor vehicle on public thoroughfare without a license tag," he said.

I looked and discovered to my dismay that the car had no license tags on it. I asked him to help me push the car to the curb to get it off the street, and told him how I happened to be driving it. He helped me park it, and then took me around to the Judd Brothers office to verify my story. We found Lloyd Judd and I was quickly released.

Zinc and lead mining was booming in Oklahoma during World War I. All the mines were going full tilt and thousands of men were employed. Housing was a difficult problem. Many people were living in tents and shacks, while some were doubling up with two or more families in one small house. We found that a house made of rough lumber containing only three or four rooms could be built for $200 and would rent for $20 a month.

A lawyer, the president of the bank, Lloyd Judd, and one or two others (knowing there would be no difficulty in renting them) had the idea that much money could be made by building a group of cheap houses near the mines. I was persuaded to join the group. It seemed to be a good way to get an income even while I was in school. I knew I didn't have enough money to pay all my expenses while in medical school.

Consequently, we formed a corporation which was called The Strain-Judd Investment Corporation. We each put up $500 which represented the down payment on lumber, brick, and other building materials, and the lease on some land on the prairie not far from Pitcher. We started at once on the construction of fifty small residences, a building which would serve as a commissary, and a small school house. We named the town we were building Maxwell, Oklahoma.

It was a thrilling experience for me to watch our buildings

grow and to feel that the investment I had made would put me through college. It was not evident until late fall, however, that the demand for lead and zinc had diminished to such an extent that mining activities came to a halt. Employees were laid off by the hundreds, and people began leaving the area by droves. The demand for housing decreased until there were more vacant dwellings than there had been for years.

The result was that almost before our housing development had been completed, there was no longer need for it. We were therefore unable to keep up the payments on our loan. The lumber company foreclosed on our mortgage, and our entire investment was lost. I found all this out after being back in medical school several months. Meanwhile I went about my work proud that I was a stockholder in a "big" corporation.

I averaged about a sale per week the rest of the summer, so that I felt that my career as an automobile salesman was not entirely a failure. A young red haired lady, whose name was Mary Turner, was the stenographer in the Judd Brothers Motor Company. I had several dates with her and enjoyed her company. We met several other young people and often formed a group to go on picnics or to the open air show at Commerce.

On July 4, 1917, we went for a picnic on the Neshoba river not far from Miami. It was hot and sunny, a delightful day to be outdoors. We got to the site of the picnic about 10:00 a.m. We immediately got into our bathing suits and went into the river. It was a clear, beautiful stream with shoals near our picnic grounds. We had such a good time swimming that we kept our bathing suits on all day. I then learned a lesson I have never forgotten. I looked like a boiled lobster before bedtime. I was so badly sunburned over my whole skin area, except that covered by the swim trunks, that I actually became ill. I had fever for two or three days and my back and shoulders were so sore and tender that it was painful to wear a shirt or even to lie down.

I went to church fairly regularly while in Miami. The office manager of our firm, who had a good tenor voice, led the singing in the Methodist church. The choir was small, but excellent. I enjoyed the sermons and felt good singing hymns again. The desire to participate in religious activity had not left me.

During the summer Kathleen, Fred, and I drove up to

Wellington, Kansas. Fred had relatives there, and of course Kathleen and I wanted to visit Jennie. The distance was about 200 miles over dirt or gravel roads. Roads were not marked in those days, but a dealer in tires and other automobile accessories in Wichita had marked roads leading to Wichita. It was called the "Hockaday Highway." This marking made it easy for us to find our way to Wellington.

As the summer drew to a close I prepared to return to Tennessee. Since I had sold about 15 cars my summer had been moderately successful. My earnings certainly amounted to much more than those of the previous summer. By this time, however, I had decided that selling on commission was not for me. I returned to Tennessee, however, with enough money to take care of my expenses for my first year in medical college. I therefore left Miami for Tennessee so that I could carry out my plans for entering the University of Tennessee College of Medicine in the fall. The trip home was by the way of Springfield, Missouri. I had a wait of about three hours between trains in Springfield. There was a vaudeville theater not far from the railroad station. Here was a good place to wait for the train, I thought, so I bought a ticket and went in. The entire show was good, but standing out in my memory was the act in which a boy and girl dressed in typical country clothes danced and sang "Good–bye maw, good–bye paw, good–bye mule with your old hee haw."

After arriving in Memphis, I planned to continue my trip to East Tennessee. I also wanted to visit my brother James who was at Camp John Sevier, Charlotte, North Carolina. He was expecting to be sent overseas any day. At the Memphis Union Station I bought a "mileage" book (1,000 miles for twenty dollars), that would take care of most of my trip to North Carolina and back to Memphis. I then obtained a ticket to Bulls Gap for a visit with Blanche, and then to Wytheville, Virginia.

I had been carrying on a brisk correspondence with Winnie BeCraft since I left Wytheville and was anxious to see her before going to live in Memphis. She was the first girl with whom I had ever fallen in love. She was pretty, had a very pleasing personality, and a fine sense of humor. Her mother was not living and she and her sister lived with their father and kept house for him.

I spent two days in Wytheville, staying in a little hotel there. I spent much time with Winnie. One day she and I went with her sister and her brother-in-law, who was a veterinarian, to a farm near Galax, Virginia, on the New River where the doctor had been called to treat some cows.

On the evening I was to leave Wytheville, I promised to write often and told her I would see her again as soon as I could. We sat in a porch swing and talked until my train was due near midnight. When my train was nearly due and I had to leave, I managed to muster up enough courage to put my arm around her. She responded and I kissed her on the cheek. She hugged me and kissed me in return. We were standing at the time. The first time a girl kissed me or showed me any kind of affection was more than I could take. I suddenly felt myself growing faint and, as odd as it may sound in these days, I would have fainted completely if I had not sat down quickly and put my head between my knees. I apologized for being so silly but she was very kind and did not laugh at me. I kissed her goodnight and hurried to catch my train.

I went on to Charlotte and to Camp John Sevier. I had no trouble finding James. I did feel, however, very conspicuous among all the soldiers since I was the only person who was wearing civilian clothes. I passed a detail of prisoners working on camp streets. They hurled all sorts of insults at me as I went by. I ignored them without a reply, but felt guilty because I, too, wasn't in military service. In James' tent several of his tent mates took turns posing with my straw hat. They seemed to be a congenial bunch of fellows.

James had been in the 114th Field Artillery but when he had heard that a newly organized unit, the motor mechanics regiment, was going to France shortly, he asked to be transferred to that outfit. He was transferred but instead of going to France, his regiment was sent to Charlotte to establish a new camp in the near-by woods. Cutting timber, making streets, building roads and general facilities for a large camp kept them busy long after the 114th Field Artillery had sailed for overseas duty.

James got a pass and we went downtown together. I felt every eye watching me, a healthy young man without a uniform. We went to a movie and saw "Over There." This was a movie that had been made to stir up sentiment about the important role the United

"I did feel, however, very conspicuous among all the soldiers since I was the only person who was wearing civilian clothes."

States was playing in the war, and how noble the American soldiers were. The picture was very effective in generating patriotism in the heart of every American.

As we came out of the show I told James that I was tired going around in civilian clothes when all other young men were in uniform, and I believed I would go back and apply for active duty in the Navy. James stopped, turned around, grabbed me by the shoulders, and said emphatically, "You'll do nothing of the kind! You are where Uncle Sam wants you and you stay there. Besides this man's army isn't all that it's cracked up to be." I thought it over and decided to take his advice. I would remain in the USNRF (U.S. Naval Reserved Force) as long as the government wanted.

I returned to Knoxville and headed toward Memphis after my visit with James. I met Jim Hall from Clinton, Tennessee, on the train, the "Memphis Special." Jim had been a pre-med student a year ahead of me at the university, and had gone to the medical school in Memphis while I was a sophomore at Knoxville. I didn't know him well previously, but on our way to Memphis I found him to be a very likeable fellow. He suggested that we room together when we got to Memphis. His suggestion appealed to me since he was a sophomore in medical school and I would be a freshman. I felt sure he would be of some help to me. This arrangement resulted in my finding one of the best friends I ever had. It was a friendship which continued through the years until his death in 1970.

VIII

Medical School

On arriving in Memphis, Jim and I put our baggage in lockers at the station and caught a street car to the medical school. We knew that there were some boarding houses on Madison Avenue near the school, so we set out to find one. We walked about two blocks and stopped at a house at 1009 Madison Avenue. We told the lady who answered the door (Mrs. Craik) what we were seeking. She told us that she had two or three rooms she usually rented to medical students and served three meals a day. She showed us the rooms and we found them suitable. We went back to the station for our baggage, pleased to have quickly found the quarters we were seeking. The room and three meals daily were thirty dollars a month. Jim was six feet four inches tall and I was six one, but we had no qualms about sleeping together in the double bed available. Shortly afterwards, Charles Potts, a freshman, and Everett Archer, a sophomore, took adjoining rooms.

I was at last in medical school. I can never forget the first class I had. It was Embryology. Dr. O. W. Hyman was the teacher. As I sat listening to my first lecture I could not help being thrilled with the idea that I was starting on a career that only a short time before had seemed to be an impossible dream. Dr. Hyman proved to be my ideal of what a good teacher should be. He made his subject so interesting and so plain that with a little application any student could learn.

Anatomy was another subject that was taught in a similarly effective fashion. The professor was Dr. A. H. Wittenborg. The big book that we had to study, *Gray's Anatomy,* and the box of human bones we were given to carry home gave us a distinct understanding that we had a lot to learn. Dr. Hyman and Dr. Wittenborg both

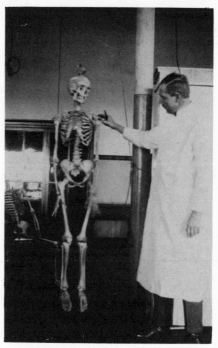

"The professor was Dr. A. H. Wittenborg."

became my close friends. Over the years to follow, they had a great
influence over my life and were the source of much help and
encouragement for me.

The freshman class of 1917 was twenty–eight in number.
Several of my pre-med classmates from Knoxville were among
them. There were also a few from various parts of the state and
surrounding area. Many of these students became my lifelong
friends. After a few weeks of school we felt that it was wise to
organize the class. A meeting was held for this purpose and to my
surprise I was elected president. That experience gave a boost to
my spirit and helped me to overcome the inferiority complex that
had plagued me so long.

During the first semester we had no classes on Wednesday
afternoons. Bill Whitehead, whose home was in Memphis and who

had been one of my Knoxville classmates, and I decided to get some recreation by attending the Orpheum Theater matinee on Wednesdays. For twenty–eight cents (three cents was war tax) we could get a reserved seat in the balcony. The Orpheum was primarily a vaudeville theater at that time, and featured the Keith Orpheum circuit. We could be found every Wednesday afternoon for the rest of the semester up in the balcony at the Orpheum where we saw the best of vaudeville. Many of the performers would later become famous in radio and T.V.

Medical school proved to be no harder than other college work except that there was much more of it. We commonly expressed the age-old complaint of students everywhere: each professor assigned us work as if he thought his was the only course we were taking. It seemed as if we never had enough time to study everything assigned. I found it necessary occasionally to get away from the constant grind. I could retain more if I rested mentally. I joined the Y.M.C.A. and often after being in school all day, would hurry down to the "Y," play handball, and take a plunge in the pool before supper. I found my mind much clearer afterward.

Memphis had a baseball team called the Chickasaws in the Southern League. The ball field was on Madison Avenue near the school across the street from the Baptist Hospital. It was called Russwood Park. After the seventh inning the gates were opened and anyone was allowed in without charge. We called it The University Hour, because there was usually a group of medical students waiting to rush in when the gates were opened. We could go to choice seats in the grandstand and see the last few innings of the game. If the score was tied, we frequently got to see several extra innings.

Medical school routine was very exacting, but a little recreation was necessary to enable the student to keep an ability to study. In talking about money spent for entertainment and recreation, Jim Hall used to say, "Unnecessary expenses are necessary."

Constant study was required to keep up with our school work. We were kept busy by classwork and laboratory exercises in anatomy, pharmacology, embryology, histology and chemistry. If we were absent for only a day or so from classes, we risked getting so far behind that we would have great difficulty in catching up. Dr.

Wittenborg made it a practice to have a written quiz on Monday or on the first day after a holiday. He said we could use the time we were out of school preparing for it. That meant we had to work harder on holidays and Sundays.

There were three medical fraternities in our school: AKK, Phi Chi and Chi Zeta Chi. Most of us were given bids to one or all three of them. I favored Chi Zeta Chi, because its members seemed to be more my type. In addition, my roommate, Jim Hall, belonged. Consequently, I joined Chi Zeta Chi.

The fraternity was strictly Southern. It was founded in Atlanta and had only eleven chapters. Several years after I finished school, it merged with a much larger national medical fraternity, Phi Rho Sigma. While we felt a little closer to our fraternity brothers, many members of the other fraternities were just as good friends. Being members of different fraternities made very little difference in our attitudes toward one another. The common bond of our professional interests and ambitions was much stronger.

At Christmas time we had a two week holiday. Through Bill Mims, a classmate whose home was in Memphis, I got a job in the mail order department of the Brodnax Jewelry store. We began December 3rd working whenever we could in the evening until midnight, and on Saturdays and Sundays. We were paid thirty-five cents an hour, which was not too bad in those days. When school was out, about a week before Christmas, we worked full time from about 8:00 a.m. until midnight. My job consisted of filling orders for all the things Brodnax sold and lasted until Christmas eve.

After Christmas Lloyd Judd asked me to come to Miami, Oklahoma, to be the best man in his wedding. Lloyd was being married to Blanche Crank whose father was a prominent lawyer in Miami. He sent me money for traveling expenses. I went downtown, rented a full dress suit, and bought a round-trip ticket for Miami. I got there in time to attend a "tea" or two and the rehearsal. I remember Lloyd getting "cold feet" about his marriage. He said to me at the rehearsal, "I wish Uncle Sam would draft me tonight." That was about a day before the wedding. However, the ceremony went off smoothly. The bride was beautiful. I felt like a dude in that formal suit with its long tails and white tie. That was the first and only time I ever wore a suit like that. Since then on formal occasions I have worn a tuxedo many times.

After the wedding a reception was held at the home of the bride. Lloyd's parents were old and they asked to be taken home immediately after the wedding. I agreed to take them. All the others went to Blanche's house. By the time I drove across town to take the elder Judds home and got back to the Crank home, all the guests had been served ice cream and cake. They were sitting around finishing their refreshments or holding empty plates when I entered. On seeing me empty handed, Blanche, the bride, came up to me and said, "Fred, wouldn't you like to have some more ice cream." I was timid in those days. I thought if I said yes, the guests would think I was a pig; if I said I had not yet had any, Blanche might be embarrassed. I merely said, "No thank you." Since then I have avoided asking guests at my house if he or she wanted any more of anything!

I learned of the failure of the Judd-Strain Investment Corporation while in Miami. I left for Memphis knowing I had enough money to finish my freshman year in medicine, but wondered what I would do for the next three years. I knew of no one from whom I could borrow. James was in the army and could not help me; Russell was unable to help, and Henry was deeply in debt buying a farm and farming equipment. I was determined to continue school for the year and prayed that somehow I could find a way. I knew that if I dropped out of medical school I would be called into active military service at once. I said nothing about the situation but continued working harder with my studies.

The chairman of the university committee on degrees was Dr. Darnell, my German professor at Knoxville. I talked to Dr. Wittenborg about my taking some extracurricular work in German to eliminate the other condition that was required before I could earn a degree. Dr. Wittenborg said he would be glad to help. I wrote Dr. Darnell and he agreed, giving me permission to take the work under Dr. Wittenborg's guidance.

I was then given a book, *Haut Krankheiten* (Skin Diseases), by Dr. Wittenborg, and instructed to read one chapter and report to him two days later. I had no difficulty with the assignment and Dr.

Wittenborg was satisfied with my recitation. He then told me that the best way to learn a language was to hear it spoken and used. He told me to come to his house the following Sunday morning and to be prepared to spend the day.

On arriving, I found Dr. Wittenborg's sister, his son and daughter (eight and twelve years of age respectively), and the maid, a young German lady who spoke very little English. Dr. Wittenborg told the family in German that there was to be no English spoken while I was there. I stayed all day long, through two meals, and during that time did not hear a word of English. I was shown through the garden, told about the vegetables and flowers there, told about the food served at both meals, and had the tableware and furniture pointed out, all in German. I soon agreed with Dr. Wittenborg: one learns a language fast in such a situation. I must admit, though, that on leaving for my room that evening I was glad to hear the English language again.

Dr. Wittenborg was kind enough to have me in his home several times, and on one occasion he took me to visit some of his German friends where no English was spoken. I recall that lentil soup was served at a Mr. Katzen's home. Dr. Wittenborg and all his family and friends seemed to enjoy helping me to learn German. After several weeks of such study he wrote Dr. Darnell that I had done sufficient work to entitle me to credit for the condition I had to get off in order to graduate. I was greatly relieved. My admiration and affection for Dr. Wittenborg continued all through my career as a medical student, and for years afterward.

As the school year drew to a close I had to decide what I would do for the summer of 1918. Lloyd Judd had joined the army, and the Judd Brothers Motor Company had gone out of business. Fred Judd, however, insisted that I return to Miami and work with him as a mechanic's helper in his garage. He promised me twenty–five dollars a week, and that was about as well as I could do anywhere else, especially when Kathleen promised me free room and board.

So I decided to go back to Oklahoma and become a mechanic, working on Model-T Fords. I soon became an expert at taking care of the ignition system and carburetor on them. The whole car was simplicity itself, having no battery, generator, or starter and being started by cranking. A magneto furnished the spark so that the engine would run. There is no comparison with the complex modern motor and its generator, starter, air conditioner, heater, windshield wiper, power brakes and steering, and automatic transmission. I certainly could not qualify as an automobile mechanic today!

Business was rather slow. Fred was not as good a businessman as his brother Lloyd. We continued for a few weeks and it was obvious that the work I was doing would not last all summer. Fred made a deal, however, with a partner in a little grocery store in Treece, Kansas, just over the line from Picher, Oklahoma. The man then failed to meet his obligation, and Fred foreclosed on the mortgage on his half interest in the store. Consequently, I was sent up to Treece to become the manager of the South Side Grocery and Meat Market.

I then got some experience in the buying and selling of groceries. The old gentleman who was the other partner stayed on, but primarily as a meat cutter and supervisor of the meat market. It was an interesting experience. I enjoyed meeting the people in the little town. Besides these customers, the salesmen for the various commodities we sold came regularly to take orders and discuss the grocery business in general. I lived in a little room in the back of the store and ate at a restaurant nearby. Fred let me use a "Model–T" Ford roadster so I could go to Miami on weekends.

After about a month of managing the grocery store, Fred sold his share to the other partner and I went back to Miami. Work was slack and I decided to go to Kansas to work on Henry Greene's farm. Wheat harvest was over but there was plenty of work to be done. Consequently, I left Miami for Kansas.

Henry had left the farm near Wellington and was farming a quarter of a section near Belle Plain, Kansas, about fifteen miles from Wellington. He was glad to see me for he was in need of a farm hand. It was time to start plowing for winter wheat. By now Henry had a large Aultman–Taylor kerosene tractor, with huge steel wheels. It could pull a four-furrow plow and do more ground in a day than we could with two four-horse teams. Moreover, we could plow longer hours, and at night when necessary. Such a schedule would have exhausted horses.

The Ninnescah River was only a quarter of a mile from the

farm on which I was working, and was a convenient place to take a good bath and swim after a day's work on the farm. It was common for another farm hand and me to take advantage of this luxury in the warm twilight after supper.

While swimming one evening, I found what I thought was a rock at the bottom of the river in about four feet of water. I knew there were no rocks in that part of Kansas and began to investigate. By diving down and digging around the "rock," I was soon able to get it loose and bring it to the surface. I was surprised to find it was a large bone at least four feet long, and four to six inches in diameter. Its shape made me think it was the tibia of a huge animal, more than likely a mastodon.

We carried the bone to the house and put it an empty corn crib. Sunday morning we took pick and shovels with us and determined to explore for more evidence of the animal which had lain buried there. Carefully digging in the bottom of the river we found part of a huge tooth and many other bones.

I was sure we had found the remains of a mastodon. We brought all the bones we found and carefully stored them with the leg bone. I made a trip into Wellington and went to the professor of biology at the Sumner County High School. I told him of my find, but he showed very little interest in it. I thought he might want the bones for the High School museum but he was not interested.

I decided to write the University of Kansas, but somehow never did. It seemed everyone I told about it, including Henry, reacted by saying, "So what?" I made a mistake in failing to tell the newspaper. By the time I was ready to leave Kansas, I found the bones had dried out, and had crumbled to a shapeless pile, which Henry insisted on throwing out of the corn crib. A few years later I heard that a mastodon skeleton had been found not far from there on excavation for the construction of a grain elevator. The story was given considerable space in the newspaper, *The Wichita Eagle*.

After plowing was done on the Belle Plain farm Henry asked me and another farm hand to take the tractor to a farm near Wellington where more plowing was to be done. The distance to the Wellington farm by the regular highway through the town of Wellington was about fifteen miles. Because the weight of the tractor was too great for some of the bridges we had to cross, and because tractors with steel traction wheels were not allowed on asphalt pavement, a long, round about way had to be mapped out. By this devious route we would have to travel a little more than twenty miles. Since the top speed of the tractor was only four miles per hour we knew it would take the greater part of the day to make the trip.

Pulling behind us two wagons on which were loaded plows and other necessary equipment, Burt, the man who accompanied me, and I started out at about 6:00 a.m. I suggested that we take lunch and a jug of water but Henry said he would catch us around noon with something to eat and drink. I drove the tractor most of the way. The driver had to stand and steer by means of a wheel that had to be turned rapidly to wind up chains going to the left and right of the front axle.

The sun came up hot, and a constant hot wind blew over the Kansas plains. No cab covered us and all day we chugged along exposed to both the sun and the hot wind. Our progress was too slow to permit our stopping to rest. We couldn't go near a store or any establishment selling food or drink. Henry didn't get to us at noon. We kept looking for him and chugging on to our destination.

Henry didn't show up until 2:00 o'clock. By that time we were very hungry and thirsty. He apologized for being late saying that he had stayed in town longer than he intended. Henry did bring a large paper sack in which we found two hamburgers and a cold bottle of beer apiece. I had never drunk beer before, but as thirsty as I was, it "hit the spot." The hamburgers were also delicious. Kansas was a "dry" state and we were surprised that he was able to find beer at all. As much as I liked it, I have never drunk more than six bottles in my life.

We continued our journey feeling somewhat better and arrived at our destination around 5:00 p.m. after eleven hours in the hot Kansas sunshine and wind. We unloaded the wagons and had everything ready to start plowing next day. Henry came for us in his car and we returned with him to the Belle Plains farm. He was buying the farm on which we were planning to plow. It was a quarter of a section (160 acres) immediately west of the farm he was renting when I first went to Kansas. It was about four miles west of

Wellington and had formerly belonged to the Cann family. My work for the rest of the summer consisted of plowing and gathering corn.

I returned to Memphis knowing that I didn't have enough money to pay my expenses for my sophomore year. Somehow I knew I would be able to manage to work part-time or borrow from some friend or relative. The school also had a student loan fund.

Soon after school started, Dr. Hyman, who was acting-Dean, received orders that because of the war the reserves among us would be called into active duty in what was called the Student's Army Training Corps, SATC, (called by regular military men "the Saturday Afternoon Tea Club"). I was in the naval section and was classified as a Hospital Apprentice, First Class (HA-IC). My pay would be $39.80 a month and I was allowed an additional two dollars a day for maintenance. This pay was more than ample to take care of my living expenses for I was paying only twenty–four dollars a month for my room and three meals a day.

We had to report for drill every morning at 7:00 o'clock, rain or shine. The lieutenant sent down to drill us seemed disgruntled because of his unglamorous job. Training a bunch of medical and dental students who had neither uniforms nor arms didn't appeal to him. As a consequence he reveled in having us "flop and crawl," and in seeing us get our clothes soiled, knowing we went directly to our classes following drill with no opportunity to clean up.

The army and navy sections of the S.A.T.C. were all drilled together. The army boys were all classified as privates and were paid only thirty dollars a month. The army also built a mess hall behind the school building (Rogers Hall) and the army men got their meals there. There were altogether about 200 men in the S.A.T.C.

I roomed that year in a private home at 44 N. Pauline Street. My roommate was a pharmacy student from Brownsville named Walter Ragland. He was a good fellow but since we had so few interests in common, he could never be the companion that Jim Hall had been. Jim had rooms with one of his classmates that year.

The subject that seemed to require the most study in our sophomore year was Pathology, taught by Dr. Herbert Brooks. Dr. Brooks was thoroughly grounded in his subject and was very serious minded. In fact, he was completely devoid of a sense of humor. We were often amused by some of his mannerisms. For example, one day we were studying the pathology of acute appendicitis. Our textbook listed a number of foreign bodies which were sometimes found in the appendix which was acutely inflamed. He asked me in class to name those objects. I named a number of them and concluded my statement with "and various other objects." Dr. Brooks said, "Mr. Strain, I can't give you 'good' on that answer. You failed to mention grape seeds." Grape seeds had been specifically mentioned in our textbook.

Then one afternoon late in October of 1918, while we were all busy in our Pathology laboratory, bells began ringing, horns tooting, and factory whistles blowing. Much excitement was evident. Paper boys were yelling, "Extra! Extra! Armistice Signed!" It was in response to the first report that the Germans had capitulated and the war was over. We were naturally very excited. Some of us ran into Dr. Brooks' office and asked him if we could take a holiday. He said, "Go ahead." We noisily began putting our microscopes and other equipment away preparing to leave when Dr. Brooks came out of his office calling out, "Wait! I thought you said you wanted to *holler today.* I have no authority to give you a holiday." We got our things out again but as can be imagined, very little work was done during the remaining hour of the lab period.

The report that the Armistice had been signed, however, turned out to be premature. It was not until two weeks later that the war was over. When the Armistice was finally signed on November 11, bedlam swept over Memphis. We went down on Main Street that night where we found the street filled with people yelling, blowing horns, making all kinds of noise, marching up and down the street, dancing, hugging one another, and behaving like a demented mob. We happily joined them and it was midnight before we came in.

With the signing of the Armistice we wondered how long we would continue in the S.A.T.C. Our discharge finally came on December 11, 1918. I thanked the Lord that the devastating, horrible war was over, even if my small income from the navy ended. I had saved enough to last through March, trusting to luck, to carry me until June 1st when school was out.

"When the Armistice was finally signed on November 11, bedlam swept Memphis."

Then matters became complicated when I had to have a tonsillectomy. I had suffered from attacks of acute tonsillitis nearly every spring for the preceding four or five years. I consulted Dr. Louis Levy, a nose and throat specialist, who advised removal of my tonsils. I asked him to do it on a Friday, but when the time came he was unable to do it until Monday morning. Consequently, I entered the hospital Sunday evening and was booked for a tonsillectomy Monday morning.

The operation was done under a local anesthetic—with one tonsil being well-anesthetized. For some reason, however, I got very little anesthesia on the left side, but that didn't bother Dr. Levy. He proceeded to remove the tonsil anyhow. He used the Sluder technique which had been recently developed by Dr. Sluder of St. Louis—and the pain was severe. It made me realize how much agony our forefathers endured by having surgery without anesthesia.

Since Dr. Levy did not charge me for his services, and my hospital bill was only twenty dollars for room and operating room, I was able to pay it without any trouble.

Dr. E. E. Francis, a general surgeon, taught us a course in applied anatomy. Our lesson one day was on the layers of the scalp. We had assembled for class that morning when Dr. Francis raced in with his hat and coat on telling us he had been called to the General Hospital for an emergency operation. Since it was a wound to the head involving the scalp and cranium, he asked us to go with him where he could demonstrate the various layers of the scalp in a living individual.

We all rushed to get our books and coats, and hurried to the hospital where most of us would witness an operation for the first time. Two patients had been brought in, a man and a woman, black, as were most of the patients in the Memphis General Hospital. It was reported that the husband of the woman had come home unexpectedly and found them in bed together. He grabbed an ax and hit both of them in the head. The resulting wounds were terrible, and had left both unconscious. Not only had the scalp been cut open and they were bleeding profusely, but the skulls had been fractured and brain tissue was protruding from the wounds.

Dr. Francis began at once to clean up the wounds (no anesthesia was needed), and discussed the layers of the scalp. The odor of ether, used to assist in cleaning the wounds, the sight of the blood, mixed with the hair, bone and brain tissue protruding, was too much for some of the boys. Curiously enough, it didn't bother me. One boy left the room and one (John Maddox) fainted. He was taken out by a nurse and some of the students and sat on the floor outside the operating room for a while. He then got up and went downstairs hoping to get some fresh air. When he was getting out of the elevator on the first floor, he passed out again. Poor John! Here he planned to be a doctor, and had passed out the first time he saw a severe, bloody wound. He wondered if he could ever get over that reaction to such conditions. He did and later became one of my fellow "interns" at the St. Joseph Hospital where we saw all sorts of severe injuries.

We called Dr. Francis, "Daddy" Francis, because he endeared himself to us by his kindness, his apparent desire to help us learn his subject, and his sense of humor. He had taught Anatomy for many years in the old Memphis Hospital Medical College which antedated the University of Tennessee College of Medicine. He told us one day that he had memorized *Gray's Anatomy* twenty times and forgot it each time, but on the twenty-first time it stuck. He certainly knew the subject more thoroughly than any surgeon I ever knew.

As the school year drew to a close I became increasingly aware that my bank account was growing smaller. I barely had enough to take care of my expenses until about the first of April. I was not certain what I would do after that time and was careful to spend as little as I could. In the meantime, I suspended all recreation that might cost a penny. As a result, I was feeling pretty despondent. I had tried unsuccessfully to borrow from every possible source. Then one afternoon as I entered the front door of the house in which I was rooming, I saw a large envelope addressed to me lying on the table where my landlady put my mail. It was from the Eighth Naval District in New Orleans addressed to Samuel F. Strain, HA-IC. I opened it and found to my surprise and delight a check for $60.00! I had heard that all discharged soldiers and sailors were to receive a sixty dollar bonus but somehow it didn't occur to me that members of the S.A.T.C. were to be included.

My first reaction was to run to the phone, call the young lady living next door (Mattie Lowery) and ask her to go to a show with me—the first date I had had in several months. She accepted. We saw a good show and afterwards went to the "Winter Garden," an ice cream parlor, for an ice cream sundae. My despondency disappeared. My prayers had been answered and I now had enough money to last me the rest of the school year.

I knew, however, that I would not be able to earn enough during the summer to pay my expenses for the next year. I was about to plan to stay out of school for a year or so until I could make enough when upon discussing the matter with Dr. Wittenborg, he told me that a position was open in the Department of Chemistry for a student assistant. The student taking the job could take half of his work in the junior year one year, and the other half the following year. That meant, however, that it would take two years to finish the junior year in medicine. He still advised me to take the job as that would be better than staying out of school a year or two. I accepted and have often wondered if that job was created for me. It began on July 1st and paid fifty dollars a month for work in the Chemistry department. In addition, I was to manage the Student Cooperative Book Store.

The arrangement was perfect. I was now able to see a way to get through medical school without any outside help. I knew I could easily live on fifty dollars a month and in addition, there was now a possibility that I might be able to save some money. Living expenses were cheap in those days. After taking that job school went on without unusual events. I had very little trouble with my studies, and was able to make fairly good grades.

Since the attack of appendicitis in Kansas, however, I had experienced a discomfort and tenderness in my right lower abdominal quadrant. I had learned something of the danger of acute appendicitis with peritonitis, and began to worry for fear that I might develop that condition. I discussed the matter with "Daddy" Francis, and he told me it might be a good idea to remove the appendix. I therefore made arrangements to enter the hospital and have the operation as soon as school was out. Dr. Francis' examination, however, had consisted only of having me lie down on his examining table, fully dressed, and pressing on my abdomen. When I indicated that I was tender in the region of my appendix, he diagnosed chronic appendicitis.

A few days after school was out I checked into the Baptist Hospital for the operation. I was put in a double room with Herbert Fossey, a junior medical student who was also having his appendix removed on the same day.

I was given an ether anesthetic by Carmen James, a senior medical student and a good personal friend of mine. The operation was done without any difficulty. The intern who assisted Dr. Francis said my appendix was the smallest he had ever seen. It had evidently been obliterated by the attack I had had five years previously, and would more than likely never have given me any trouble. In short, my operation was the result of a medical student's fear and the willingness of the surgeon to operate without careful investigation. Medical students are prone to develop symptoms of nearly every disease they study. In later years I saw many medical students who came to my office very frightened and feeling sure that they had the condition about which they had been studying. I remembered my experience and took them seriously, giving them a thorough examination. I never teased them about their problem.

I also recall how strictly I was kept in bed for two weeks following surgery. I wasn't allowed to sit up until a week had passed. I suffered considerably from dizziness and distension with gas, for which I was treated with "flatus enemata". In these days with "early ambulation," where the patient is encouraged to be up within a few hours after the operation, these symptoms rarely occur. Moreover, when I was finally dismissed on the fourteenth day, I was so weak that after walking the five blocks to my home from the Baptist Hospital in the broiling afternoon sun, I developed a severe headache. In those days there was no one in Memphis to call on for help. School was out and my friends were all gone.

IX

Life in Memphis

I was to be awarded a Bachelor of Science degree following two years in medical school and the two years I had at the university in Knoxville. Since my work in the chemistry department didn't begin until July, I decided to go to Knoxville for the graduation ceremony. Blanche and Russell had moved there when Russell was made chief dispatcher for the Southern Railway. After a week or so I felt sufficiently recovered from my appendectomy to make the trip without any trouble and arrived in Knoxville several days before the June 25th commencement. I stayed with Blanche and Russell who lived in an apartment on West Vine Street just about two blocks from Gay.

James S. Hall, my good friend and former roommate who lived at Clinton, a small town about twenty miles from Knoxville, invited me out for a visit with him. His father was a very popular general practitioner there. I spent the night with them and thoroughly enjoyed my visit. Jim and I returned to Knoxville the next day. He was to get a degree also. We arranged for our caps and gowns and when the time came, we got in a procession and marched to the hall where the commencement exercises were to be held. After a long and uninteresting address by a dignified and solemn gentleman, we were awarded our diplomas. At last I had received my college degree even though I had never graduated from high school.

After the ceremonies were over, Jim and I met his parents and we were taken to Goode's Restaurant where we had lunch. I then bade them goodbye and went to Blanche's apartment. When I arrived I found Blanche somewhat upset because she had been thinking that I was bringing Jim Hall with me to have lunch with her. She had therefore prepared a lovely lunch for us. I was apologetic but could not understand her irritation. I don't recall ever telling her we would come, but I must have said something that gave her that impression. She was kind enough to let me out of "the doghouse" in a short time.

July was approaching and it was time for me to return to Memphis. Because I was short on cash, Blanche let me have a one hundred dollar war bond for which I received ninety dollars at a local bank. In those days a trip from Knoxville to Memphis could be made by boarding a train, "The Memphis Special," at about 7:00 p.m., and arriving in Memphis at 8:00 a.m., with a good night's sleep in the pullman.

On arriving in Memphis, I found that my landlady could no longer take boarders so I moved to 699 Jefferson Avenue where I secured room and board, and began my work at the college in the Chemistry Department. I was to keep the laboratory in good order and have everything ready for the students when school began.

Chemistry was used very little in clinical work in Memphis. Dr. DeShea, the professor of chemistry and my supervisor, decided to make clinical chemistry available to the hospitals and doctors in Memphis. We let it be known that this work was available and we soon had calls for the service. I believe we did the first chemistry for diagnostic purposes ever done in the city. Blood sugar, blood urea, non–protein nitrogen, and blood creatinine were soon being done by us for a number of the best doctors. It is hard to realize that those procedures had not been used in Memphis before. The Resident Physician of the Memphis General Hospital became very much interested in the work and was soon bringing me blood samples for analysis every day. I was kept busy doing these studies after a few weeks.

Since I was to run the Student's Cooperative Book Store, I had to contact each instructor to learn what text he planned to use and how many he thought he would need when school began in the fall. This information was obtained so that the books could be ordered early enough for them to be received before school began. I had to order books needed for dental and pharmacy students, as well as for medical students. We ordered them to be sent on consignment, which meant we would pay for them as they were sold, and give a monthly sales report to the publishers. The Dean's secretary, Miss Mary Turner, was kind enough to do my stenographic work and assist me with the bookkeeping involved.

After the Chemistry Department was put in order and ready to receive students, and the bookstore work was completed. I had little to do. I was then asked to serve as "Camp Doctor" for the Boy Scouts camp—Kamp Kia Kima—on the Spring River near Hardy, Arkansas. This was the camp for the Chickasaw Council and had been established only a year before. My duties were to serve as a glorified first aid man. My expenses would be paid and I was to receive a salary of fifty dollars a month. I discussed it with Dr. DeShea and found that he thought I should go.

I enjoyed living at the "Kamp" for the next six weeks. There were about two hundred boys there and I found them to be a wonderful bunch. I slept in a screened enclosed "shack" which was called the infirmary. There was a space for me to take care of minor injuries and illnesses, and there were three cots in another section for boys sick enough to require care at night.

I had a number of "patients" suffering from cuts, bruises, poison ivy, bee stings, and similar afflictions. If they became seriously ill I would call their parents in Memphis and send them home. One day a little boy about fourteen years of age remained in his bunk and wouldn't come to mess. One of his lodge mates asked me to see him. I found him with high fever and having a chill. It was obviously malaria, and I took him some quinine. He refused to take any medication insisting that he was not sick. When I urged him to take the quinine he said, "Here is all the medicine I need," and pulled from under his pillow *Science and Health with the Key to the Scriptures,* by Mary Baker Eddy. I then realized that he was a Christian Scientist. I talked to "Chief" Crowe, the camp director, and we decided to send him home to Memphis. Although I admired the boy for his courage and did not try to change his way of thinking, I did not want the responsibility of allowing his malaria to go untreated.

Kamp Kia Kima was a well-ordered camp. There was a regular schedule with set times for getting up in the morning, breakfast, straightening up lodges, inspections of lodge, recreation, noon meals, rest period, and so on. Each period was signaled with a bugle call. The flag was raised in the morning and lowered in the evening with a formal camp–wide ceremony. The regular time for swimming was strictly enforced with no scouts allowed in the river at other times. The "buddy" system was always practiced with the scout in swimming always watching his friend. If he couldn't he had to come out of the water. The camp also had a number of fine canoes, and canoe trips were planned at intervals. Canoe tilting was a common and popular sport.

About a mile down the river was a Girl Scout camp and another camp for the Y.W.C.A. One day I was asked to go quickly to the girl scout camp. When I got there I found that of the forty–two in the camp including the camp directors, thirty–five had gastroenteritis (food poisoning). They had contracted it by eating beef that had been kept several days. It had been cooled only by spring water as no refrigeration was available. I felt sorry for those poor little sick girls. Some of them were very miserable. I prescribed the treatment advised in the medical books which I had taken with me to Kamp Kia Kima and they all recovered promptly. From that time on, my reputation among them was unimpeachable!

The Girl Scouts occasionally would put on a show and invite the Boy Scouts, and the Boy Scouts would then reciprocate by having a show for the girls. At the Girl Scouts' show about a week after the food poisoning episode, they had a chorus singing a parody on the song "Take it slow and easy if you want to make a hit with me." One verse went: "We know a doctor and his name is Strain/He knows how to cure spoiled beef pain."

On another occasion I was called to the Y.W.C.A. camp to see a girl named Annie Laurie Burton who had fallen and received a wound in her leg below the knee. A stick had penetrated about an inch into the flesh. I cleaned the wound, applied antiseptics, and a dressing. I saw her several times afterwards and dressed the wound each time. It healed without infection.

At a later show the girls had for the Boy Scouts a group sang a song with one stanza saying: "Annie Laurie got a splinter in her leg, If the doctor hadn't come, she'd have to have a peg."

Sitting around the campfire at night in the cool Ozarks was a delightful experience. The boys would sing, tell jokes, ask riddles,

"The Girl Scouts occasionally would put on a show and invite the Boy Scouts. . . ."

and give speeches. One night at the campfire Perry Pipkin, a scout (who later became prominent in Memphis—the Pipkin Building at the Fair Grounds was named for him) said to me with his characteristic stuttering speech, "Doc–doc–doctor Strain, wu–wu–we don't want you any longer." "Why not, Pip?," I asked. "K–K–cause you're long enough," he replied.

I have never enjoyed a summer more than the one I spent at Kamp Kia Kima. The friends I made there, and the simple, but pleasant experiences I had have been the source of pleasant memories. Some of my Boy Scouts became leaders in civic and political affairs in Memphis later.

On my return to Memphis I found a letter in my room telling me that Blanche, James, and Mary Evelyn would be coming through Memphis. The train on which they were coming was to arrive at the exact time I was reading the letter. I rushed out and caught a street car to the station where I thought they were probably waiting. As I went south on Main Street I looked carefully at the pedestrians on the sidewalk to see if I could find them. Sure enough I saw them there walking slowly north on the sidewalk. I got off the street car at the next block and rushed to catch them in front of the Gayoso Hotel.

It was good to see them. James was now out of the army and on his way to Kansas to work on Henry's farm until he could find something else to do. We enjoyed our visit as we walked to Confederate Park where we watched the river traffic and other activities of the city. Mary Evelyn had a great time feeding the pigeons and squirrels in Court Square. I stayed with them the entire three hours until they caught their train for Kansas.

I once again began my work at the school book store and in the Chemistry Department. We had everything ready to go in both places well before the school year began. Clinical Chemistry also was resumed and I soon had plenty to do. I was occasionally called upon to analyze body tissue and organs removed at autopsy from subjects who had died from suspected cases of poisoning. These studies proved to be interesting exercises in chemistry. Moreover, I began to develop a reputation as a physiological chemist. I seriously considered the suggestion of Dr. Morrow, who took Dr. DeShea's place as Professor of Chemistry, that I take up physiological chemistry instead of medicine as a profession. The idea appealed to me but I also thought a degree in medicine would be a good foundation for such a profession.

Dr. McElroy, the Professor of Medicine and one of the city's leading internists, sent his technician out for me to teach her how to do some of the most frequently used procedures in clinical chemistry. She came for several hours every day for about two weeks. She had very little knowledge of chemistry but I was able to teach her the techniques of the most important procedures. The Pathologist of the Baptist Hospital, Dr. Leake, also asked me to make out a list of all the equipment needed to set up a chemistry laboratory in the hospital. I did this and can claim that I got clinical chemistry started in Memphis. I have seen many advances in the development of tools for studying the functions and malfunctions of the human body. It is difficult for modern medical students and young physicians to realize that commonplace instruments and methods were nonexistent only a relatively short time ago.

During the few weeks before school began, I indicated my willingness to do night duty as a male nurse by registering with the Nurses' Registry. Male nurses were often needed and there seemed to be a scarcity of them in Memphis. I was called on several cases for night duty lasting from 7:00 p.m. to 7:00 a.m. for which I was paid the standard five dollars.

I had one case which was considered infectious, and therefore was paid ten dollars each night. He was a young man who had a compound fracture of the tibia with a severe infection which was diagnosed erysipelas. The treatment involved the use of Dakin's Solution which was injected into tubes extending through the dressing. It was a chlorine solution which had been developed by a Dr. Dakin in France during the war and had to be injected every two hours. I was on this case about ten nights. I was able to do my work at the college but I didn't get as much sleep as I needed. After all, my work at the college was only a part–time job, and I didn't have to be at the school all day.

When school started I took as many units of instruction as I thought I could handle with my other duties. It turned out that I was taking nearly two–thirds of the subjects required for the junior year student, but I was able to keep up with my studies and also take care of my other work.

Since my part-time jobs in the Chemistry Department and with the student book store prohibited me taking a heavy schedule in my school work, I had less studying to do and more time for recreation. I began spending time with Rose Ballard during my freshman year, and started dating her more frequently. We not only went to shows but particularly enjoyed dancing. Public dance halls were popular in Memphis with "The Roof Garden" on top of the Falls Building being one of our favorites. Rose and I spent many an evening there dancing to such tunes as "Sweet Little Alice Blue Gown," "Three O'Clock in the Morning," and "The Missouri Waltz." The principle dances were Waltzes, Fox Trots and the One Step. The "Dark Town Strutter's Ball," "Shake It or Break It and Hang It on the Wall," "The St. Louis Blues," and The "Memphis Blues" were our favorite melodies.

Rose went to school at Tennessee College in Murfreesboro

and therefore was not in Memphis during the school year. We corresponded regularly, however, and were together during the Christmas holidays when she came home.

Rogers Hall had a large lobby with a tile floor which was an ideal place for dances. Frequently the dental and medical students would get together and hire a three to five piece orchestra from W. C. Handy and have a dance there. In those days it was not uncommon for outsiders, "Jelly Beans" we called them, to come and crash the dance. Joe Gronauer, a dental student, and I were usually appointed "bouncers." Joe finished dentistry but he married a Goldsmith girl and gave it up to become manager of Goldsmith's, the largest department store in town.

At Christmas time A. B. McCreary, a classmate, who worked at the Home for Incurables, asked me to take his place there while he was on Christmas vacation. Consequently, I served as an attendant there for about two weeks. The inmates of that institution were hopeless cripples, paralyzed, deformed with arthritis, poliomyelitis, and various conditions which caused them to be helpless. Yet I found their cheerfulness to be surprising. It was indeed a pleasure to help them in any way at all because of the gratitude they expressed. I made rounds seeing all of them at least twice a day, and would frequently sit and visit. This seemed to give these people a great deal of pleasure. Many had few or no outside visitors, and it was evident that they were hungry for someone to show them some attention.

I was inspired and blessed with the opportunity I had in my work there. All my troubles and worries seemed insignificant as I visited with these dear people. The lessons I learned in my care of people who needed help later became invaluable to me in my practice of medicine. I learned how much empathy and sympathy on the part of a doctor or anyone who cared for unfortunate people really meant to them. I tried to explain it to my medical students and interns years later. Empathy is a trait too often lacking in those who care for the sick and afflicted.

School work, my work in the Chemistry Department and in the book store throughout the early months and spring of 1920 went on smoothly. My health remained good and I was able, by being careful, to live within my meager income. Rose was off at school and my social life was minimal.

I attended church regularly at the Alabama Street Presbyterian church. A fine old gentleman, Dr. Curry, was pastor, and Horace Hull was my Sunday School teacher. We had a small Sunday School class, and on several occasions when Mr. Hull was absent, I was asked to teach the lesson. I was once again beginning to feel the need of spiritual food, and I liked going to church.

I had taken my heaviest subjects in school and by the end of the year I was finished with surgery, obstetrics, gynecology, and medicine. Only specialties such as dermatology, neurology, ophthalmalogy, otolaryngology, and urology were left. I had done well in the subjects I had taken and knew that the second half of my junior year would be easier.

About the time school was out I received a call asking me to serve another summer as "Camp Physician" at the Boy Scout camp at Hardy. I arranged with my chemistry professor to take six weeks off and accepted the invitation. After getting the book store business in order, and the work in the Chemistry Department cleaned up, I left for Kamp Kia Kima on July 1st. I once again spent a delightful six weeks. The business of taking care of the boy's boils, chigger bites, poison ivy, sunburns, and small wounds was not too time consuming, and I had plenty of opportunity to take part in many of the camp activities. Baseball, canoeing, swimming, hiking over the mountains, fishing, and frog gigging gave us plenty to do.

Time passed rapidly and this summer was as enjoyable as the previous one. We again exchanged visits and entertainment programs with the girl scouts and the Y.W.C.A. girls. With some of our camp counsellors I would occasionally walk in to Hardy, about three miles, to the "Wahpeton Inn" and dance with girls vacationing there. Near the end I was asked to serve as Camp Director for the next summer.

On August 7th I left the camp for Memphis after turning my work over to a classmate, Charles Potts. The weather was hot with absolutely no wind. The train I was to catch came through Hardy at 10:00 p.m. so I started walking toward town alone at about 6:30 p.m., carrying a heavy suitcase. The sun went down behind a very dark cloud. The path I took was narrow, crooked and through a dense forest over some very rocky and hilly terrain. Before I got half way to town it was pitch black with zero visibility. I was able to see where I was going only by virtue of frequent flashes of "sheet lightning" that lasted until I got to the Wahpeton Inn which stood on a hill across the river from Hardy. I could outline my path for a few yards at each flash and hurry to make as much distance as possible for fear the lightning would stop. As a consequence I became dripping wet with sweat. I took off my coat and shirt, and carried them with my suitcase on my shoulder. Fortunately, the almost constant flashes of lightning enabled me to make the whole three mile trip. Without these flashes the trip would have been next to impossible.

Just before going up to the hotel I put on my shirt and tie. Since it was two or three hours until train time, I decided to wait there instead of at the depot. I found the usual activities of vacationers, many of whom I had met before. An orchestra was going and they were dancing. Air conditioning as we now know it was unknown, but the large overhead fans furnished enough air currents to help us tolerate the heat. After cooling off, I joined the others and danced until nearly train time. I then headed back to Memphis, sorry that such a delightful summer's experience had come to an end.

Back in Memphis, I began checking with professors to get their textbooks ordered by the first day of school at the end of September. There had been some changes of the faculty during the summer. Dr. Desha had left us to become Professor of Chemistry at Washington and Lee University while Dr. Morrow took his place. I was sorry to see Dr. Desha leave, but I found Dr. Morrow to be likeable.

I was also busy in the Chemistry Department receiving and cataloguing supplies, preparing the reagents that were to be used by students, and doing clinical chemistry for the Baptist and Memphis General Hospital. After the first week or two I began to have more time for other activities. I served as a night nurse in a few cases and managed to increase my income. The school even gave me a welcome raise in my pay to sixty-four dollars a month.

I also had time to play tennis with some of the hospital interns, and frequently played hand ball at the "Y." I saw Rose often and we went to shows, parties, and danced on "The Roof," at East End or in private homes. Still, I found myself subject to spells of "loneliness" occasionally. I keenly felt the need for homelife. I envied boys that had homes to which they could go, and parents upon whom they could depend for counsel and encouragement. When I registered for another school year I could give no permanent address. I found a remedy for these spells by counting my blessings and thanking God for the opportunities that had come my way. After school began in the fall I was no longer lonesome and rarely had time to think about myself.

A short time before school began I was offered a job as an orderly in the Baptist Hospital. I was to be given my room, board and laundry for taking care of calls at night. I accepted the job, moved in, and took a small room with a comfortable bed, dresser, table and chair, and ate in the nurse's dining room. I had only a few

"A short time before school began I was offered a job as an orderly in the Baptist Hospital."

calls at night so I could get a fairly good night's rest. My work was mostly catheterizing male patients, "prepping" patients for surgery, and giving enemas. Not a dignified occupation, it was still profitable for me at the time.

I had been at this work for about a week before school began, when Aubry Lewis, a senior and former classmate told me that St. Joseph Hospital was seeking student interns. I applied for the position and was accepted at once. I felt that I could enjoy work as an intern more than as an orderly, so I left the Baptist Hospital to go to St. Joseph's.

Because of the war, and small classes in medical schools, graduate interns were still not available. The hospitals had to depend on medical students for their interns. No pay was given, but the hospital furnished room, board, and laundry. Our work consisted of assisting in operations, in obstetrics, answering calls in the emergency room, giving anesthetics (ether was about the only general anesthetic given then), and doing such things as applying postoperative dressings. We also took care of charity patients under the supervision of visiting physicians and surgeons. These duties were performed any time we could be in the hospital.

The experiences I had there were worth a great deal to me. It was a good introduction to what the practice of medicine was all about. I saw many interesting cases and learned much that wasn't in our textbooks.

I also saw the difference between good skilled surgery, and poor surgery attempted by untrained "occasional operators," as Dr. Frank Smyth called them.

I also learned about the rigid discipline of the Catholic sisters who ran the hospital. Some of the finest, most lovable women I have ever known wore the habit, but a few were very unlovely. Many of the sisters looked upon interns as untrustworthy creatures of low morals. Student nurses were forbidden to carry on any conversation with interns except in the line of duty.

The food we had was unusually good. There was a small private dining room in which we ate. The sisters would put the food on the table and leave it for us to get anytime that was convenient for breakfast, lunch, and dinner. There was always a pitcher of good, cold buttermilk, a pitcher of tea in the summer, or a pot of coffee at breakfast time during cold weather. There were only six of us. Four of us, John Maddox, Ralph Monger, Aubrey Lewis and I, stayed in one big room with four beds, a bathroom on the side, and suitable furniture. The four of us were congenial and we got along well together most of the time. We walked hurriedly back and forth from the hospital to school, making the one mile trip both ways at lunch time.

This was a very pleasant although a busy period for me. I was carrying a light load as far as my studies were concerned for I had completed more than half my Junior work the year before. I could therefore easily take care of my work in chemistry, the Book Store and the hospital, as well as my classwork. Since I was getting my room, board, and laundry in exchange for my work in the hospital, I was able to save most of my pay from the jobs at the Chemistry Department and Book Store. For the first time in my life I was able to buy clothes, shoes and other things I wanted. I had the pleasure of seeing my bank account grow. At Christmas I slipped off for a few days and took the place of an intern at the Gartly-Ramsy Hospital.

With the coming of 1921 work in the hospital, the school, the Chemistry department, and the Book Store continued uneventfully. I found some time for recreation at the Y.M.C.A., and on the local tennis courts. I also went out with a friend, Dr. R. S. Vinsant, for my first game of golf at the Overton Park golf course.

I was making plans to take the position of Camp Director at Kamp Kia Kima the next summer and was meeting occasionally with members of the Scout Council. I knew it would be a responsible position and a real challenge for me. The camp was to open June 1st. I was to go about a week before, taking my staff with me.

Mr. Ramsay and Dr. George Gartly arranged a dance for the student nurses of the Gartly–Ramsay Hospital to be held on May 16th. They asked a number of medical students and interns to attend and dance with the girls. Frayzer Hinton of the J. T. Hinton & Son Funeral Parlor offered to furnish a chauffeur driven car—a big Pierce Arrow Limousine—to provide transportation for those who had no other way to get there. I chose to go with this group. The dance was to be held at a house out on Macon Road.

The party was a great success. We had a good orchestra, and

many of the girls were good dancers. The party ended with the band playing "Good Night Ladies" and we left to go home around 1:00 a.m. Our chauffeur seemed to be in a hurry to get back to Memphis as he drove well beyond the speed limit. After going a few miles we came to a right angle turn in the road which he attempted to negotiate without slowing down. The right front wheel of the heavy car couldn't stand the stress and collapsed with its wooden spokes. The car turned over and for a brief period we were tossed about in complete darkness. When it came to rest I found myself in a ditch unable to breathe. I thought the car was on my chest. I struggled for my breath and quickly realized that it had been knocked out of me. I was able to lift the weight off my chest, however, as it was the car door.

Almost immediately cars following us arrived. I could see from the light of their headlights that my left leg had an abnormal angle at mid-thigh, and that my left foot twisted inward. I also felt the back of my head and realized I was bleeding. We were immediately surrounded by our friends who had left the party. Dr. Conley Sanford was the first one to me and tried hurriedly to evaluate the extent of my injuries. I told him I had only a broken leg and suggested that he make sure the others were not more severely injured. I was having considerable pain which seemed to become greater as things quieted down a bit. Someone brought a bottle of whiskey and said that a few drinks might help relieve the pain while we waited for the ambulance. I had never drunk whiskey before and upon taking a sip, I was unable to swallow it. I learned that of the five other passengers in the car, one boy did not have even a scratch, the other two had only slight bruises. The two girls on the back seat not only had several ribs broken, but also had back injuries requiring a few weeks hospitalization.

I was taken to St. Joseph's hospital where I was scolded by the sisters for being with a group from another hospital — and drinking! They smelled my breath. I was given morphine for pain, the wounds on the back of my head and left buttock were treated and dressed, and my left leg was put in a Thomas Splint. I asked that Dr. Willis Campbell take care of me. For the next week I was in a great deal of pain. The sisters allowed me only one hypodermic for each twenty-four hours. That would relieve pain for about three hours and allow me to sleep that long. I remained awake the remainder of the day or night.

My left thigh was so badly swollen that Dr. Campbell delayed setting the broken bone and applying a cast until the swelling was reduced. After about ten days I was given an anesthetic and the fracture was set. A "Spika" cast was applied. I was in a cast from my arm pits to my left foot and to my right knee. As had been my experience when my appendix was removed, the ether anesthetic resulted in causing intense nausea. For more than twenty–four hours I had nausea and vomiting, unable to retain anything I tried to swallow. The administration of intravenous fluids was seldom resorted to in those days and as a result I became very severely dehydrated.

With the retching I experienced, I could feel the bones in my thigh slipping and I knew that the fragments were again out of alignment. Dr. Campbell was out of town and his young assistant, Dr. J. S. Sneed, refused to do anything about it until Dr. Campbell returned. When he returned two weeks later, my cast was removed, I was given ether again, and another cast was applied. Another spell of intense nausea followed. I recall how delighted I was when I could retain a few sips of ginger ale.

The bone slipped again but not as much. The x–ray examination showed the fragments together with the anterior cortex of the lower fragment in alignment with the posterior cortex of the upper fragment. Dr. Campbell was very sympathetic and tried to comfort me. He said if we left it alone it would heal and again be strong, but it would take longer. Otherwise, he said, an open operation could be performed, but there was always a risk of infection with osteomyelitis developing. In the days before antibiotics, osteomyelitis was a chronic, almost incurably crippling disease. We agreed not to operate. I was fairly comfortable in the cast. I could lie on my back or left side, but was held rigidly straight. I also had the head of my bed elevated so that reading would be easier.

The nurses and my friends were good to me. I was in that hospital from May 16 to September 16th, and there were very few days that I failed to have a visitor. Rose Ballard came to see me every day that summer except in stormy, rainy weather. A young lady, Edith Henry, whom I had met at Hardy, worked at the Cossitt

Library. She kept me supplied with books, bringing a new supply every Saturday, and taking back those I had read. I read almost constantly. On several occasions Mariam Drane and a laboratory technician, Jess Thompson, came to see me. I enjoyed their visits more and more as I became better acquainted with them.

This experience presented some real problems. My injury occurred only four days before final examinations were given. Moreover, I had to give up the idea of being Camp Director of Kamp Kia Kima; my income had stopped, and though I had nearly a thousand dollars in the bank, I knew much of my savings would be gone by the end of summer. I was told by my professors that I could take my examination in the fall in time to start school as a senior. Since my school work had been very light, I felt that I could manage that all right.

During the summer my brother, James, came from Kansas to see me. My fellow interns took him in, let him sleep in my bed at the intern's quarters, and entertained him royally. He stayed three or four days. My cast was changed twice during the summer but no further anesthetic was needed. I can never forget how hot the cast was. There was no such thing as air conditioning in those days, and Memphis can get mighty hot in the summertime.

I looked forward to the time when the cast could be removed and I could take a good, warm tub bath. When it was finally taken off, however, I was miserable. My back, hip, and knees were stiff from having been in a fixed position for sixteen weeks, and the slight sag in the hospital bed caused much discomfort. I was so stiff I couldn't reach my knees with my hand. A brace was made for me when I was discharged from the hospital. It had a strap around the hips, and metal strips down both sides of the left leg which fastened to my shoe. It was to be worn all the time I was up. A thick cork sole was built under my right shoe to make it easier for me to swing my left foot when I walked with crutches. After about two weeks, during which time I became accustomed to using crutches, and my joints began to improve in movability, I made arrangements to leave the hospital and to go stay with Blanche until school began. She lived in Bristol, Virginia, at that time.

I had a lower berth in the Pullman but still couldn't take off my pants or shoes so I got the porter to help me. I still slept very little that night. The train left Memphis at 8:00 p.m. and did not arrive in Bristol until 11:00 a.m. the next day. I rested at Blanche's and by gradually increasing exercise became more able to take care of myself.

Winnie BeCraft, from Wytheville, with whom I had corresponded regularly, came down to Bristol to see me. She came with her sister and spent the day with us. It was good to see her, but somehow she did not appeal to me as much as she had before. I had changed more than she had, I suppose. She did not seem to be as interesting as some of the girls I had met more recently. I realized that my affection for her had been more like the infatuation of a teenager with his first love. When I saw her board the train, and told her goodbye, I knew it would be the last time I would ever see her. The parting was a painful experience.

While I was in Bristol I received a telegram from Jarrell Penn, a junior medical student from Humboldt, asking me if I would room with him during the next school year. I replied I would be delighted. Jarrell also said that he would find a place for us. Jarrell's offer certainly appealed to me, especially since I was still on crutches, wearing a brace on my left leg, and was unable to take it off or put it on.

After about two weeks at Blanche's, I boarded the "Memphis Special" for Memphis. Jarrell Penn was at the station to meet me when I arrived. He took charge of my baggage and helped me to the taxi stand. We went by taxi to the place he had found for us. It was a good room in the home of Mr. & Mrs. Bateman Fite on Keppel Place, about two blocks from the school. I received the best of care because I was still crippled. Jarrell would help me take my clothes off at night, and get dressed in the morning. If he went out on a date, or for other reasons happened to be late getting home, Mr. Fite would help me or I would just lie across the bed fully dressed until he came in. Needless to say, I found Jarrell Penn to be one of the best roommates I ever had. He and Jim Hall were to remain my very close friends in subsequent years. Jarrell ultimately became the leading orthopedist in Knoxville.

I gradually increased the range of motion of my spine, hips, and knee joints with the help of physical therapy, until I was able to reach my foot so that I was no longer dependent on such valet service. The task of going to school on crutches, however, was quite a problem. I was tired after a day at school, moving from class to class, and building to building. On more than one occasion, I was too tired to make class and would cut it. As time went on, however, I grew stronger and was gradually able to move without much fatigue. By Thanksgiving I was able to leave off the brace, and a few weeks later I threw my crutches away and started using only a cane.

My bank account, however, was not faring as well as my injuries as it gradually grew smaller. Neither the hospital nor Dr. Campbell charged me for their services, but other expenses seemed to erode my balance pretty far. At the suggestion of the owner of the car, Frazier Hinton, I and the two girls who were injured in the wreck sued him. After months of waiting our lawyer told us that the matter had been settled out of court. We were awarded $2,000. The lawyer got half of that, the two girls got $250 each, and I got $500. I could not help but believe we could have gotten more if the matter had been taken to court. I asked Dr. Campbell and the hospital to send me a bill before the case was settled. Dr. Campbell's bill was $700, and the hospital bill was $1,900. Both told me I didn't need to pay anything unless the insurance company allowed that amount.

The $500 helped considerably, but I still didn't have enough to take care of my expenses until graduation. My cousin, Walter Remine had been successful in his business ventures and was kind enough to loan me $200. His father, Uncle Cal, let me have $100. With this amount I was able to take care of my expenses until graduation in June.

My senior year of medicine was most interesting. We were taught how to apply the knowledge we had acquired in our "pre-clinical" years. We saw patients, took medical histories on them, and did physical examinations. We also observed operations, assisted in obstetrics, and participated in the care of sick and injured people. We were learning what the practice of medicine was like.

We studied hard and had little time for recreation except for occasional dances in Rogers Hall, and attending football games. A number of boys in Medical, Dentistry, and Pharmacy schools had played football on the teams of schools they had attended before coming to U.T. Several had been outstanding on their previous college teams so they organized a squad and called themselves the "U.T. Docs." They played four years without losing a game.

By Christmas I was walking without a cane and was even able to dance some. During the vacation Lloyd Judd, who had moved from Miami, Oklahoma, invited me to visit him at his new home in Little Rock. I spent several days at his home and enjoyed seeing him and his wife, Blanche, again. His father and her parents were living in Little Rock at the time of my visit.

The final months of school passed without incident. I had no trouble with my studies and my health was good. Because of my automobile accident I decided to remain in Memphis for internship instead of going on to Philadelphia General with two of my former classmates, Bill Mims and Harry Brown. Moreover, at that time the lawsuit still had not been settled. Because of subsequent events, I have concluded this was the most fortunate decision I ever made.

Since I had applied for internship in the Memphis General Hospital, I was asked by the Superintendent if I would come April 1st, even before my graduation in June, 1922. I accepted the invitation and therefore had my room and board furnished the last two and one–half months of my medical school years. This situation was certainly a boost to my dwindling financial situation.

I was assigned to the "Receiving Ward," as the emergency room was called. Every patient entering the hospital passed through the "Receiving Ward." The intern was given the responsibility of sending the patient to the appropriate service (Medical, Surgical, Gyn., Obs.). This required a medical history with a summary of complaints, a complete physical examination, and a provisional diagnosis. This activity was splendid experience. Naturally the admitting intern wanted to have a good "batting average" on his diagnoses, and was anxious to do his best. Diagnosis became a game, and diagnosis of a patient's illness continued to be the most interesting part of practicing medicine for me.

We also took care of emergencies. We saw every imaginable kind of emergency in the emergency room of a hospital like the Memphis General which was primarily for poor people, white as well as black. Injuries from fights with blunt instruments, razors, knives, scissors, and ice picks, in addition to gunshot wounds, varying from minor to fatal and all degrees between, were common. The victims were drunk or sober, male or female, black or white. There were automobile accidents, industrial injuries, burns, poisoning, dog bites, snake bites, bee stings—no end to the list of types of emergencies. No matter how gruesome the injury, the nurses and interns took care of it without the least excitement. I found that serving in the Emergency Room was a duty that taught a doctor or nurse to remain calm in any situation.

My work in the hospital varied in amount. We were especially busy on weekends, but I could arrange my time so that it did not interfere with my school work. I found living in the hospital to be very comfortable. I was given a room in intern quarters which was suitable for studying without interruption by the other interns. The other interns for the most part had been those classmates of mine who had graduated a year ahead of me because I worked part-time during my junior year. The food was good, but it quickly became monotonous because they served the same meals every Monday, Tuesday and so on, for each day of the week. We could tell what day it was from the food we were served.

Graduation finally came on June 12, 1922 with commencement exercises being held in the auditorium of Rogers Hall. This auditorium would accommodate from two hundred to three hundred and was well-filled. June 12 turned out to be a hot day, and the auditorium was sweltering that evening. There were no ceiling fans, and air conditioning was only a dream at that time.

There were eleven medical, eleven dental and eighteen pharmacy graduates. Many had parents, wives, and sweethearts attending this great event in their lives. My sister, Blanche, came all the way down from Bristol for the occasion. Rose Ballard had insisted that she stay at their house while she was in town, and Rose brought her to the graduation exercises. Jess Thompson also came.

We graduates sat sweltering in our caps and gowns during the inevitably long, dull speech by a prominent Memphis lawyer, Israel Peres. His address was totally inappropriate and aroused the resentment of us medical graduates, by congratulating us on our completion of "three long years of hard study." Three long years indeed! For us it had been from six to eight years!

I was called to march up the steps to the platform three times: once for my diploma, once for an honor certificate, and finally for the faculty medal as I had the best average in my class.

The whole occasion was a solemn one for me. I had at last achieved the goal I had been struggling toward for seven long years. I had at last earned an M.D. degree and was now Doctor Fred Strain! Blanche was proud of her brother, and Jess Thompson seemed to understand what it meant to me. Rose, on the other hand, could hardly wait for the ceremonies to be over, for she was in a hurry to get to a dance being held at the home of a friend out on Peabody Avenue. I reluctantly consented to go with her. Although she seemed to have a most enjoyable evening, I never went to a party I enjoyed less and told her so on our way home. From that evening on I began to realize that Rose and I were not as compatible as I initially thought. Jess Thompson seemed to be more "my kind of folks."

Soon after graduation came the State Board Examination. This examination was required for a license to practice medicine in the state. I thought it was surprisingly easy and passed it without difficulty. Still, I realized that there was much about the practice of medicine I hadn't been taught in school. The value of a good internship was beginning to be realized by me. I chose the Memphis General Hospital for several reasons: I needed to stay in Memphis until the law suit against the J. T. Hinton and Son was settled; it was the teaching hospital for the University of Tennessee College of Medicine and I would have the opportunity to attend lectures, ward rounds, clinical pathological conferences and to participate in the teaching of medical students; and I was becoming romantically interested in the laboratory technician, Jess Thompson.

X

Intern

We were short of interns. Medical Schools all over the country had turned out small classes because of the war, so graduates in medicine had no difficulty in 1922 in getting an internship at almost any hospital in the country. I turned out to be the only member of my class that stayed in Memphis. All the others took internships elsewhere.

My first assignment was to Internal Medicine. For awhile I was the only intern on that specialty and, with ninety or more patients to look after, was far too busy. It was my responsibility to see each patient at least once daily. Some had to be seen several times. The Resident Physician, Dr. Omar Smith, a classmate of mine at the University of Tennessee at Knoxville, had gone to Vanderbilt Medical School where he had finished the year before.

The search for interns almost grew desperate. Two medical students were engaged to take care of the Receiving Ward, but I still got no help with my hospital work. I told Dr. Haas, the Medical Director, that unless assistance came soon that I would apply for an internship in a hospital where I could get some training as well as experience. He promised to give me the month of August as a vacation if I would stay.

I had little time for recreation that summer although occasionally I managed to play tennis with other interns. Jess Thompson, who often played with us, was about the only girl capable of beating us and was always welcomed on the court for both singles and doubles matches. She was nicknamed "Tommy" by all the interns. In the meantime, my dates with Rose were fewer and farther between. Besides, she had more dates with John Leigh than with me. One evening I went with Rose to the home of Carrol

White and his bride, Elizabeth "Dit" Leigh. Carrol had made a little "crystal set" radio. There was only one radio station in town in 1922, Reichman-Crosby's Station W.K.N. I was thrilled to hear my first radio program through the headphones on his set that evening. Receiving sets with loud speakers were rare and very expensive at that time. All of them were run by batteries that needed charging frequently.

The following day I bought a crystal set with head phones and put up a long aerial on the roof of the hospital. One night while I was listening to the weak signal of the W.K.N. station, a booming voice broke in, "This is station W.M.C. of Memphis, Tennessee, testing–testing." This was the first radio transmission from W.M.C., the first real station in Memphis. It was much stronger than the Reichman-Crosby station and completely blotted out the weaker station's signal. I enjoyed listening to W.M.C. and when it began to get programs from New York "by remote control," I would listen with one earphone and hold the other to the phone for Jess to hear. One night she and I listened to *The Mikado* in this manner.

Rose and I saw less and less of each other as the summer went on, and by the time she returned to school in Murfreesboro that fall, we had broken up entirely. I never felt that she loved me. Our backgrounds had been so different with her being raised in the city, and my being a country boy.

Jess Thompson appealed to me more and more as time went on. We played tennis often, occasionally went to a picture show together, and often enjoyed a date in the porch swing at her rooming house. She did not care much for dancing, but we did go to a few parties where dancing was the principal activity. We had many interests in common, and the more I saw of her, the more I realized that she was the kind of companion I could enjoy for an indefinite period.

When I was an intern I developed "acute catarrhal jaundice," which is what we called hepatitis in those days. Jess felt sorry for me when I told her I had completely lost my appetite. She went to the market, bought a fryer, and took it to her rooming house to fry. She brought it to me in the hospital, fried perfectly, and convinced me she was a good cook. The sight of anything greasy, however, increased my anorexia and actually caused nausea. I thanked her and told her I would eat it after she left, as I did not want our visit to be disturbed by my eating while she was there. After she left, another intern, Jack Kazar, came in my room. I gave the chicken to him, and he sat and ate every bite of it, licking his fingers and throwing the bones in the waste basket.

True to his promise, Dr. Haas let me take the month of August off. My sister Kathleen was then living in Denver, Colorado. The railroads advertised a special reduced rate on round trip tickets between Denver and Memphis, so I bought one for forty dollars and left for Colorado.

By the first of September I was back in Memphis. I found that the hospital had recruited several more interns so that my work was more easily accomplished. I was assigned to surgery for three months. Surgical specialties included ear, nose and throat, opthalmology, urology and orthopedics. I still had not decided which field was the most interesting. I assisted in all the operations, and took care of the patients postoperatively. I decided that I liked surgery and that I should become a surgeon.

After surgical service I was assigned to "Obs and Gyn." During my three months there I delivered more than 100 babies, including three sets of twins. My chief, Dr. Toombs, had been doing obstetrics for nearly thirty years and had delivered only four sets of twins. After only three months I decided that "Obs and Gyn" was the specialty for me. All of my patients would be young, usually healthy, and for the most part happy. Only a rare complication or illegitimate baby brought unhappiness.

Pediatrics was also great. I found the time spent in this field to be interesting and enjoyable. I had another "hitch" on the receiving ward which included riding the ambulance. Another intern shared this service with me. The two of us were on call twenty-four hours a day, but then my partner, Dr. Edwin Shepherd, got sick and I had to take care of the Receiving Ward by myself for two weeks. During this period I averaged four hours of sleep a night.

My final service was in Internal Medicine. This specialization also proved to be interesting. Dr. J. B. McElroy, Professor of Medicine at the University of Tennessee, made this specialty exciting by his abilities to diagnose diseases from symptoms and physical findings. He used to tell us that if we listened carefully to

"... When I was asked to serve as Resident Physician
the following year, I accepted."

what the patient told us we also could make an accurate diagnosis.

I became more interested in this specialty as I continued, so
that when I was asked to serve as Resident Physician the following
year, I accepted. I would be paid two thousand dollars a year and
was made Assistant Professor of Medicine in the University
College of Medicine. At the end of my one year's internship on
June 30, 1923, I took over as Resident Physician. At that time the
Memphis General Hospital had only two Residents: Medical and
Surgical. While the interns were paid only twenty-five dollars a
month, the year I served as an intern was the first year they had
been paid anything. An internship was considered a part of the
young doctor's training. With an income of two thousand dollars a

year plus my board, room, laundry and a furnished uniform, I was able to save a little. I not only paid the debts I owed Uncle Cal and Walter Remine, but in the fall was able to buy a second hand Model–T Ford coupe.

I also had some extra money to spend on recreation. By this time Jess Thompson and I had become more than just friends. We were together as frequently as my time off duty would allow. We played tennis, went to shows, parties, and when the weather was suitable, swimming at Lakeview or on Wolf River. "Tommy," as she was called, was also popular with the tennis players about the hospital as she was an excellent player. She was runner-up in the city tournament which determined the championship for women's singles.

"By this time Jess Thompson and I had become more than just friends."

Life did not continue to go smoothly, however, for Miss Thompson was found to have pleurisy with effusion. This condition is nearly always due to tuberculosis. We sent her home to Alabama for treatment which consisted principally of bed rest. Although the prognosis was usually good in such cases, a long period of rest was required. I was greatly disturbed and felt completely lost with her being away so long. We corresponded regularly, but I missed her very much. It was nearly three months before her doctor thought she was ready to return to Memphis. Her recovery seemed to be complete, and she never had a return of any kind of pulmonary disease. I was deeply in love with her, and certain that she was the girl for me. She accepted my proposal for marriage, and we instantly began to plan a wedding that would follow the completion of my residency.

Work in the hospital was pretty heavy most of the time. Our interns varied in number, and we often would have only a medical student to cover one of the Medical Services. I did much of the so-called "skutt work" of an intern because the student intern had to be in school or on some other assignment.

It was my responsibility to see that Internal Medicine and all the medical specialties were properly covered, including Pediatrics, Neurology, Dermatology, Isolation, and Drug Addiction. We also had to give treatments for syphilis two afternoons a week in the out-patient department.

Miss Thompson (I called her Jess) did Kolmer Wassermann tests for the hospital, and for physicians of the city and county. She had an average of 150 tests to make daily. I often helped her get blood from her sheep, inject the sheep's blood in a rabbit, and later bleed the rabbit—for amboceptor—and bleed guinea pigs for "blood complement." The Wassermann test has long since been discarded for a much simpler test for syphilis.

An interesting event occurred one weekend when I was Resident. A rather obese young Negro woman was brought in to the hospital unconscious and with high fever. She had been seen in the Emergency Room about a week previously when a large carbuncle on her neck was incised. She was not examined further and was allowed to return home. She developed fever, however, and on the day she was readmitted to the hospital, became unconscious. Examination with appropriate laboratory studies revealed the fact that she was suffering from blood stream infection and diabetic acidosis with coma.

It happened that we had received a complimentary supply of insulin which had not been put on the market as it had just recently been discovered. I had heard of this long awaited discovery and had read all I could find on its use. Here was an opportunity to try it out. The Intern on Medical Service was out and the laboratory technician was off for the weekend. I got busy. I gave insulin, examined the urine, took blood for estimation of sugar doing the chemistry myself. I recall her first blood sugar estimation was 600 mgs. per cc. Evidence of severe acidosis was confirmed in the tests for acetone and diacetic acid in the urine. I gave insulin every hour until her blood sugar returned to below 150 mgs. per cc., and the amount of sugar in the urine was very much reduced. I worked with the patient all night, but in spite of all I could do, she died the next day from her blood stream infection (Staphylococcic septicemia).

This was the first patient treated with insulin at Memphis General Hospital. I still have not heard of any insulin being used in Memphis previously. Its discovery has been a God-send for diabetics and many lives have been saved by it.

I am fascinated by the fact that in my short life I have witnessed the beginning and development of so many important, and now indispensible things: the electric light, the phonograph, the automobile, the air plane, wireless telegraphy, radio, clinical chemistry, insulin, and many other "miracle drugs," the electrocardiogram, and blood banks.

Jess and I made plans to get married June 7th. I would be finished with my residency by then, and she would be able to get off from her laboratory work for a two weeks' vacation. I had already accepted a job as the Director of the Division of Tuberculosis with the City of Memphis Health Department.

The last few weeks in May were hectic. By that time the rotation of services had resulted in all the medical services being covered by medical students instead of graduate interns. This situation doubled my work, for I had to check more closely on my students. Moreover, the students were about to have their final examinations, and were inclined to give their school work priority over their hospital duties.

In addition, Jess wanted me to go with her to select a place to live, and to buy furniture. These trips, of necessity, had to be brief. To make bad matters worse, more than a thousand Confederate Veterans were in town. Their 1924 reunion was being held, and the second floor of the Isolation Hospital was to be arranged to take care of those who might get ill or injured during the convention. My duty was to take care of them. They evidently had a rip–roaring time marching, singing, and making merry, but many of them fell out from heat and exhaustion and were rushed to the hospital for care. Several became quite drunk and were rushed out to us. One old soldier got out of the ambulance waving his arms and yelling, "Whoopee, we'll whip them damned Yankees yet!" Another old gentleman, age ninety, was brought in unconscious with a 104 degrees fever. I stayed up with him until midnight expecting to see him dead by morning. On going to the hospital early the next day I found him sitting up in bed, reading the morning paper without glasses and being perfectly rational.

By the time the Veterans Reunion was over, I was pretty well exhausted. With all my other hospital duties to take care of, and all the arrangements for our wedding to be made, I felt like I was really under a lot of pressure. I managed to make it, however, and was ready when the day came.

Jess and I also managed to find a little apartment at 940 Faxon Avenue. We had furnished it and were ready to start housekeeping. Neither of us had any money left, so we planned on spending our honeymoon in our own apartment. I truly looked forward to having a home for the first time in twelve years.

Jess had been living in the home of Mrs. Budeke on Claybrook street, and across the street was the Madison Heights Methodist Church. She was a Baptist and I was a Presbyterian, but when I had a date with her on Sunday evenings we usually walked across the street to hear Dr. Lewis preach. This arrangement was convenient and took less of our time. We met the Pastor, Dr. Lewis, and liked him very much, both as a preacher and as a friend. He used to tell us we should join his church because, "Baptist plus Presbyterian equals Methodist."

One evening I called Dr. Lewis and began my conversation by saying, "Dr. Lewis, Miss Thompson and I are thinking about getting married." His immediate reply was, "You must be thinking about it pretty seriously to call a preacher." He consented to perform the ceremony in his home. A formal church wedding was out of the question since neither Jess nor I had parents in Memphis and our circle of friends was rather limited.

So on Saturday afternoon, June 7, 1924, at about 5:00 p.m., we were married at the home of Reverend Lewis, Pastor of the Madison Heights Methodist Church. We invited several of our friends: Dr. William Kraus, director of the laboratory in which Jess worked, Dr. "Red" Kennedy, an intern in the Memphis General Hospital, Dr. J. F. Hamilton who worked in the laboratory with Jess, and several others. After the ceremony we got in our little Ford coupe and took a devious route to the Gayoso Hotel for dinner.

I have never been happier, nor has Jess looked more beautiful. It all seemed too good to be true. I was at last an M.D., had a good job, and—best of all had a dear, loving companion. In addition I was about to have a place I could call home. Only those who have been as homeless as I had been can realize the significance of this new experience to me. We went home after dinner at the Gayoso.

The next morning Jess went to the kitchen to prepare our first breakfast. She wanted to satisfy her new husband, I suppose, and to impress him with her culinary skills, so she suggested that I go for a Sunday newspaper while she got breakfast. I walked to a drug store about four blocks away and got a Sunday issue of *The Commercial Appeal.* When I came back she told me to wait, that breakfast would soon be ready. I sat on the porch and had read the paper almost from cover to cover when she called at about 10:00 a.m. She had made biscuits, fried chicken, and gravy. She confessed she had boiled the coffee dry once before breakfast was ready. I bragged on the breakfast, and, after asking the blessing, kissed her. Jess soon learned to cook more than one thing at a time and to serve a more conventional breakfast with ease. By the time I had to go to work we had adjusted to life as a married couple.

I found the work in the Health Department not difficult, but it was much less interesting to me than clinical medicine. Dr. J. J. Durrett was Director of the Health Department. He had been brought to Memphis by Mayor Rowlett Payne. A graduate of the Harvard School of Public Health, he was the first real specialist in that field who had been Chief of the City of Memphis Health Department. Prior to his coming to Memphis, the city had no milk ordinance and any kind of milk could be sold in Memphis. Dr. Durrett had a real fight with dairymen in trying to enforce the ordinance which allowed only pasteurized milk, or raw milk produced and marketed under very rigid conditions, to be sold in the city.

Tuberculosis was prevalent throughout the region at that time. The death rate from tuberculosis in Tennessee was higher than that in any state in the Union except Colorado. It was high in Colorado because so many people suffering from the disease went to that state for treatment, thinking climate was an important factor. Oakville Memorial Tuberculosis Hospital had been opened a short time before. My responsibility was to locate every case of tuberculosis in the city, see to it that the patient obtained the best care possible, and that measures for preventing the spread of the disease to others were taken. I visited every case reported, and urged them to enter the Sanatorium at Oakville for treatment. The institution was soon filled and the waiting list grew long.

I succeeded in getting the Memphis General Hospital to convert the second floor of the isolation hospital into a facility for taking care of advanced tuberculosis patients. This facility would make it possible to take hopeless and highly infectious cases out of homes and help prevent the spread of the disease to others in the family. The sanitarium at Oakville could be used for the treatment of patients who had a good chance of recovering. Beds could be used to a better advantage and would not be taken up by those advanced and hopeless cases. I saw all these patients daily and assumed the responsibility for the medical care of patients in the Isolation Hospital.

I still recall finding one Negro woman with terminal tuberculosis on a bed in extremely unsanitary conditions in a room where nine other people slept. She was moved to the Isolation

Hospital but died in about two weeks. Within a year six of the nine occupying that room, women and children, were found to have active tuberculosis.

I assisted Doctors Price and Townsend and the doctors of Oakville with tuberculosis clinics in various locations about the city and county. We had no field x-ray equipment but we gave physical examinations, and sent all those we suspected might have tuberculosis to the out-patient x-ray department of the General Hospital.

I cooperated in every way I could with the local office of the Tuberculosis Association, and participated in programs of education in the schools and before various groups. We tried to point out the importance of early diagnosis and prompt treatment, and to dispel the idea most Negroes had that Oakville Sanitarium was a place where people went to die. Among the blacks it was only the far advanced, hopeless, and helpless ones whom we could ever get to go to Oakville!

Meanwhile, Jess continued her work at the City Laboratory. Her salary was $140 a month while mine was $250. We lived on my salary and put hers in a savings account. From the beginning we had a joint checking account and never had the least dispute over money matters. We made it a practice to live within our income, and have never bought anything or made a debt that we couldn't promptly pay. Our furniture, bought on the installment plan at Goldsmith's, cost sixty dollars a month, and was paid without missing a single payment. We valued our credit rating very highly.

We also enjoyed recreation together—tennis, swimming, picture shows, and good musicals which frequently came to the Lyric Theatre. We had many friends, and frequently had them over for dinner. On our first Thanksgiving together we invited Dr. and Mrs. Jospeh Hamilton for dinner. They also had been married only a short time. We bought a turkey and Jess did it justice with dressing, cranberry sauce, mince pie, and all appropriate Thanksgiving dishes. We had a delightful dinner and then went to the Lyric Theatre to see Al G. Field Minstrel. The only difficulty was that we ate such a small amount of turkey that for a week or so afterward, Jess and I had turkey at nearly every meal: turkey sandwiches, turkey hash, and turkey in every conceivable other form until we used it all up.

When Christmas came we decided to have a goose instead of turkey. We had the Hamiltons again, and again found we had much more goose than we needed for one meal. The only difference between goose and turkey was the former seemed to get more greasy as the days went by.

The apartment in which we were living was one of three in the building. It was owned by an elderly, retired Methodist preacher who lived upstairs. His two old maid daughters lived in the other downstairs apartment. Although the building was heated by a coal furnace in the basement, cold weather came and our apartment was never warm. The problem was that the owner was too stingy to use the coal. Consequently we rarely had hot water in our bathroom or kitchen sink. One night the plumbing froze and water leaked from upstairs into our apartment. After expressing our dissatisfaction without satisfactory results, Jess and I decided to move.

We were fortunate in finding a bungalow at 1437 Jefferson Avenue which just suited our needs. It had two bedrooms, a good floor plan, and was in a fine location. Moreover, there was land in back of the house which we could use as a vegetable garden. We certainly found ourselves more comfortably situated than in our first apartment.

In May of 1925 I was asked by the Tuberculosis Society of Shelby County to attend the Trudeau School of Tuberculosis at Saranac Lake, New York and was given $200 to pay my expenses. Except for the fact that I hated to leave Jess, I was glad to take advantage of this opportunity. The "school" was to last six weeks, beginning May 15 and lasting until June 30.

On May 12 I left Memphis wearing a stiff brim straw hat, as it was "straw hat day" in Memphis. I arrived in Chicago early next morning. It was a damp, cloudy day there and the temperature was in the low forties. I had three hours layover before I changed to a New York Central train. So after a bus ride to the New York Central Station, I took a walk up Michigan Avenue. This was my first visit to Chicago, and I wanted to see as much of it as I could.

Everywhere I went—at the railroad station, on the bus, or on the streets—people gazed at my straw hat and made remarks about it. Some even asked me why I was wearing a straw hat so early in the year. In the three hour stay in Chicago I only saw one other straw hat. It was worn by a man who had arrived with me on the train.

As I traveled east I was careful to put my straw hat in an inconspicuous place on the train. I was pleased, however, as we went through Toledo to note headlines in the Toledo paper announcing that it was "straw hat day." But I did not see anybody wearing a straw hat. Next morning in Utica, N.Y., where I had to change cars again, I was able to walk out and see Utica greet the day. It was about seven a.m. and the day was cold and cloudy. Overcoats were worn by all the people hurrying to work. I saw one man who had a new straw hat on and followed him a block or two down the street. He stopped in front of a haberdasher, the show windows of which were filled with new straw hats. He pulled out his keys, opened the door, and turned on the lights. He was the manager, opening shop.

I arrived at last after an interesting ride through central New York at the village of Saranac Lake. A taxi took me to the boarding house which was reserved for me, on Church Street. The landlady who was running this house also was taking care of her son who had come to Saranac Lake for treatment of his tuberculosis. They had come from "down–state" New York. It was said that everyone in Saranac Lake either had tuberculosis, had had it, or was there with some member of his family who had it. And I am sure that statement was not far from the truth.

My landlady was a lovely lady. Her son had been a law student at Cornell University when he developed tuberculosis. When I showed him *The Commercial Appeal* which I received daily, he was very much surprised to see such a good newspaper in the South.

I had my meals next door where I found that the lady running the boarding house had a daughter who was a patient at one of the tuberculosis hospitals there. Next morning I went over for a breakfast which consisted of eggs, bacon, toast, and coffee. Jess had asked me to let her know what the Yankees served for breakfast, as she still could not cook anything except eggs, bacon, and toast. I had to tell her that the Yankees ate the same thing that we did.

The lady told me that a doctor had come in the evening before to attend the School of Tuberculosis and that he would be down for breakfast soon. It wasn't long before he came down, and introduced himself, "Smith is my name, Cha'leston, South Ca'lina." I told him I was glad to see someone from below the Mason Dixon Line. We enjoyed our breakfast together and began a friendship that lasted for years. We were constant companions during our stay in Saranac Lake.

May 15th was a bright morning with the sun shining brightly on a heavy frost, although the temperature was below freezing. I had purchased a cap and therefore did not have to wear my straw hat. A limousine came to pick us up and to take us to the Trudeau Sanitarium where we would attend an intensive course on every phase of tuberculosis. Smith and I, and a young doctor from Windsor, Ontario, joined two or three other doctors in the automobile. Dr. Baldwin, who was the director of the school met us at the entrance to the grounds and said, "Well, boys, you have a beautiful day to start your work, haven't you?" As we drove through the entrance, a doctor in the middle of the back seat who was snuggled down inside of a leather jacket said, "So he calls this a beautiful day! Hell, when I left Phoenix it was 105 and pleasant."

There were about twenty–eight students in the class who came from all over the United States and from several foreign countries. They were from their late twenties to their fifties in age. All worked in either tuberculosis hospitals, public health, or in private practice specializing in tuberculosis.

The faculty was made up of men who were from Saranac Lake, but several came from other sections of the country. All were leaders in the field, and were nationally and internationally known as authorities. Without exception they were first rate. Dr. Baldwin was the director. Dr. Lawrason Brown, Dr. Soper, Dr. Gardner, Dr. Petroff, and Dr. Alexander from New York City were on the faculty, while Homer Sampson was in x-ray.

The course was thorough. Every aspect of tuberculosis was discussed: the bacteriology, pathology, x-ray diagnosis, symptomatology, physical findings, prevention and treatment. The latest methods in the 1920s such as pheniceotomy, pneumothoraz, surgery, rest and diet were discussed. Complications were also covered. Six weeks of intensive study and lectures resulted in our being saturated with the subject of Tuberculosis.

On the day after I arrived in Saranac Lake, I went to the bank (there was only one in town). I took $200 in Travelers Checks and a $100 check on a Memphis Bank to open a checking account. I explained to the teller that I was a student in the Trudeau School of Tuberculosis and that while I was in town I wanted to be able to pay my bills by check. He accepted my deposit and said he was glad to open the account for me. On the following day, a fellow student, Dr. Davenport from Ohio, asked me what I was doing about my fianances. When I told him I had opened a checking account at the bank, he said he would like to do the same.

I went with him to the bank. Dr. Davenport was about fifty years old. He was the director of a Veterans Administration Hospital in Ohio. He went to the bank teller, the same one with whom I had dealt the day before, and told him that he wanted to open a checking account. The teller asked Dr. Davenport if he could give any references. When the doctor responded that he knew no one in town, the teller replied that he was not eligible to open a checking account. Hearing the argument, I stepped up to the window and told the teller that I had a checking account there and would be glad to endorse his customer. Although the teller allowed Dr. Davenport to open the account, we left the bank. Dr. Davenport was very angry! Why had he accepted me, just a thirty year old boy without a reference, and turned down a mature man in his fifties? I told him I didn't know, but now I am sure the answer to that question lies in the approaches we had made.

Dr. Davis, a student from Johnson City, New York, had brought his car so that he could go home at frequent intervals. He, Dr. Billy Smith, and I took frequent tours around the area to Lake Placid, Tupper Lake, Ausable Chasms, and other nearby places of interest. One evening the Chamber of Commerce of Saranac Lake entertained us with a "Flap Jack Fry" on upper Saranac Lake. It was a delightful occasion, but I have never seen mosquitoes more vicious. If we had not had a screened area in which to enjoy the occasion, I don't believe we could have tolerated it. One member of the Chamber of Commerce introduced himself to me saying, "And where do you live?" I told him, "Memphis, down in Dixie," using the same advertising slogan for the Memphis radio station WMC. He said, "Memphis, Dixie, eh? Memphis, Dixie. I've never been further south than Pittsburgh, myself." It was obvious to me that he had not.

When I told another gentleman that I came from Memphis, Tennessee, he said, "I have a friend down that way. You may know him." "What is his name and where does he live?," I asked. "His name is Jones, and he lives in Washington, D.C." I told him I did not know him, but I skipped telling him how far Washington, D.C. was from Memphis!

One Saturday my friend, Dr. McKenzie from Windsor, Ontario, and I took a bus trip over to Plattsburg. There we saw Lake Champlain, the monument commemorating the Battle of Ticonderoga, and other interesting sights.

The weather of that area of New York was interesting. Frequently we had a killing frost as late as June 25. Once a two inch snow fell on May 25. I was amused at the appearance of many men on the streets wearing white linen suits, white shoes, stiff brimmed straw hats, and overcoats. It was a common saying that "Saranac Lake has three seasons: July, August and winter." The only vegetables that grew there were Irish potatoes. Nevertheless we had several days in June when the weather was hot and, with the high humidity, the nights hot and sultry.

There were three churches in the village: a Catholic, an Episcopalian and a Presbyterian. Dr. McKenzie, my Canadian friend, and I attended the latter. One Sunday a special collection was taken to send missionaries to the South! The preacher told the congregation that there were more than 900 communities in the south, east of the Mississippi River, without Sunday Schools. He also stated that the Mississippi River "region was the most God-forsaken country he had ever seen." You can imagine how McKenzie ragged me about that. I told him that, because I could speak the language, I might apply for the job.

I wrote to and heard from Jess almost every day. Never had I been so homesick to see anybody. It seemed sometimes that time dragged on extremely slowly. On June 7, our first anniversary, we were hundreds of miles apart. I found a florist and sent her a dozen roses by F.T.D. She was still working, but we agreed that she would give up her job on July 1st. July 1st came finally. School was out and we were headed home. This time I packed my cap and wore my straw hat. Instead of going back through Chicago, I decided to go through New York City. I had a friend there who was interning in Flowers Hospital, and I wrote him that I was coming through. He was Joseph V. Caltagirone, a former student at the University of Tennessee College of Medicine and, later, a student intern in Memphis General Hospital when I was a resident physician.

The trip from Albany down along the Hudson river was an interesting, scenic trip. On my arrival in Grand Central Station, "Cal," as we called him, was there to meet me. When he insisted that I spend the night at his home, we took a taxi to Troutman Street in Brooklyn where he and his family lived on the second floor of a large apartment house in a solidly Italian community. Signs on windows, advertising, street directions and newspapers all were in Italian. The family was jolly, very friendly and extremely hospitable. They had moved to America from Sicily when Cal was thirteen years old. His mother spoke only Italian. His father spoke very broken English, and a sister who was older than Cal spoke good English but with a definite Italian accent. A brother and sister younger than Cal spoke English with no accent at all.

The following day Cal took me on a tour of New York City. We traveled by surface cars and by subway and saw Rockefeller Institute, Columbia University, City College, Central Park, Mulberry Street's Chinatown, Wall Street, the Battery, and even the Statue of Liberty. We arrived at the latter after the elevator had quit running for the day, and we climbed the winding stairs to the top. We looked out the windows in her crown. What a sight! Next day we went to Coney Island. There I rode on the highest and most frightening "Roly Coaster" I have ever seen. I said a silent prayer on that ride, promising the Good Lord that if I got off it alive, I would never ride on it again. We also visited Harlem and the Harlem General Hospital. Nearly all the patients there were black, but a few whites were seen in some of the wards. A white here and there among many blacks seemed odd.

We arrived back at Cal's home about 6:30 p.m., tired, hot, and thirsty. Dinner was ready for us. Here I met the whole family at the dinner table. I could speak to the mother only through an interpreter, but she was a most gracious hostess. The father, who sat at the head of the table, was in a gay mood. For drinks only beer and wine were served. I was dry and thirsty and, therefore, asked for beer. Mr. Caltagirone laughed and said, "Why you no drinka da wine. Wine make biga strong muscles." He flexed his arms to demonstrate. "Beer makes too biga da bell," he said, patting his abdomen.

We started eating at about seven p.m. First we were served anchovies on a sweet pepper, covered with olive oil. Next came a large plate, heaped with spaghetti which was sprinkled with grated, sharp cheese. Here I learned to eat spaghetti as Italians eat it by gathering a fork full of spaghetti and twisting it against a large spoon into a ball that would fit the mouth. Thinking this was the main course, I ate it all. To my surprise we were served a half chicken, broiled, after the spaghetti. As we ate, our host became more jolly and even broke into song, repeating the chorus of "Why did I kiss that girl?" many times.

I found that a sip of wine occasionally made it possible to eat what was served without discomfort. For dessert we were served blocks of ice cream and cake. Two blocks of ice cream were put on my plate. What a meal! It finally ended at 10:00 p.m. I was afraid such a feast would keep me awake that night; however, even though I slept in the bed with Cal's ten year old brother, I slept soundly all night.

Next day we planned to go to the station to catch the train home. About the time we were ready to go, there came a downpour of rain which continued all morning. Because of flooding streets, surface street cars were not running, and although we tried running from one street to another, we could not hail a taxi. When we finally caught one, we had less than a half hour to make it from Troutman Street in Brooklyn to the Pennsylvania Station in Manhattan. We got in and Cal told the driver that our making it on time would mean an extra tip. The ride following was a hair-raising one. It was evident that the New York police paid little attention to speeders, for of all the rides I ever took, this one was the most exciting. The taxi driver rushed through wet streets, dodging traffic, skidding around corners, and barely missing pedestrians at break–neck speed — all to no avail. We arrived at the station ten minutes after the train had left.

I wired Jess, who was in Bristol with Blanche, to tell her that I would be a day late. Then I went with Cal to Flowers Hospital to spend the night with him in intern quarters.

Next day I arrived by subway at Pennsylvania Station a half-hour or more before the train left and caught it that time. After another all-night ride on a train that I thought was mighty slow, I arrived in Bristol at about 11:00 a.m. on July 3. There on the platform with Blanche was Jess!

It was a joy indeed to be with Jess once more. It seemed so long since we had been together. I was glad also to be in East Tennessee again and to be with Blanche and her family. It was Jess's first trip to East Tennessee. That afternoon when we were all leaving the house to go for a drive, Jess remarked that we had better take umbrellas because that big black cloud in the east certainly indi- cated rain. We laughed, because "the big black cloud" was the mountain in the distance. She hadn't seen the mountains before.

Next day, after a good visit with Blanche, Jess and I caught the "Memphis Special." It was good to be home at last, and at our little home on Jefferson Avenue we started all over again: I went back to work with the Health Department; Jess, who was no longer working, enjoyed housekeeping. Joe (Dr. J. F.) and Ruby Hamil- ton, who moved into the bungalow next door, were our closest friends, and delightful neighbors.

Work at the Health Department was very much the same until Dr. Cummings Harris, Director of Communicable Disease Con- trol, became ill. He had a large, non–toxic goitre removed and was away from his office for several weeks. During Dr. Harris' absence, I was given the responsibility of taking care of communicable disease problems, spending much time while I was at the office immunizing school children and supervising the nurses. We also had many children brought in for anti–rabies inoculations. Twenty–one daily injections were required in each case. We could hear the poor kids crying out on the street as their mothers dragged them in for their "shot" daily for three long weeks.

At this time a small pox epidemic occurred. Within a period of about three weeks I saw, personally, 150 cases. We vaccinated every contact we could find, including all persons who might have been near the patient where he worked. I would take a nurse and have every employee of the plant in which the patient worked sent to a designated place in the plant for vaccination. At the Uneeda Biscuit Company Plant, we vaccinated 200 employees in one day. The importance of vaccination in preventing infection was well publicized, and, as a result, there was a constant line of people coming to the Health Department for vaccination. The epidemic was soon over and smallpox only returned rarely afterward.

One of the duties given to me during this period was taking care of students in "The Lions Open Air School," which was supported by the Lions Club. The students were children whose health was below par and who had been exposed to tuberculosis, many having reacted positively to tuberculin tests. I visited the school once or twice weekly and checked with the principal on any problem pertaining to the health of the pupils. These children were given well-balanced diets and required to take rest periods in open air (on screened porches) twice daily.

From the time we were married, Jess and I attended church regularly. We agreed that we should both belong to the same church, and, because I was a Presbyterian and she was a Baptist, one of us would have to change church membership. At the beginning we would go one Sunday to a Presbyterian Church and the next to a Baptist, trying to decide which we would both eventually join. It occurred to me that I was a Presbyterian because my father and his family belonged to that denomination. I thought then that the more intelligent way to decide was to learn in detail what the various denominations actually believed and what they stood for. I read several books and pamphlets on the subject and found that the Baptist belief was in accord with my own. I remember a statement attributed to a Negro man when he was asked why he was a Baptist; he replied, "I'se a Baptist because I believes in de Bible." Therefore I decided to join the Baptist church where Jess and I could worship together.

Jess was a member of the Central Baptist Church in Memphis. The pastor was Dr. Ben Cox, an Englishman. Somehow I did not think his sermons were nearly as good as those I heard Dr. A. U.

Boone, Pastor of the First Baptist Church, preach. During my medical school days I had gone to Sunday School at First Baptist Church on the invitation of one of my teachers, Dr. John McIntosh. The teacher of that class, Mr. Sam Holloway, was one of the best I had ever heard, and I told Jess that if she would move her membership to First Baptist Church, I would join that church with her. She was glad to do so, and in the fall of 1924, we joined the First Baptist Church. I was baptized by immersion by Dr. A. U. Boone. Jess joined by letter. We became active in the church at once. Jess took a class in the Primary Department of the Sunday School. I became a member of the choir, singing bass (thanks to my old High School Glee Club training), and I attended the Baraca Class regularly. I soon began teaching in the Intermediate Department, a class of 15 year old boys. Bob Sanders, Duke McCall, and Milton Duncan are a few I remember belonging to the class then. Later I consented to teach the Berean Class in the Young Peoples Department.

Teaching the Bible stimulated me to study it, and the more I knew of the Bible, the more I was convinced that it was truly the Word of God. I was happy in my church activities and got much pleasure from the fellowship with Christian people. We soon made friends with many people, and we have enjoyed their friendship many years.

About this time I read a book by Dr. E. Stanley Jones, *The Christ of the Indian Road.* This book was just what I needed and was looking for. I wanted more from being a church member than the pleasure of association with good people. I wanted real faith with a complete relief from doubt. This book helped me regain the faith that had weakened so much during the preceding years. From then on I took part in church activities not so much because I liked the fellowship, but because I felt I was doing God's will. My love for Christian activities was motivated by my love for Jesus. I wanted to do His will.

XI

The Polyclinic

My desire to do clinical medicine continued. While public health work is a noble profession in that by preventing disease many people are benefitted, the physician practicing clinical medicine sees the results of his work at once. The physician who is doing public health work must measure his success in terms of months or years by watching the decline of the incidence of disease in the total population. He can get great satisfaction from statistics indicating the number of deaths prevented by controlling typhoid, tuberculosis, small pox and other diseases, by better water, sanitary milk, immunization programs, stricter isolation and such measures.

Nevertheless, I wanted to practice medicine. Consequently, when Dr. Henry Rudner came down to the City Health Department offices and asked if I would join his practice, I was immediately interested. Dr. Rudner had about the biggest practice in Memphis. Moreover, since he was Jewish and spoke Yiddish as well, he was especially popular among the Jews of the city. He also spoke Italian and was therefore very popular among the Italian people of Memphis. After talking the matter over with Jess and Dr. Durrett, I finally accepted Dr. Rudner's offer.

I turned over my work with the Health Department to a schoolmate, Dr. Obersmith, and joined Dr. Rudner on October 1, 1925. The work with Dr. Rudner turned out to be interesting and rewarding, but I encountered many unpleasant experiences. For example, the Orthodox Jews often refused to see me, even when Dr. Rudner sent me on house calls. "Vare is Dr. Rudner? If we can't have Dr. Rudner, we call somebody else," and slam went the door.

The Italians liked me and I found them to be the most appreciative patients I ever cared for. However, when one would tell Dr. Rudner, "You don't needa come to see us. We lika Dr. Strain alla right," I never got to see that patient again.

To augment my limited income, I accepted a job as insurance examiner for the Life and Casualty Insurance Company. This proved to be unprofitable. I found if I filled out the form accurately noting heart murmurs, high blood pressure, and other physical abnormalities that would result in the rejection of the applicant for insurance, the agent would never refer another applicant to me. Needless to say, the word got around quickly.

The insurance office then gave me the job of checking on policy holders who claimed disability for more than a week. I visited several sick policy holders, most of whom were black. If I found the poor soul sitting up and reported it, the insurance benefits would be stopped because the policy, in small print, said that the disability must be such that the disabled must be "confined to bed."

On one particular case I was sent to see a patient who was claiming disability because of "an infected thumb." His doctor, who was black, had sent in claims for disability on that diagnosis. On examining the patient and taking a good history, I found that he had been a cook in a restaurant on Beale Street. He had injured his thumb while preparing wild rabbits for cooking. I immediately thought of a disease described recently in the Journal of the American Medical Association by Dr. Edward Francis of the United Public Health Service—Tularemia.

I had seen two cases a short time previously, one previously diagnosed as Military Tuberculosis (whose recovery gave me a clue), and the other with an infected thumb, and abscesses under the arm and near the elbow. Both of these patients worked in meat markets and handled rabbits. I had sent serum from these patients to Dr. Francis in Washington, and received a report from him by telegram and a letter. He confirmed my diagnosis by telling me that I had discovered the first cases of Tularemia in the state of Tennessee. Consequently, I sent serum to Washington from my latest patient so that it could be tested. The results showed that he too had Tularemia. In a short time I discovered nine cases, all associated with wild rabbits. I reported them before the Tennessee

Medical Association and my paper was published in the *Journal of Tennessee Medical Association,* 1926.

One evening while I was completing some records of patients at the Baptist Hospital Dr. R. L. Sanders came up and put his hand on my shoulder. "How are you getting along, Fred?" he said.

"Very well, I suppose," I answered.

"Are you happy in your work?"

"I can't say that I am, Dr. Sanders," I said.

"I didn't think you would be. How would you like to come over and join us at the Polyclinic?" It sounded too good to be true, a real answer to a prayer.

"I can't think of anything I'd like better," I said at once.

The Polyclinic was a group of the best doctors in the city. Dr. Sanders had been trained at the Mayo Clinic and had visions of building such an institution in Memphis. He had secured several doctors who had also trained at the Mayo Clinic: Dr. C. H. Heacock, a Radiologist, Dr. W. C. Chaney, an Internist, Dr. H. W. Hundling, a surgeon and Dr. T. D. Moore a Urologist. Dr. Carl Sanders, the brother of R. L. Sanders, and Dr. J. P. Henry Internists; Dr. C. D. Blessingame an Otolaryngologist, and Dr. O. S. Warr, a classmate of Dr. R. L. Sanders, were also members of the group. I had worked with most of these men when I was an Intern, and several of them had been my teachers in medical school. Without exception there were none better in Memphis, not only professionally, but also in terms of integrity and personality.

That evening I told Dr. Rudner about Dr. Sanders' offer, and that I would like to accept it. Dr. Rudner's reaction pleased me. He said, "Freddy (that's what he always called me), I knew you weren't happy here. . . . I can't help being selfish. I'm not accustomed to working with someone else. I think you would be happier if you were with that group. I'd like for us to remain friends, for I have always admired and liked you." My friendship with Dr. Rudner has continued throughout the years since.

So after two weeks I became a member of the Polyclinic. Not only were the working conditions more pleasant and stimulating, but my income was better. All the doctors in the group were delightful companions, generous in their relations to me and Jess, and sincere, conscientious men. All remained among my dearest friends in the following years.

From the beginning I worked closely with Dr. Warr who with Dr. R. L. Sanders was an organizer of the group, and who was the Professor of Medicine at the University of Tennessee Medical College. We had weekly staff meetings at which the program was made up of a short report from our business manager, B. H. Shawhan, reviews of journals in three specialties by three specialists in our group; and an original paper by one of the doctors.

I was made program chairman and secretary of these meetings. I was also assigned three journals to review for the staff, periodically. They were the *Journal of the National Tuberculosis Association, The Archives of Internal Medicine,* and *The American Journal of Medical Science.* That meant I was supposed to read these three journals thoroughly as they came each month, and be able to give a summary of important articles in them to the staff when my time came to be on the program. These staff meetings resulted in our keeping abreast of all new developments in every specialty of medicine. It was a valuable process of continuing education.

One of the duties assigned to me a short time after I joined the clinic was electrocardiography. Dr. Henry had been doing this work, but because he wanted to give his entire time to allergy, he wanted me to assume this task. Electrocardiography was a new diagnostic procedure at that time. When I began there were only two other doctors in Memphis who had electrocardiographs. The instrument at that time was not as highly developed as are the modern ones. The clinic owned the Hindle Electrocardiograph which was as large as a piano. The tracing was made by recording on photographic paper the shadow of a fine silver covered quartz filament which vibrated with each heart beat, as the minute electric impulse flowed through it. It was stretched tightly between the poles of a powerful magnet which caused the vibrations.

At that time only three leads were used: leads I, II and III. Today twelve leads are routine. The film on which the tracing was reflected had to be developed like any photographic film. This was done as a rule, and certainly by us, in the same solutions in which X-ray films were developed.

Since electrocardiography was such a new science we had to learn the principles of it from the beginning. The interpretations of the tracings with only three leads was just being developed. This new responsibility called for much study and research from me. In fact, by my hesitancy in saying, "No," I soon found myself overloaded with many activities. In addition to teaching a Sunday School class and singing in the choir, I was ordained a deacon in the church. I also became a member of the Medical Staff of the Memphis General Hospital, and before I knew it I was made secretary of that organization. I also accepted the job of lecturing to the senior dental students twice weekly on "Dental Medicine." This course covered those diseases of the mouth that had systemic effects, and general systemic diseases with manifestations in the mouth. On top of all of this I became attending physician on the Charity Service at the Baptist Hospital. I also became a member of the Memphis and Shelby County Medical Society and I did some teaching in the Out-Patient Medical Clinic.

Each of these duties required my attendance at weekly or monthly meetings so that I soon found that Saturday evening was my only evening at home. I was foolish to accept so many responsibilities as I had practically no time for recreation. Jess encouraged me in my activities and cooperated with me in every way. I was fortunate indeed that she was not very much interested in social affairs.

Because of my continued interest in tuberculosis, I expressed a desire to attend the meeting of the National Tuberculosis Association that was being held in Washington, D.C. in October of 1926. When Dr. "R. L." heard about it, he told me that I should go. The Clinic would pay my expenses. A policy of the Clinic was to send members to national or state meetings of various medical organizations. A report of these meetings was then made to the staff. This was another way that the clinic staff could be kept informed about progress being made in the medical profession.

So I attended the meeting of the National Tuberculosis Association in October. It was my first visit to Washington. I stayed at the Mayflower Hotel on Connecticut Avenue. I was delighted to find there, without a hotel reservation, my old friend of Saranac Lake days, Dr. Billy Smith of Charleston, S.C. I told the room clerk

I'd take a double room and let Dr. Smith share it with me. We had four more days together, attending the meetings and seeing the sights.

On this trip to Washington I saw traffic lights for the first time, and for the first time saw women smoking cigarettes in public. Times were changing! Dr. Delmar Goode a medical schoolmate, was working with the Veteran's Administration in Washington. He was kind enough to take us for a long drive over the city. I saw a number of my acquaintances from the Trudeau School of Tuberculosis, both faculty and students at this meeting.

During my stay in Washington I called Dr. Edward Francis of the "Hygienic Laboratories" (now called the National Institute of Health) and asked him if I could see him and discuss Tularemia. He was the discoverer of the disease while studying a plague-like disease in rodents in Tulare County, California. Tularemia is the only disease first discovered, described in detail, and completely worked up in the United States.

Dr. Francis invited me out and when I asked him if he would get someone to show me over the Laboratory, he said, "Get somebody, Hell! I'll show you myself!" When I got to the laboratory he met me as if I had been his long lost brother. "Old Tularemia Strain!" he said as he grabbed my hand and slapped me on the back. He then took me to his laboratory where he introduced me to his staff as if I had been someone important, and showed me the work he had done, and was doing in the study of Tularemia. He then took me all over the laboratory building. He introduced me to Admiral Stitt whose textbook on Tropical Medicine I had studied in school, and who was at that time revising the book. After leaving the laboratory I returned to my hotel feeling elated from the delightfully interesting experience I had enjoyed.

On my return to Memphis, Jess met me at the station. When I asked her who drove the car, she proudly told me she had herself. After I left the City Health Department we used the money we had saved from Jess's salary and bought a Dodge "Business Man's Coupe." It had four cylinders, disc wheels, chrome plated radiator, a motor-meter, and cost $1,385.00. Jess had never driven a car before and decided that while I was gone she would learn. She had a friend go with her a few times while she drove until she felt confident she could drive. Back in Memphis, I took up my busy schedule again. Some changes came, however, as Jess and I had planned and hoped for children. Consequently, we were delighted when it became evident that our wishes were coming true. When we found that our first child was on the way, Jess thought that living in an apartment would be easier for her than living in the bungalow on Jefferson Avenue. Accordingly we looked at several apartments and finally decided to move to 891 Maury. This apartment building was new and very satisfactory.

On February 1, 1927 about 11:00 a.m. one of her friends, Ethel Wiersema, who had a month old baby, was visiting Jess. She called me at the clinic and told me I had better get Jess to the hospital for she was having pains every ten minutes. Jess did not realize what the pains meant and was practically disregarding them. I rushed out to get my car and there it stood with a flat tire. I ran back in the clinic and found Dr. Alf Mason, who had recently joined us, and got his car, a Plymouth "Pathfinder."

I called our obstetrician, Dr. Percy Toombs and got Jess and her things to the Baptist Hospital. We got to the hospital at about 12:00 noon and the baby came at 2:00 p.m.

The child was a boy and we named him Samuel Frederick Strain, Jr. He wasn't a pretty baby, but he was active and healthy. I cannot imagine how parents could be more proud of a baby than we were. He weighed six pounds and twelve ounces, and nobody could have persuaded me that he wasn't the finest baby in the world. I think I know what David meant when he said "My cup runneth over!"

Jess got along well after delivery. It was customary in those days to keep mothers in bed longer than has been found to be necessary. She was discharged on the twelfth day. We both felt a great sense of responsibility taking home a tiny new baby. Staying in bed twelve days had left Jess very weak. We were fortunate in securing a very competent and reliable Negro maid, "Sarah," who was able to do the housework as well as take care of the baby and Jess. One day Sarah's husband came by to get her. He looked at little Fred and since he could not honestly say he was a pretty baby, he said, "Dat boy sho is got a head fur a heap o' sense!" His prediction proved very true in later years.

Jess proved to be an ideal mother. Taking care of her baby and her household responsibilities took precedence over every other activity. I do not recall our ever hiring a baby sitter. Taking care of our child was more important to us than any show or party.

When Fred was five months old I got a two week's vacation. There had been much talk about the Memphis-to-Bristol highway, and part of it was completed. It was called State Highway No. 1. I had always thought that driving the entire distance would be most interesting, especially since I wanted to see East Tennessee again.

We decided to spend our vacation taking such a trip. Our sturdy Dodge was in good condition, and we thought the tires were good enough. We knew we couldn't drive the entire distance to Bristol in one day, so we planned to spend a night at the Sedberry Hotel in McMinnville, Tennessee.

We got away early on our great adventure. The old auto ran well, but on a smooth, straight road the top speed I could get was only forty–five miles per hour. Moreover, the highway varied a great deal from county to county. Some stretches were well graded and concreted while in another area the road was under construction and very rough. It also could be the old, original, county road, narrow and crooked.

As we approached the Tennessee River east of Camden, the road became sandy across the river bottom. At this location we had a flat tire. A thunder storm was approaching when I got out to jack-up the car to change the tire. While I was jacking-up the car a rather severe thunder storm came. The lightning struck a tree ahead of us that stood near a fence by the side of the road. The charge ran along the barbed wire near me and I got a jolting electric shock. I recovered quickly and got in the car immediately where I sat until the drenching rain was over, and the storm had moved away from us. When I got back out of the car to finish the job of changing the tire, I found the highway covered with ankle deep water. I had to feel in the water to find my tools. After about an hour's delay we finally got started again.

Since there was no bridge across the river, we took a ferry. There was not much traffic in those days and consequently there were only two other cars on the boat.

We had brought a picnic lunch so we would not have to stop at a restaurant for lunch. At noon we found a shady grove along the highway where we stopped for lunch. It had rained some and the ground was wet, but it was cloudy and the temperature was pleasant. Fred seemed more content when we stopped as the constant noise, jolting and swaying of the car seemed to make him restless.

After a lunch of sandwiches, fruit, and tea from the thermos jug we continued our journey. The rain began again, however, and we soon found ourselves on a very rough detour around several miles of highway that was being constructed. The road was muddy and rocky and when we finally came to the end of the detour and were again on the pavement, we discovered we had a flat tire. Not only was it flat, it had been ruined by the rough rocky road. It was another hour or more before the car was ready to go as I had to repair the flat spare tire by patching the innertube and pumping it up before we could continue. It was growing late, but fortunately the days were long. Poor little Fred was getting more fretful, and Jess was worried and nervous. We did not realize that we should have brought bottles with us for a supplemental feeding.

We finally drove up to the Sedberry Hotel in McMinnville at about 8:00 p.m. A young Negro boy in a uniform came to the car as I was getting out and said, "Is this the doctor from Memphis?" When I told him it was, he said "We're waitin' supper on you." After going into the hotel, registering, and taking our baggage to our room, we were escorted to the dining room. We were assured that they were glad to have us, and were received most cordially. We were the only guests in the dining room. The negro boy came, took Fred, and entertained him by walking him around the dining room while we ate. We were seated at a table with a white tablecloth, and without asking us what we wanted, the waiters began bringing in the food. It was a most delightful dinner.

The Sedberry Hotel was an old institution owned and operated by three unmarried Sedberry sisters. It had the reputation of serving the "best meals between the Atlantic and the Pacific," and I was inclined to believe that statement. I had heard the praises of the hotel and been advised that it was the best between Memphis and Bristol. Our stay was all that we could have asked.

We felt much better after a good night's rest and prepared to leave next morning for Bristol. Before I left McMinnville, however, I had to buy a tire. There was only one service station open on that Sunday morning and they had only one tire that would fit my car. It was a "United States" tire that cost thirty-two dollars. That transaction depleted my finances considerably, but punctures were so common that I could not think of driving without a spare.

We had a puncture, too, before we got halfway to Knoxville. I certainly had plenty of experience changing tires by the end of the trip.

The journey to Knoxville was over roads that were as rough as these we had encountered on the first day. Highway 1 which was to cross the Cumberland plateau and mountains was unfinished, and had sharp curves over steep grades, narrow roads, and gravel roadbeds. In addition, roads that were still under construction made traveling somewhat slow. We were still struck by the beauty of the Cumberlands around Sparta and when we passed through Cookeville, Monterey, Crossville, and Rockwood. We crossed the Clinch River at Kingston and saw large peach orchards there. We finally reached the "Kingston Pike" which we followed into Knoxville. This road was newly "McAdamized," but was still hilly, crooked, and narrow.

It had grown late by the time we reached Knoxville and little Fred was getting fretful. We therefore decided to spend the night there. I drove through the grounds of the University of Tennessee to show Jess where I had attended college. Seeing my old Chemistry professor, Dr. Hill, standing by Science Hall, I stopped the car, got out, and spoke to him. I told him who I was and that I had enjoyed his course.

Since motels had not come into existence yet, we went to the Farragut Hotel where we found lodging for the night. The Farragut was relatively new and was built on the site formerly occupied by the old Imperial Hotel which had burned while I was a student in Knoxville. It was in Knoxville that we discovered Fred was cutting his first tooth, a lower incisor.

We got away fairly early next morning knowing that we had only about 140 more miles to go. We took U.S. Highway 11–W out of Knoxville and went up through Rutledge, Rogersville, and Kingsport. I had wanted to go by 11–E through Morristown,

Greenville, Limestone, Jonesboro and Johnson City, but because of our experience traveling with Fred, I thought the quickest route was the most desirable.

The road was not too good, but our trip was uneventful. We stopped at Tate Springs, once a famous resort because of the mineral spring there. The water from the spring was recommended as a cure for rheumatism, anemia, and a host of other causes of poor health. I got a thermos jug of the water to tease Blanche, as I knew it was foul tasting. Sure enough when she tried the water, she found it to be terrible.

At last we arrived in Bristol around the middle of the afternoon. It is hard to think that trip of only five hundred miles took us most of three days to make. The journey had been very tiresome and taught us how foolish we had been to take it with an infant. Poor Jess and Fred were both pretty well worn by the time we completed the journey. After a few days rest we all felt much better. After a delightful and restful visit with Blanche and her family we left for a blessedly uneventful trip home.

XII

Sanatorium, Mississippi

We resumed our usual routine back in Memphis. I was busy constantly as I had been before, but I seemed to tire unduly and I began to have long periods of insomnia. I noticed also that my pulse was high and I was losing weight. One day my temperature reached 99.8 degrees and I had Dr. Carl (Sanders) examine me. A chest X-ray revealed a small infiltration in the upper lobe of my left lung. There was no question in my mind that I had active tuberculosis of the lung!

My parents had both died of the disease and being intimately exposed to them during childhood, it was a wonder that I had not developed it sooner. Four of my brothers and sisters had developed active tuberculosis with two, Lucy and Annie Jackson, having died from the disease. I was the fifth to get it.

I knew it was minimal but wanted to do something to prevent its becoming more advanced. Carl Sanders and Dr. Otis Warr tried to minimize the situation and to relieve my mind by telling me not to worry. I knew enough about tuberculosis, however, to know that it was not a disease to be disregarded. It is treacherous and requires the greatest care in preventing its spreading. I also knew that recovery could be brought only with proper rest. My greatest fear was that I might expose Fred to the infection at an age when he was most susceptible.

My two doctors insisted that I get as much rest as possible while I continued my work. I therefore stopped all other activities except my work in the clinic, taking a rest period after lunch every day, and stopping all house calls. I also took general ultra-violet radiation daily.

These measures were so effective that within a few weeks I had

172

gained weight, my pulse rate became normal, my temperature was no longer fast, and I did not readily tire. After about two months an X-ray examination of my chest showed considerable clearing. I was greatly encouraged but knew such a routine would have to be continued until complete healing was assured. I gradually increased my work at the clinic, but was careful to avoid undue fatigue. I gradually began to feel that my health was good again, and I resumed normal living.

We had planned to have several children, but I was now somewhat apprehensive because of the threat of tuberculosis which hung over me. When it appeared that I was all right again, Jess and I agreed that it might be safe. We were happy to find in the summer of 1928 that another child was on the way. We decided to move into a larger house with a spare bedroom so that Jess' mother could come and live with us. We therefore moved to 659 Dickinson Street. Jess' second pregnancy went just as smoothly as the first. She had no trouble at all, and we looked forward to the day when our little family would increase.

Fred was growing and developing normally in every way. He was as active as a squirrel, doing unbelievable things like putting his little dog in the ice box (we didn't have an electric refrigerator); feeding the remains of a baked hen to his dog; pouring a box of borax in the skillet in which sausage was frying; and similar stunts. One day our next door neighbor found him standing on the wash basin in their bathroom attempting to shave with a straight razor! He was only about two years old at that time.

In December of 1928 an epidemic of influenza struck the city. I constantly made house calls, doing little else beyond seeing five to ten patients in their homes every day. The weather turned bitterly cold around Christmas and to our surprise the epidemic came to an abrupt halt. But to our dismay Jess came down with the disease within a few weeks before her delivery was expected. Jess' mother came to be with us and she was a great help in taking care of Fred. No man ever had a dearer, more lovable mother–in–law than I had.

On the night of January 1, 1929 Jess began having pains. They were very light and rather infrequent but we got ready to take her to the hospital. At the same time I received a call telling me that one of my patients, an old lady, was apparently dying from pneumonia

174

following influenza. I rushed out to see her, hoping that Jess would be alright until I got back. I found the patient in critical condition, obviously dying. I explained to the family my situation at home and that there was nothing I could do for the patient. I asked them to let me rush home and I promised I would keep in touch with them. They were sensible people and agreed.

I hurried home where I found Jess' pains closer together and more severe. I left Fred with "Mama Tom," as Fred called her, and took Jess to the hospital. We arrived about midnight with the baby coming at about 8:00 a.m. on January 2, 1929. It was another boy. He weighed 7½ lbs., and was in perfect condition. We named him James Edgar. In spite of her weakness due to the recent attack of influenza, Jess recovered splendidly.

We were delighted with our little family and prayed daily that our two sons would grow up to be honorable, God–fearing men. Our prayers were answered—and we have always been proud of them both.

Things continued as usual in my work. Jess and her mother took excellent care of our boys and our home. We had lots of friends who were a pleasure and comfort and our future looked bright. We were trying to save enough money to make a down payment on a house, and looked at several in hopes that we could buy one.

At this time, however, a cloud began to appear on our horizon. My previous symptoms began to reappear. In spite of the slowing of my activities, they continued. In desperation, I had another chest x–ray film made. To my dismay the previous signs had reappeared, and if anything the infiltration was greater than revealed by the previous examination. This development was a blow. I now knew that I must give up my work and take the "rest cure" for a period long enough to insure complete recovery. Dr. Warr and Carl thought I could recover by resuming the routine I had followed before, but I knew enough about tuberculosis to realize I could no longer take any chances.

At Dr. Warr's suggestion I went to Cincinnati to consult a widely known authority on the disease. Dr. Kennon Dunham was the author of a book on the diagnosis and treatment of tuberculosis, and had lectured to us at the Trudeau School of tuberculosis.

After checking my x-ray films and examining me he advised that I give up work, and apply myself full time to the business of "taking the cure." He gave me a tour of the Hamilton County Tuberculosis Hospital, of which he was the Medical Director. He told me he would take care of me until I was ready to work part-time, and would pay me seventy-five dollars a month and full maintenance for myself. He introduced me to Dr. Lydia White who was in charge. Dr. White then took me all over the hospital. It was well equipped and would have been a grand place to work, but I could not support Jess and the boys on such an arrangement.

I went back to Memphis considerably depressed, but determined to make the best of it. I prayed for courage and guidance in taking the right course. Of all the difficulties I had experienced, this was the greatest. Now my troubles involved the most precious persons in the world: Jess and my two sons. I gave up work at the clinic and went home to take the "rest cure." In those days the treatment for minimal tuberculosis of the lungs was simply bed rest. No special diet, no climate change, and no medication were necessary. Just bed rest.

This routine was somewhat difficult for Jess and the children. I spent nearly all of my time in bed and got up only for meals, the bathroom, and occasionally to sit in a rocking chair on the porch in the cool of the evening. We had no air conditioning then. I read almost constantly and went through the Bible entirely in one month. I remember that I read Genesis in one day. I maintained this routine for about three months.

A few years before, Dr. Henry Boswell, the superintendent of the Mississippi State Sanatorium had seen me in Memphis and had offered me a place on his staff. I had not been interested at that time. Now that I had an active disease, however, I thought it might be wise to talk to Dr. Boswell again. I called him by phone and told him my problem. He suggested that I bring my x-ray films and come down to see him. I caught a train that evening and was in Sanatorium, Mississippi, by the next morning.

Dr. Boswell met me at the station and then took me to his home on the sanatorium grounds for breakfast. He looked at the x-rays and told me he would first like me to come down as a patient. He would keep me under close observation for a month and if I improved he could put me to work, part–time at first, and then full time. Full time pay was two hundred and fifty dollars a month with living quarters for me and my family. This appeared to me to be the best solution to my problem. I accepted his offer and returned to Memphis to arrange the move.

My dream house had come tumbling down over my ears. The hope of buying a home, the joy of practicing medicine like I wanted to, the pleasure of raising my sons in a town with so many advantages, the satisfaction of active participation in Christian service in the First Baptist Church, and my fellowship with so many dear friends—all these had to be given up. In addition, the thought of being unable to support my family as they deserved, and the dark prospects for the future, brought me many sleepless nights. Trying to be cheerful when I was deeply depressed was indeed an effort.

In spite of it all, Jess and I tried to make the most of it. We decided that she would take the boys and go to her mother's home in Wilton, Alabama. I would go to Sanatorium and send for her as soon as arrangements could be made.

We left our furniture and household goods to be stored with the O.K. Storage Company. We took only our clothes and essentials in suitcases, or packed in boxes, to be taken in the trunk of my car. After saying good–bye to Jess and the boys as they left on the train to Alabama, I sat in my car and cried like a baby. Only a prayer that we could be happy together, and the faith that God answers prayer gave me any comfort at all.

I spent the night at the home of Dr. and Mrs. J. F. Hamilton (Joe and Ruby) who had been so kind and helpful during the ordeal. The next morning I got in my car and headed for Mississippi. I kept quoting Romans 8:28 as I drove down the gravel road that was Highway 51, and praying that this experience would bring some good for all of us. "All things work together for good to them that love God," I said, over and over again, even as tears frequently dimmed my vision.

I decided to break the trip, rather than to drive the entire distance in one day in order to avoid too much effort and fatigue. I found a good hotel at Winona and stayed there for the night. I had driven about 130 miles, or nearly half way to Sanatorium.

Feeling rested the next morning even though I slept rather fitfully, I left Winona to continue my journey southward. The roads were all gravel as there was only two hundred miles of paved highway in the state at the time, and that ran across the lower end of Mississippi near the coast, with other short stretches from Jackson to Vicksburg, and from Canton to Jackson. The trip to Sanatorium (a train stop and a post office by that name) was uneventful.

I was welcomed at the sanatorium and given a private room on the second floor. I was made comfortable and it seems that the nurses and other hospital personnel were all intent on being cheerful. When I was left alone, however, I developed a severe case of "the blues."

I was lying there trying hard not to pity myself when someone knocked on my door. At my request to enter, Dr. James Emmett Walker, the assistant director of the Sanatorium appeared. He introduced himself and sat down for a little visit. He said he had heard that I was a specialist, and he thought I might be interested in a book on that subject by Chick Sales. He stayed about a half hour and I found him to be charming. A friendship began at that time and lasted until his death several years later.

When he left I picked up Sales' little book, *The Specialist.* Having neither seen nor heard of it before, I thought it might be a scientific book on the subject of specialization. I had not finished the first page, however, before I found it to be the most hilariously humorous book I had ever read. Before I had read two pages I was laughing out loud and tears were running down my cheeks. I was afraid someone would come in and find me laughing by myself and recommend a straightjacket. The book was a quick antedote for my "blues."

The Mississippi State Sanatorium was built in south Mississippi in the long–leaf pine country among rolling hills. The campus must have been about forty acres in area. The pine trees had been cleared except for just enough to make the grounds beautiful. The Sanatorium itself consisted of a main building (the "infirmary") which was three stories high, about one hundred yards long, and housed about one hundred and fifty patients besides the business offices, the post office, the laboratory and x–ray equipment, several private examining offices, and a large lounge for visitors.

There was also a kitchen and dining hall behind the main building, and behind these facilities there were about a dozen cottages which housed four convalescing patients apiece. When a patient was transferred from the infirmary to one of these cottages it was called being "sent to the country." There was another building for Negro patients about one hundred yards from the main building. It had a one hundred patient capacity. Several small houses, also on the grounds, were for the superintendent and his staff, and there was a well-built nursing home. Moreover, an apartment house was being built for the doctors. The Sanatorium also had its own power plant and water supply. Altogether it was a remarkably well-planned and well-built institution. It certainly was a monument to Dr. Henry Boswell whose persistence, political knowledge, and impressive personality were responsible for its construction.

My daily routine at Sanatorium initially consisted of complete bed rest except bathroom privileges. Meals, which were excellent, were also served in bed. I spent my time reading and entertaining visitors. One by one the doctors on the staff came in to get acquainted with me and to discuss some of their problems: Dr. Kemp, Dr. Wesley Wiemers, Dr. Hugh Anderson and, of course, Dr. Boswell. I found all of these middle-aged gentlemen to be very likable. They had all had tuberculosis themselves, except for Dr. Wiemers. Dr. Wiemers had been practicing in Columbus, Mississippi when his wife developed tuberculosis and at the time I arrived she was a patient in the Sanatorium. He had given up his practice to be with her.

After I had been there two or three days, Rev. Lewis Ferrell, pastor of the Baptist church at Magee, only three miles away, came to see me. He was about my age and from the beginning I became fond of him. He visited the patients of the Sanatorium regularly, and on each visit he called on me. I told him I looked forward to the time when I could get out and attend his church.

After a few weeks I was allowed to go to the dining room for meals. This was a great pleasure for it meant I could get out of the building and walk outdoors to another building. At first I felt a little weak, but as I improved I felt like running to my meals, and hurdling the hedge along the walk. In spite of my feeling of increased energy I continued the slow pace to conserve my strength.

Winter came before I could send for Jess. I heard from her nearly every day, and of course wrote her as frequently. One of her letters told me that Edgar was not well, and the doctor had advised

"After being at the Sanatorium for about two months, I improved so much that Dr. Boswell thought I might be able to do some part-time work."

her to give him melba toast and Cambric tea. I had never heard of this diet, and knowing that Wilton was a small village, I told her if she could not get melba toast and Cambric tea, she could phone a friend in Memphis and have them sent to her. I was somewhat embarrassed to learn that melba toast and Cambric tea were simply dry toast and hot water with milk and sugar.

After being at the Sanatorium for about two months, I improved so much that Dr. Boswell thought I might be able to do part-time work. He therefore asked me to take care of one ward of thirty patients. The routine for the patient was a rest period of one hour before and after each meal and a "recreation" period between times. The rest periods were to be quiet, no visitors and not even nursing activities with the patients, unless absolutely required. Between rest periods the patients could have visitors, sit up or if able, stir about in their rooms. The nurses could straighten beds and do other tasks for the patient doing this time of day.

I was to take rest periods like other patients, and during recreation made rounds, examined patients, and did other things for them. I became acquainted with my patients after a few days and really enjoyed taking care of them. Some had been there for as long as two years or more and most had felt a great need for attention which they believed they had not been getting. I examined them more frequently, spent some time visiting with them, and discussed their problems. I tried to attend to their every need as well as I could since they knew that I also was a victim of their disease, and could have a great deal of empathy for their human predicament. I found many of these patients (all women) to be charming and interesting people.

My finances were getting low. I had received the last check I was to get from the Polyclinic, did not know where I would get money to take care of Jess and the boys. I did not think I would be paid for taking care of my ward. I was disturbed by this situation. One day I encountered the bookkeeper for the Sanatorium, Mr. Lowry, after I had been working for more than a month. He told me he had a check for me and wondered why I hadn't been around to get it. I hurried around to the office and there was a check for one hundred dollars! What a relief! I was on the payroll! My fortunes were taking a slight turn upward.

I began to plan to send for Jess and the boys. The apartment for the doctors was not quite complete, but a room for Jess was offered us in the home of Luke Everett, the taxi driver, just off the sanatorium grounds. This seemed satisfactory for a short time. I wrote Jess telling her and she agreed to come. To reach Sanatorium from Alabama she had to come by train to Hattiesburg, spend the night, and catch a train to Sanatorium the following morning. I arranged to meet her in Hattiesburg and to help with the boys. Fred was nearly three years old at the time, and Edgar was about one. While Fred was active and quick, requiring close supervision, Edgar was fat and a real load to carry.

I drove the forty-five miles to Hattiesburg and was there when the train arrived. It was wonderful to see my little family again. The next morning we drove to Sanatorium.

The room for Jess was not ideal, but she said she could take it for awhile. While I could not stay with her, I could at least see her every day. Moreover, she could get all her meals at the Sanatorium dining room. She also could use the car. The wives of the staff, and others, were most friendly to her, and quickly became delightful friends. We have never been anywhere where we found such lovely people.

Just before Christmas we moved into a little building that had once served as a dormitory for nurses. It had been converted into a two apartment building and proved to be very satisfactory. We could all live as a family again.

My health improved rapidly so that I began working full time. I had three wards to take care of: Ward E for women, Ward H for men. Each of these had thirty patients. I also took care of the top floor on which was a solarium. On this floor the so-called extrapulmonary tuberculosis was cared for. This included tuberculosis of the bone, tuberculosis peritonitis, and lymph gland tuberculosis.

The doctors who had taken care of the patients in the Sanatorium had been general practioners and had no special training in internal medicine, or in tuberculosis. When I studied my patients I found conditions which had not been recognized previously. Two had a chronic lung disease known as bronchiectasis which was not of tuberculosis origin. They responded rapidly to treatment for this condition which did not require the months of bed rest they had been getting. I also found some cardiac problems, diabetes, and other conditions which responded to proper treatment.

There were patients suffering from other conditions in addition to their tuberculosis of the lungs. These could be greatly helped by special attention to these problems also. In addition, I had a surprising number of patients with painful and often infected ingrown toenails. I learned to cure their problem by a simple operation. Moreover, I started pneumothorax on several of my patients who I knew would be benefitted by it. I soon had a number of "pneumo" patients, and many were referred to me by other doctors on the staff. The news travelled fast among the patients and many asked to be considered for the treatment.

When pneumothorax was not possible, a minor operation causing paralysis of one leaf of the diaphragm proved to be beneficial. I requested Dr. Jack Barksdale, a surgeon in Jackson who came down to help the Sanatorium when surgery was necessary to perform the operation on one or two of my patients. He had never done the operation before, but was confident he could. He got no beneficial results on any patients, however, as he clipped the wrong nerves. The effects, to put it mildly, were unsatisfactory. In one case, he clipped the recurrent laryngeal nerve causing paralysis of a vocal cord. In the other, he clipped the cervical sympathetic nerve causing Horner's syndrome (the recession of the eyeball and constriction of the pupil of the same side).

I determinded to learn to do the operation myself. With Dr. Boswell's permission I studied the anatomy of the phrenic nerve carefully and performed the operation on each side of six unclaimed bodies soon after their death. I also read books on the subject and found that the phrenic nerve was easily identified in the neck. It lies across the "belly" of the scalenus muscle and is the only nerve which runs downward and inward in that region. All the other nerves run downward and outward.

I needed more narrow retractors to hold the wound open but instead of ordering them from a surgical supply house I decided to make them. I got two ice tea spoons from the kitchen which the man in charge reluctantly let me have, and took them to the shop at the power house. There with the help of the engineer I flattened them, bent one end in a curve, and the handle end at a right angle. In this way I developed two perfectly useful retractors. I then arranged for two patients to have the operation. I had considerable training in surgery during my internship and was confident I could do it. When the head nurse asked me who was to do the surgery and I told her I was, she said, "Good Lord!" I operated on both patients under local anesthesia and took about twenty minutes with each. I found the phrenic nerve at once, cut it, and sutured the wounds without difficulty. Both operations were a success and the nurses changed their attitude toward me. I told them I would never attempt anything unless I knew I could do it. The word got around, and I soon had calls for several other phrenicectomies, as the operation was called. I did twelve or fifteen within the next few months.

I found on the top floor a young lady with tuberculosis peritonitis. She had been taking heliotherapy (sun light) for some time without benefit. I had learned at Saranac Lake that intra–abdominal oxygen was effective in the treatment of this condition. I therefore treated her with weekly injections of oxygen into the abdomen. A remarkable improvement was achieved and eventually a complete cure resulted. Two other patients were treated the same way with good results.

I also tackled the problem of treating tuberculosis of the larynx. I found a dust covered, water cooled Kromayer light with several quartz applicators in a cabinet in the operating room. I knew this equipment was made to apply ultraviolet light directly to the lesion. The curved quartz applicator was designed to apply light directly to ulcers in the larynx.

I secured a monograph, "Tuberculosis of the Larynx" by a Laryngologist in Denver. I also discussed the problem with an oaryngologist, Dr. W. D. Stinson of Memphis.

After I had learned all I could about the subject, I decided to give the treatment to the patients at Sanatorium. The only treatment employed prior to this time, was silence. Conscientious patients would go months without saying a word, and without having their throat examined. It was a great psychological boost to them to have someone give special attention to their problem, and they were more than cooperative in my plans to treat them.

I started treating patients on my wards but soon word got around and I was treating patients with tuberculosis of the larynx from all over the hospital. I had from ten to fifteen patients whom I treated weekly. In addition to the Kromayer quartz light, I also used local application of Chaulmoogra oil which was recommended by some authorities for the more acute ulcerative lesions. Definite improvement was noted in those patients whose pulmonary involvement was not too far advanced. I was seeing and treating more tuberculosis of the larynx than most laryngologists see in a life time.

The other doctors of the staff all cooperated with me in the various activities and procedures I had started, and Dr. Boswell was more than helpful. He purchased any equipment I suggested, and seemed proud of the treatment patients at his hospital were receiving. He bought a bronchoscope for me, which I used on frequent occasions, and also provided any nose and throat equipment I needed. In addition, I secured a supply of Lipiodol. This is a bland oil containing iodine, which when instilled into the bronchi cast shadows on the x–ray film outlining the contour of the bronchi. This diagnostic procedure is known as Bronchography. It was especially valuable in the diagnosis of bronchiectasis. We frequently performed this examination with the cooperation of the x–ray technician. It was especially valuable in studying chronic, productive coughs in patients whose sputum tubercle bacilli could not be found.

All of these innovations were developed gradually over two or three years of my four year stay at the hospital. They were promoted by my desire to do all I could for the poor victims of a chronic, disabling, and sometimes hopeless illness. I felt a great sympathy for them. They had come from their homes, their families and friends, giving up their work, and their pleasures with the hope that they could regain their health. Many of them were there for more than a year, some three or more years. They often received very little attention, and felt they were being forgotten by family and friends, and even by the doctors who were supposed to

treat them. Depression was common among them. One of the
pleasures I got from my work was helping my patients overcome
this feeling. This concern was why I saw each patient every day,
examined them often, and tried to give attention to their slightest
need. Headaches, indigestion, constipation, ingrown toe nails, sore
throat, insomnia—all these symptoms were considered serious to
the patient, and I did what I could to relieve them.

I recall a young man whose wife had been a patient in the
Sanatorium three years. It seemed she started having fever
everytime she felt well enough to sit up and was allowed to do so.
Her husband came to see her nearly every weekend from his home
in north Mississippi and always brought his son, about eight years
of age. On one visit he asked to see me. "Doctor," he said, "I want to
talk to you about my wife." He looked out the window and into the
distance and added, "I wish she would either get well—or something." Great tears rolled down his cheek, and my eyes also filled
up. How I prayed that some day we would find a way to cure
tuberculosis. Now, after all these years antibiotics have finally been
found to cure the disease.

Life at the Sanatorium wasn't all unpleasant. The doctors
apartment was finally completed and we were permitted to move
in. It was strictly modern in every respect and we were most
comfortable there. Jess' mother soon came to live with us and Jess
was given some relief from the house work. We found friends
among the members of the staff and at Magee. Several of them had
children who were about the same age as our boys. We were
anxious, however, for Fred to go to kindergarten but there was no
such facility at the sanatorium. Jess then read about The Calvert
School of Baltimore, which furnished the material and instructions
for teaching any grade from kindergarten through high school.
This facility was especially designed for missionaries, or parents in
the foreign service who wanted to teach their own children.

We ordered it and it proved to be ideal for our purposes. We
soon received all the material, books, charts and equipment along
with explicit and easily understood instructions. Jess discussed the
matter with other mothers and as a result she had a kindergarten of
eight pupils. Fred was four when it started and this training made
schoolwork easy for him when he later went to elementary school.

Dr. Boswell loved to play golf. The Sanatorium grounds were ideally suited for a golf course and a group of Sanatorium employees and friends from Magee formed the Sanatorium Golf Club. They raised enough money, and with some help from the state which Dr. Boswell succeeded in getting, built in a beautiful nine hole golf course on the grounds.

I was not able to play of course, but Jess, athlete that she was, soon became quite good and played several times a week. Dr. Boswell found a young man who had become an expert in the game, starting as a caddy on the golf course at Laurel, Mississippi, and gave him a job in the laundry. He became our "golf pro," and gave lessons to all who wanted them. There was also a swimming pool on the grounds and our boys were able to learn to swim at an early age. Of course the patients were not allowed in the pool.

I was soon able to be up and about and began going to church in Magee, a little town of about two thousand inhabitants that was only three miles from the Sanatorium. We joined the Baptist church there, soon became very active, and I was made a deacon. The pastor was Rev. Lewis Ferrell.

We made many wonderful friends in that church. The membership was about 300, but there was only one Sunday School class for men and this class was only for men over twenty. Most of its members, however, were more than fifty years old. A class for young men was needed. Rev. Ferrell and two or three young men asked me to teach such a class, and as usual I could not say "no," so I accepted the job. We started with five and they insisted on naming themselves "The Strain Bible Class." After a few weeks and some work on the part of the organizers, the membership was built to about thirty-five, with an average attendance of about thirty. I enjoyed teaching this group of fine young men and got a great deal of pleasure out of my membership in that little church.

We did have some problems at Sanatorium. Theodore Bilbo was governor of the state and while we were there the Great Depression occurred. The State of Mississippi was in financial distress and was unable to pay her employees. Governor Bilbo tried to borrow money in the East but Mississippi was not considered a good risk so he was not able to sell any state bonds. As a result all state employees could no longer be paid. Teachers and some other state employees were paid in "script." The so-called "script" was essentially a promise to pay that could be cashed by banks and departments stores at ten percent discount.

Sanatorium employees, however, were not paid at all. We borrowed money from the Bank of Magee at eight percent interest and some of the stores extended credit. But they soon had to discontinue this practice because the creditors were demanding their money. The doctors of the Sanatorium were being paid only $200 a month plus living quarters, utilities and laundry. I had been unable to save any money on that salary, and had even been forced to borrow in order to pay my insurance premium.

This situation lasted ten months during which time we built up a sizeable debt. Our creditors were beginning to let us know that they were wondering whether it was wise to extend additional credit. We were able to get small amounts of cash occasionally from the business office at the Sanatorium on an "I.O.U."

State elections came, however, and Bilbo's term of office expired. Mike Conner was elected and had a reputation for being a young man with integrity and unusual intelligence. On becoming governor he immediately introduced into the legislature, and got passed, a bill creating a three percent sales tax. This was the first sales tax in the United States. Mississippi had no trouble borrowing enough money to pay off all her debts as soon as the law passed. We received our back pay after ten months and were able to pay all our debts. I paid out more than eighty dollars interest, but we began to breathe more easily.

At about this time, however, Fred was playing "garage man" (he said) and pretending to fill my car with gasoline. The problem was, however, that he poured a coca cola bottle full of sand into my gasoline tank. Soon afterward my car stopped suddenly. I found I could get it started by disconnecting the carburetor and blowing hard in the pipe leading back to the gas tank. This procedure was troublesome and could not be done easily without my getting my hands and lips soiled.

One day Jess, the boys, and I were all dressed and going to a church social in Magee when the car stopped about a mile out of town. Not wanting to get my hands and clothes soiled, I decided to hitch a ride into Magee and get a friend at the filling station to come out and get my car started. I got out of my car to thumb a ride. I saw a Ford coupe coming down the road at a fairly rapid rate. A lady was driving it. She apparently decided not to stop but when she saw Jess and the two children in the car she decided that it might be safe to stop for me. She slammed on her brakes, and skidded to a stop in the gravelled road just in front of my car. Her auto was immediately enveloped in smoke and flames, and in spite of all we could do, burned completely about fifteen feet in front of mine. I was afraid her gas tank might explode but could not move my car. I got Jess and the boys out and had them run a safe distance. Several cars soon came up and we did what we could to save the lady's car. She had had a can of gasoline in the back of her car and when she stopped suddenly, the can turned over spilling gasoline down through the floor on to the red hot exhaust pipe. Someone picked her up and took her in to Magee. I never learned her name and never heard from her. I got my gas line blown out and went on to church.

I decided I must get a new car as my family seemed to have outgrown a one seated car. Consequently, I traded my old Dodge for a new 1932 Chevrolet sedan. We had saved a little money and, with the allowance on our Dodge, were able to pay for the new car without any trouble. Having at last attained an arrest of my tuberculosis, I was feeling well enough to take a trip. So we planned to take a trip to Kansas during our two weeks vacation for the summer of 1932.

We drove on U.S. Highway 80 from Jackson, Mississippi, through Vicksburg, Ruston, Louisiana, and Shreveport to Marshall, Texas. The trip was uneventful but interesting. We were rather tired of driving all day, although the roads were good for the most part. At Marshall we found a good hotel for the night. When we got to our room Jess and I fell across the bed, tired from the long drive, to relax. Fred, who was five years old then, came over and tugging at me said, "Daddy, get up. Let's get in the car and ride around to see the town." After being in the car all day that was the last thing I wanted to do. I did feel the need of some exercise, however, so I got the boys and took them for a walk around several blocks in downtown Marshall.

We got started early the next morning and drove west to

Dallas, and then turned north. We saw lots of activity in the oil fields near Longview, and were thrilled at the acres of roses around Tyler. As we went northward through Denton, Texas, we crossed the Red River into Oklahoma just south of Ardmore. We spent the night in Ardmore where we sweltered in our hotel room and battled constantly with mosquitoes.

We continued our journey north the next day through Oklahoma City, Guthrie, Ponca City, and finally arrived in Wellington, Kansas, in the mid–afternoon. We stopped first at my brother James' home, and after a short visit we drove out on the farm to Jennie's. The boys had a great time running around on the farm and were fascinated with the chickens, ducks, calves and other livestock. They were especially excited whenever they saw a Jack Rabbit jump up and run away.

After a few days in Kansas visiting with James and his wife, May, and Jennie and her family, we left for Mississippi. Ruth, Jennie's eighteen year old daughter accepted our invitation to return home with us. This time we returned through Fort Smith, across Arkansas and down through Little Rock and Memphis where we spent the night in the King Cotton Hotel. The next day we drove all the way to Sanatorium. Ruth had spent all her life in Kansas and was impressed with the hills, forests, and rivers we encountered on our trip. After a few days in Sanatorium she returned home by train. She was a lovely girl and we enjoyed her visit.

One of our recreational activities while we were in Mississippi was fishing trips to the coast. We were only about one hundred miles from the Gulf Coast and with the road conditions could make the drive in about four hours.

On one occasion we had Dr. and Mrs. Hamilton (Joe and Ruby) drive down with us. They brought their children, Joe Frank, and Margaret Ann and we followed them into Biloxi where we rented a cottage in which we all stayed. Joe and I went fishing the morning after we arrived. We rented a boat and guide, and spent all morning fishing in the Sound off the coast in front of the Edgewater Gulf Hotel. We caught more than eighty white and speckled trout using shrimp for bait. During the morning we hung six tarpon but our tackle was too weak to handle them. The line

"We caught more than eight white and
speckled trout using shrimp for bait."

snapped in each case, but they gave us some excitement. I did not
want to get my shoes wet, so I took them off, rolled my trousers up
half way to my knees, and fished gayly all morning. When I
attempted to put my shoes and sox on, however, I discovered that
my ankles and feet were badly sunburned. After a few days and lots
of fun we returned to the Sanatorium.

Some of my friends from Magee, including my pastor, Rev.
Lewis Ferrell, Lawrence Duckworth, Fordie Smith, and I made
several trips to the gulf to fish. Our favorite spot was the Gravellene
Bayou just east of Biloxi. We would drive down before noon one
day, and come back the next afternoon, spending the night, and
fishing two half-days. Sometimes we would drive down leaving
Magee at about 4:00 a.m., fish several hours, and return the same
evening.

While I worked at the Sanatorium I was a member of the

Mississippi Medical Association. When the annual meeting was held in Jackson I read a paper before the Association on "Pneumothorax." At another meeting when I was on the program I gave a paper on "Bronchography." I met doctors from all over the state at these meetings, many of whom had sent patients to the Sanatorium.

There were many pleasant features in the work at the Sanatorium. The climate in that region was delightful the year round with temperatures falling to freezing or below only once in the four years we were there. There was nearly always a pleasant breeze in the summer, and the days were seldom uncomfortably warm. My work was interesting and I felt that I was really rendering a service to the poor victims of such a dread disease. Moreover, we had many friends whom we enjoyed. I have never enjoyed membership in any church as much as I enjoyed my belonging to the First Baptist Church of Magee.

There were two aspects of my work at the Sanatorium, however, that I did not like. In the first place, I was afraid to raise my boys in that environment. They had the run of the grounds and I was afraid they might go places where they would be exposed to infection from tuberculosis. I saw patients who were "on exercise" walking through the grounds, call the boys, play with them, and give them candy.

Then, too, our pay was very poor. My salary was two hundred dollars a month plus living quarters. With that pay we were unable to save any money and there was no prospect that our salary would ever be increased. I wanted to own a home, educate my boys, and to give Jess more than a bare living.

XIII

Depression and the T.V.A.

A return to Memphis as an alternative to Sanatorium did not seem advisable. The Great Depression had begun with the crash of the stock market in 1929 and came on the heels of a disastrous flood on the Mississippi River in 1927, and a severe drouth in the Mississippi Delta in 1928. The consequences for the Polyclinic were equally disastrous. With more than a quarter million dollars in uncollectible accounts, it went broke. The doctors split up and went out on their own, every fellow for himself.

I went to Memphis to investigate the possibility of establishing a practice there, but met with discouragement. The manager of the Medical Arts Building told me when I was inquiring about renting office space there, that he would not initially push me for the rent. He said there were doctors in the building who had not been able to pay their rent for over a year, and he was not putting them out. I realized that if established doctors were having that kind of trouble, it was no time for me to come to Memphis.

I wanted to go to East Tennessee as I still considered that part of the country to be my home. I took a trip up that way hoping that I could get started in Johnson City, Bristol, or Kingsport. The result of my investigation was that I saw no way I could make a go of it. I did stop off in Knoxville, however, where I was encouraged.

Dr. Herbert Acuff, Knoxville's leading surgeon, told me that Knoxville needed Internists and he would help me get started. He would let me share his suite of offices without cost, if I came. That sounded good to me. I returned to Sanatorium resolved to move to Knoxville.

After definite plans to move to Knoxville had been made it occurred to me that I would be wise to brush up on the diagnosis

192

and treatment of allergic conditions. Allergy was becoming a specialty that was proving to be very valuable in the treatment of sufferers of such conditions as asthma, hay fever and other allergic conditions. Dr. Acuff informed me that there was no doctor in Knoxville who was doing that type of work.

I made arrangements with Dr. J. P (Jack) Henry in Memphis who was limiting his work to allergy, to spend some time with him. I had been associated with him in the Polyclinic and I was familiar with his capabilities.

I therefore went to Memphis where I spent a week or two to study under his direction. I spent the time in his office observing his routine in caring for patients. After taking a careful and thorough history he had his technicians make the skin tests to find the offending allergen, the substance to which the patient was allergic, and which was the cause of the symptoms from which the patient suffered. A solution was then prepared from this substance with which the patient could be desensitized. After about ten days of observation and study I felt I had obtained the information I needed for a start in this work.

The municipal airport had been opened in Memphis in 1929, and American Airlines had regular planes on a flight from Chicago to New Orleans with stops at Memphis and Jackson, Mississippi. It occurred to me that this would be a good time to try travelling by air. I could get home much faster and would not have to spend the night on the train.

I called for a reservation, and Dr. and Mrs. Henry took me to the airport. When I bought a ticket I was given a supply of chewing gum. In those days the planes were not pressurized. The passenger was advised to chew gum while in flight, so that he could swallow frequently to adjust the pressure on the ear drums. Without this activity marked changes in altitude caused much discomfort in the ears.

The planes in those days were nothing like our modern passenger planes. The one I boarded was a "Tri–motor Ford." The fuselage was covered with corrugated metal. Because of its appearance it was often spoken of as "the flying washboard." It was also referred to as "the tin goose." It was equipped for carrying twelve passengers, with a single row of seats on each side and a narrow aisle between. There was no partition between the pilots and the passengers. Hostesses had not been made a part of the crew yet.

After starting the three engines, the plane took off from a bumpy runway and was soon airborne. I then experienced for the first time the thrill of watching the scene beneath me grow farther and farther away as we gained altitude.

No attempt was made to dampen the noise of the motors. Ears popped as we chewed gum vigorously and swallowed often. I discovered that conversation with fellow passengers was almost impossible. This became apparent after we had been up a short while when I attempted to say something to the passenger in the seat in front of me. I had become so accustomed to the noise I had almost forgotten it. When I tried to say something I could not even hear myself. Only when we yelled at each other could we carry on a conversation.

The pilot told me at Jackson that we had flown at an elevation of 5,000 feet. I was glad to realize that I had no sense of acrophobia. I recall that as we flew over Greenwood we had a marvelous view of a very disastrous flood on the Yalobusha and Tallahatchia Rivers that caused great damage there.

On arriving in Jackson I "deplaned" with a feeling of elation, feeling lucky to be among the passengers arriving there by air. I caught the afternoon train to Sanatorium, arriving there much sooner than anyone had expected.

We felt bad when we told the patients and friends in Sanatorium and Magee that we were leaving. They begged us to stay, but we had made our decision to go. Dr. Felix Underwood, the State Commissioner of Health, offered me a position as Director of the Division of Tuberculosis of the State Health Department but the pay was still meager and I longed for the opportunity to do internal medicine again.

I wrote my old Limestone friend, Charles Biddle, who was at that time vice president of a bank in Knoxville and asked him to find a house which we could rent. He wrote that he had found one which he thought would meet our needs. It was located at 2901 Magnolia Avenue.

After making all necessary arrangements, and telling our friends good–bye, we left for Knoxville. We left Sanatorium with mixed emotions. We hated to leave our friends, and it was a rather sad experience for me to leave my patients. But we were optimistic about the future, and I was looking forward to the privilege of living in East Tennessee again. We could only hope that we were making the right move.

Our trip to Knoxville was on U.S. Highway 11. We had the O.K. Storage Company move our furniture and household goods from Memphis. Knowing they would arrive in Knoxville the next day, we decided to spend the night at Rockwood about fifty miles west of the city. In this way we could arrange to be at our new home before the furniture arrived. We went on into Knoxville the next day. Since I had lived in Knoxville previously, I knew how to find 2901 Magnolia. We arrived there at about 9:00 A.M. and the van came shortly afterwards.

We found our new home suitable. It had two bedrooms and a sun parlor, besides the living room, dining room, and kitchen. It was only two or three blocks from Chilhowee Park, the site of the Appalachian Exposition which I had attended in 1910.

We were hospitably received. Charles Biddle came soon after we arrived. The lady across the street brought us a large pitcher of ice water. My cousin, Walter Remine, and his wife, Ila, came at about the time the moving van arrived. He was wearing overalls and brought a pair of pliers, a claw hammer and a screw driver. He welcomed us, saying he came to help us move into our new home. He and Ila lived only two blocks from us. The second day we were there the "Welcome Wagon" lady called on us. She gave us lots of coupons and tickets to entitle us to articles and services and made us feel that Knoxville welcomed us. Within a few days after her visit we had callers from five Baptist churches inviting us to worship with them. The Welcome Wagon lady had given them the information that we were Baptist and the churches were prompt in visiting prospective members.

I went to Dr. Acuff's office soon after getting settled in Knoxville and found the situation to be satisfactory. He let me have an office and examining room in his suite, and his receptionist-bookkeeper–secretary was at my disposal. In addition, his nurse was available to assist me any time I needed her. Dr. Acuff also asked me to interpret all electrocardiograms and chest x–ray films.

I had to buy a desk and some other office equipment, but was soon ready for work. Dr. Acuff had me make some house calls for him, and I helped with some of his medical problems in the hospitals.

I began having a few patients of my own, but days often went by without a single patient coming into the office. I began to wonder if I had made a move at the right time. I had not realized when I came to Knoxville in 1933 the depth of the depression throughout the nation. This fact was made more evident when my collections for the entire month of September amounted to only seventy-five dollars. It became clear that I was seeing patients who had seen other doctors whom they owed, but could not pay. I was new, so they came to me. I had thought I was doing reasonably well from the number of patients I was seeing, but realized differently at the end of the month.

I seemed to be doing better in October as I was seeing more patients. I joined the Knox County Medical Society and met many doctors who became good friends. At the end of the month, however, the story had not changed. My collections were only $150 and were not enough to pay for living expenses. Moreover, my meager savings were dwindling.

Jess and I enjoyed living in Knoxville and made many good friends. We joined the First Baptist Church and were received warmly. I was soon made an usher and was even asked to serve as toastmaster for a banquet the men of the church were giving to honor Dr. James D. Hoskins who was president of the University of Tennessee. I and other alumni still called him "Dean" Hoskins. This assignment was pleasant for me. I had a nice visit with the "Dean," as I sat at the head table with him. Our pastor, Dr. Fred Brown, was one of the best preachers I ever heard. Every sermon was soul-stirring.

Jess was as active as she had been elsewhere. She had made many friends amongst the ladies of the church and also was taken out for golf regularly. Moreover, Fred started school and, because of the Kindergarten training under Jess at Sanatorium, was promoted to the second grade after three months.

Although strangers thought Knoxville was dirty, ugly, and non-progressive we considered it a grand place to live. The city was filled with hospitable people who were friendly and lovable.

Moreover, East Tennesseans do not tolerate criticism. They say they are no better than anyone else, but "by Ned, they ain't nobody better than we are!" "Dean" Hoskins said East Tennesseans kept the Ten Commandments and everything else they could lay their hands on.

The area around Knoxville was also beautiful. When time was available, we often took short trips to the scenic Smokey Mountains. We even drove over good roads up to Limestone for visits with relatives and friends in my familiar childhood haunts.

Despite all these attractions, November of 1933 came and passed with no increase in my practice or income. My total income for that month was still less than $200 and my savings were about gone. I knew I could not go on much longer as things were. I was not alone, as the depression was deepening. President Roosevelt was attempting to combat it with the formation of the P.W.A., the C.C.C., and other such agencies. Most importantly for me, however, was the Tennessee Valley Authority which was at work building the Norris Dam just thirty miles from Knoxville on the Clinch River. T.V.A. headquarters were in Knoxville.

One day I ran into Walter Stromquist, who had been a good friend of mine in Memphis. Walter was now in the Health and Safety Department of the T.V.A. He had been the City Sanitary Engineer with the Memphis Health Department when I was associated with that organization. When he asked how I was doing, I related some of my problems. He then told me that the T.V.A. was planning to use some doctors to examine employees. He suggested that I get some part-time work with them.

On the following day I went to the T.V.A. office to see about the possibility. I talked to Dr. A. E. Russell, Assistant Director of the Health and Safety work. Dr. Russell was very interested in using me and handed me an application blank. I was accepted at once. My job was to drive out to Norris Dam to give physical examinations to the employees. A rough lumber building was built about one hundred yards below the site of the dam for the use of the medical department. Adequate supplies and materials were made available for the examinations and treating any minor injuries.

I went out the the dam every morning and worked a half day. It was 2:00 P.M. or later by the time I got back to my office. My pay was $180 a month from the T.V.A., but my office practice was reduced to the point where many days passed when I failed to see an office patient all day. The income from my office practice was very meager. I looked out the office window many days watching workmen building a new post office and envying them because I knew they would have a check waiting at the end of the week. I began to regret I had left Sanatorium.

Dr. Bishop, the Director of the Health and Safety Division of the T.V.A., called me in one day and asked if I would take a full time job. The pay would be $4,000 a year and I would have a car to drive. This meant that I would have an assured income during the Depression that would be sufficient to take care of our living expenses. I also thought that I could continue to work until Norris Dam was complete. By that time, I would be able to save a little money and could then start practice in Knoxville again. I accepted the job and started full time work as "Medical Officer" for the T.V.A. on December 11, 1933. I also gave up my office in Knoxville and thanked Dr. Acuff and the bookkeeper for their kindness.

My initial work with the T.V.A. was not very interesting. It consisted of examining employees, treating minor injuries and illnesses, and sending those more severely injured to "Designated Physicians" in Knoxville. There was an enormous amount of paper work to be done. There were reports of injuries (even minor ones), and filling out forms in quadruplicate for the U.S. Employee Compensation Commission for all employees who lost time because of on the job injuries. There was a form to report the accident, another form with the doctor's description of the accident with signatures of the employee's immediate superior, forms authorizing the designated physician to treat him, forms every two weeks reporting the status of his condition until he was able to return to duty, and a form reporting his return to duty. All these forms were made out in quadruplicate. I was also responsible for the first-aid stations which we had at the construction site.

The whole matter of massive construction was new to me. I became rather closely associated with an entirely new world. The constant, amost frantic (it seemed to me) grind of bull dozers, rock drilling, blasting, rock crushing, trucks running to and fro, work-men with picks, shovels, jack–hammers, saws and all kinds of tools, building a structure that was beyond my comprehension. The mud, the noises, the whistles and loud voices giving signals, kept up constantly. This activity went on through rain, snow or fair weather. I bought a wool shirt, a heavy jacket and a pair of corduroy trousers. This attire was more appropriate in the atmosphere and the weather in which I was working. The village of Norris, Tennessee arose in the matter of a few weeks. Bunk houses, mess hall and cottages had been erected and a well planned village was built where only woods had existed before. This village was about two miles from the dam site. Meals were available to all the employees in the mess hall for a small fee. One of my responsibilities was checking on the sanitation in the mess hall, the dormitories, and general environment. We had a young sanitary engineer to help with this work.

My work went on at a constant pace. The thirty mile drive out to Norris and back to Knoxville through all kinds of weather was sometimes rather difficult. The ground was covered on several occasions with four to six inches of snow. Then in February, Dr. Bishop called and requested me to come in a little early and meet him in his office. He told me after I arrived that a medical office was being opened at Wilson Dam, Alabama, and he wanted me to go down to get it started. I got a round trip railroad ticket and went to Sheffield, Alabama, the following day.

I found space available for a medical office but no equipment except for an old examining table and a few other pieces of furniture which had been salvaged from the army hospital which was in operation during the construction of Wilson Dam. A first aid man had already been employed. Milton Dunn, recently discharged from the Navy where he had served as a corpsman, was superbly well trained for the work he was to do. He was indeed a great help to me. We set up two medical offices: one in the Fertilizer works and one at "First Quarters," near the personnel and other offices. I was given space for the doctor's office, and a secretary was also provided for me.

I had been told that a medical officer would be secured to take over the Wilson Dam unit, and I would be allowed to return to Knoxville. Two weeks had expired with no word of a medical officer who would replace me. I called the central office in

200

FROM THE NOLICHUCKY TO MEMPHIS

Knoxville and told them my round trip ticket would expire within two days, and I would have to have it renewed if I could not get relief. Dr. Bishop told me to come back to Knoxville at once.

I went directly to the T.V.A. office when I arrived. Dr. Bishop called me into his office. He was putting on his top coat, closing a briefcase, and getting ready to leave immediately for Nashville where he was still the State Commissioner of Health. He patted me on the back and said, "You've done such a good job down there we have been unable to replace you. We are therefore transferring you to Wilson Dam to take over." He then put on his hat and left at once.

What a blow! I also found out that Dr. Bob Watson had been employed to take my place at Norris. In spite of my real desire to stay in East Tennessee I was denied that privilege. I had not been able to save any money. I could take one of two actions: go to Alabama as ordered, or leave the T.V.A. This meant there was nothing left for me to do but to go to Alabama. To try and borrow enough money to start practicing medicine during the Depression was out of the question.

Again on the move. Engaging a moving company, we helped get our household goods packed for the van. We sadly left Knoxville for Alabama. Jess was wonderful through it all and often stated that she was always ready to do what was best wherever we might have to do.

Jess and I drove to Sheffield, Alabama, and arrived on the evening of March 1, 1934. We spent the night in one of the large rooms of the old Sheffield Hotel. Next morning we went to house No. 54 in Village One; the house which had been assigned to us.

Sheffield at that time was pretty much run down following the crash of the boom which resulted from the rumor that the Ford Motor Company was planning to take over Wilson dam and establish a major plant there. Everywhere were evidences of a deep depression. To move into such a town was depressing to contemplate.

Village One was a government village originally built by the army for officers during the construction of Wilson Dam and the nitrate plants in 1926. In spite of the fact that the houses had not been occupied since 1926, they were in remarkably good condition. They were built of hollow tile, stucco, and covered with a heavy tile roof. The T.V.A. was renovating them, painting the walls inside and making the necessary repairs.

The village was laid out with the upper part being in the shape of a large liberty bell. Even the crack in the bell was represented by a short street with three houses on it. The handle of the bell was a short street with a hairpin curve at the end, and a grassy strip in the middle with two houses on each side facing the street. The center of the bell was a large, grassy "common" with a few gum trees in it. Houses were built all around the bell facing the "common." Numerous shade trees, gum, oak, hackberry and elm stood in the backyards or between the houses. Below the "bell" streets were laid off straight east and west, or north and south. There also was a good school house, as well as a larger house which had been built as a dormitory for unmarried officers.

We had been assigned a house which was in the lower portion of "The Bell" houses. It had only two bedrooms. We were promised a larger house higher up on "the bell" when its renovation was completed. Our house had a large coal burning range in the kitchen which had been there for several years. It was fortunate for us that the stove was available. The stove we had brought with us was gas burning, even though gas was not available in the village. Jess enjoyed cooking on the old range, however, even if keeping it fired up was a troublesome chore. We sold our gas stove to some T.V.A. people who were moving to Chattanooga, and when we eventually moved into house No. 94, we bought an electric stove.

House No. 94 was much better. It was larger and was placed on a lot deep enough to permit us to have a large vegetable garden. The house also faced the "common."

The professional T.V.A. people for the Wilson Dam district lived in this section of the village. Our neighbors were all well-educated and delightful. We found some of the best friends we had known. There was Charlie Young from Washington state, a chemist at the fertilizer plant; Fred Gray from Alabama, also a chemist; John Heffernon from New York state, in charge of transportation; C. C. Kiker from Texas, a Sanitary Engineer in charge of Malaria control; Joe Work from Missouri, engineer at the fertilizer plant; D. O. Dugger from Kentucky, Reservoir Property Manager; Dr. Kelly Elmore from North Carolina, a chemist and

"House No. 94 was much better. It was larger and was placed on a lot deep enough to permit us to have a large vegetable garden."

Dr. John Raulston from East Tennessee, medical officer. Then there was Dr. Frerer from Connecticut, a chemist; Arthur Miller from Long Island, Superintendent of the fertilizer works; and Dr. Harold Hinman from Canada, in charge of research in malaria control work. All were new to the community, and all were eager to find new friends.

From the very beginning we had bridge parties, song fests, and simple good fun. It is notable that no alcoholic beverages were ever served or used with all these good people. We found many congenial friends in Village One whose friendship we enjoyed for years. In spite of our reluctance to move from Knoxville to Alabama, we found Alabama to be a delightful place to live.

My work still consisted mostly of administrative details. I was to supervise administratively the activities of the various sections of the Health and Safety Division of the T.V.A. in the "Western Division." This included the Medical Section, with offices at the Wilson Dam Power House, the Fertilizer Works and at First Quarters (where the principal offices were located including the Personnel Office). The medical facilities at Pickwick Dam, Wheeler Dam, Kentucky Dam, and the Guntersville Dam—all under construction, were later included. At each of these dams we had small hospitals with ten to twenty beds to take care of the employees living and working on the projects, as well as dependents living in the villages that had been constructed at each dam site.

It was my responsibility to staff each hospital with doctors, nurses, clinical laboratory personnel, and first aid men. The requisitions for personnel needed were sent to the personnel department which would secure them. Fortunately for us we had more applications for positions than we could use because of the depression which was still plaguing the country.

We maintained medical offices for reservoir clearance activities on the area to be inundated when the dams were closed. These offices were located at Scottsboro, Alabama; Decatur, Alabama; Iuka, Mississippi; Parsons, Tennessee; Camden, Tennessee; and Murray, Kentucky. The personnel in each Reservoir Clearance office consisted of a doctor, a clerk and several first aid men.

I also had administrative supervision over the sanitation section which looked after water supplies, sewage disposal, and food handling at all T.V.A. offices and activities. The Malaria Control Unit was also in this section. This unit was responsible for the massive undertaking of controlling mosquito breeding in the T.V.A. lakes. It required many employees to spray the shore line where grass or weeds were partially inundated at times. They sprayed from boats, airplanes, or on foot. The section was headed by Dr. R. B. Watson who had a staff of entomologists, botanists, and laboratory technicians. The field work was headed up by Mr. C. C. Kiker, malaria control engineer. My responsibility was "administrative;" Dr. Watson's was "technical." It was my job to see that the work had the necessary personnel, equipment, and supplies. The Safety Section was also under my supervision as safety engineers were employed at all the major construction projects. All of these activities resulted in my having to travel over the territory from Kentucky Dam to Guntersville and visit all the stations in between at frequent intervals to help solve problems. I also checked on personnel, and helped formulate budgets for each activity. I often had to make frequent visits to the central office in Knoxville, and to Chattanooga and when it was moved.

I learned the problems of many divergent professions, trades, skills and occupations. I also learned about labor problems by my dealings with union representatives, shop stewards and T.V.A. "Labor Relations" personnel. I was chosen to sit on a panel which drew on an "Employees Relationship Policy." This duty required me to attend weekly meetings of this panel which alternated between Knoxville and Wilson Dam. We spent about six weeks writing the Employee Relationship Policy.

The train trip between Sheffield and Knoxville was convenient. I could get on a pullman at Sheffield at 11:00 P.M., sleep soundly all night, and awaken in the morning with my pullman car sitting on the side track at the Knoxville station. The return trip was also by night, allowing a good rest on the pullman. I learned to sleep well on the train and am sorry such traveling is no longer available.

I had contacts also with construction engineers, construction superintendents, foremen of carpenters, excavators, concrete men, sheet metal workers, plumbers, electricians, and all the disciplines on a big construction job. I had frequent meetings with one or the other of these groups concerning health, medical, or safety problems.

After four years I was transferred to Chattanooga. I was then given the wider responsibility of covering the whole T.V.A. operation. My area of activity extended from the dams being constructed in North Carolina and Georgia (Hiawassee, Notely, Chatuga, Appalachia and Fontana) and to the Loudon, Watts Bar, Chickamauga Widow's Bar, Guntersville, Wheeler, Wilson, Pickwick and Kentucky Dams. I visited all these projects on matters concerning medical problems, industrial hygiene and sanitation. I became friends with Dr. M. F. Langston, from the Central Health and Safety office, who frequently accompanied me on these trips.

I was also called upon to make several trips to various cities in other states. For example, I went to Cincinnati twice; once to consult scientists about the danger of phosphorus to workmen (our employees at the Fertilizer works were exposed to phosphorus fumes), and again to attend a school conducted by Civil Defense on the various poisonous gases used in warfare to which civilians might be exposed. I recall going to Cleveland, Ohio, to attend a national meeting of personnel officers where I was on a panel discussing employee health; to New York City to hear a discussion of "Acute Iritis" which was spreading among industrial employees and was very difficult to control, and even went to Washington, D.C. two or three times to meet with U.S. Public Health Service personnel and other agencies. I attended the meeting of the Southern Medical Association in St. Louis, Missouri, where I read Dr. Watson's paper on malaria control, and attended a meeting of the same organization in New Orleans, as well as a meeting of the American Social Hygiene Association in Atlanta to discuss venereal disease. Several visits to the State Health Departments of Alabama at Montgomery and of Tennessee at Nashville were also made. These institutions, in themselves, signified the advanced degree that public health organizations in the United States had reached by the 1930s.

In April of 1936 before I moved to Chattanooga a very destructive tornado struck Tupelo, Mississippi, at 10:00 p.m. I was called by Mr. John Neely, the chief of the T.V.A. activities in our region who told me about the destruction it caused. He asked me to get as many T.V.A. doctors, nurses, and first aid men as I could, and go to Tupelo as soon as possible. After a few minutes on the telephone I was able to get several doctors and first aid men and we were off to the stricken area. We arrived early that morning with a good supply of bandages, gauze, and other materials. We found indescribable destruction. The streets were blocked by trees, utility poles, houses, and all kinds of debris, so that we had to park at the edge of town. We hurried on foot into the area of destruction.

The Civilian Conservation Corps had been called in and with many T.V.A. employees, and others, were busy trying to clear streets and search for dead and injured. I hurried toward the court house where a first aid station had been established and where doctors from Tupelo and the surrounding area, including Memphis, were busy taking care of the injured. I was stopped on my way several times to help an injured man or woman, or to pronounce someone dead. I was hailed on one occasion and asked to see a Negro baby which had just been found. It had lain in water under a plank since the tornado struck at 10:00 p.m. until it was found at about 7:00 a.m. When I saw it, the infant was cold, and barely breathing. It died while we were trying to get it out. By the time I got to the court house I had run out of supplies completely. A large table in the lobby of the Court House was being used as an operating table. Dr. Carl Feemster, a Tupelo surgeon, had been working at that table since before midnight. He saw me and said, "Strain, please take over this table, I'm about to give out."

I took over and as fast as I could get one injured person taken care of, mainly by temporary dressings, splinting fractures and suturing wounds, another patient was waiting. I had two nurses helping me. We would dress the wounds, give the patient anti-tetanus serum, and then the patient was tagged and sent to hospitals in Oxford, or Memphis. The roof of the Tupelo hospital had been blown off and rain had left the operating room on the top floor unusable. Another emergency room had been set up in the lobby of a theater nearby. I was busy for an hour or so when I saw Dr. Sam Williamson from Memphis. I called for him and let him take over my work. Tupelo ladies were busy serving coffee to us as we worked, and also prepared lunch for us.

It was reported that about 200 people lost their lives, and more than a thousand had been injured in the disaster. I shall never forget that experience, and I will believe any tale I hear about what can take place in a tornado.

Just ten months later in February, 1937, we were again called out for disaster relief. This time it was to Memphis to help take care of the refugees from the great Mississippi River flood. This flood was the most severe in history. Water spread over Arkansas and Mississippi and drove thousands of people away from their homes and caused immeasurable damage. Sixty thousand refugees (they called themselves "rivergees") came into Memphis. Most of these were black and brought little more than a few clothes tied up in a small bag. The Red Cross, the National Guard, and various city and Federal agencies were called upon to help. City schools were discontinued for the emergency. The Central High School was converted into a dormitory for whites while two negro schools were made dormitories for blacks. Fairview High School was converted into a hospital to take care of the many sick refugees. Flu and pneumonia were rampant among the refugees.

The T.V.A. sent men and equipment. A T.V.A. camp was set up in Hodge's athletic field. This field was north of Jefferson Avenue and west of Bellevue where the Veterans' Hospital is now located. The T.V.A. employees lived in this camp. All of their equipment, including trucks and automobiles for transportation, were distributed from there. The medical unit we brought was assigned a tent to be used as headquarters and we quickly began taking calls for ambulance service to pick up sick refugees and carry them to an appropriate emergency hospital.

I was responsible for supervising all medical personnel. This group consisted of laboratory technicians, ambulance drivers, nurses, and doctors. They had brought enough equipment to set up and run a hospital. The Technical High School on Poplar Avenue had been assigned to us. The demand for hospital beds did not increase, however, so that the opening of another hospital was unnecessary. Our personnel, therefore, were distributed to hospitals where they could be used.

I increasingly became a liaison between the various agencies involved in caring for refugees. I had my technicians, medical officers, nurses, and ambulance drivers report to me every evening by phone. I stayed at the Claridge Hotel, but was busy throughout the city during the day. I met daily with a committee of the Memphis and Shelby County Medical Society to keep posted on the activities of this organization, and I visited the emergency hospitals. I also had dealings with the United States Public Health representative, and the City Health Department.

One day I was asked to accompany a colonel from Fort Oglethorpe who had been sent over. He wanted to inspect the housing provided the refugees. I took him to the Central High School which was being used as a dormitory for white women. These women were all poor from the country, and were greatly worried because their homes had been inundated, and their only possessions probably destroyed. Many of them had children, and some had small babies.

The colonel entered one large room filled with army cots on which the women slept. He quickly found that one woman had pulled her baby's cot up against her own. The colonel demanded in a rough voice that the cots be at least three feet apart, and ordered the woman to separate the cots immediately. A little English teacher who probably weighed no more than one hundred pounds, was accompanying us on the inspection. She was serving as the matron for that part of the dormitory. At the colonel's demand that the poor frightened woman move her baby's cot, the little English teacher jumped in front of the officer, her eyes flashing fire, her whole being bristling with rage, and said, "Look here, colonel, all this brass you're wearing doesn't mean anything to me. You are not dealing with soldiers, you are dealing with women and children. This cot stays where it is so this mother can take care of her baby, regardless of what you say!" The Colonel's face turned several colors. He turned on his heels and walked out without saying a word. I admired the little lady, and gloried in her spunk. I am sorry I have forgotten her name.

After about two weeks, the flood had subsided, so that the refugees began to return to their homes. The problem was over and we all prepared to return to our work with the T.V.A.

Dr. Otis Warr who also had worked with me at the Polyclinic, was the president of the local medical society, and had acted as chairman of the committee which had regular daily meetings at lunch. Since I was leaving Memphis I drove to his office to say goodbye. "I'm glad you came, Fred," he said, "I have been trying to get in touch with you. I wanted to tell you that we want you back in Memphis. If you want to come back to Memphis and specialize in treating tuberculosis, I'll finance you until you build up a good practice. "Or," he continued, "I'd be glad to have you work with me again." He added, "You don't have to give your answer now. Go home, talk it over with Jess, and return in about two weeks and let me know your decision."

Although I didn't tell him, I had already made my decision. I would jump at the chance to work with him again. I thanked him, and told him I would let him know in two weeks. Two weeks later I returned, this time with Jess and the boys. On arriving, I called Dr. Warr's office to ask if I could see him. I was told that he was on vacation in Gatlinburg. We spent the night in Memphis, and the next day after shopping awhile, we had lunch at the Sears Roebuck Cafe. While we were eating, Dr. Sam Williamson, an old friend from medical school days came through and saw us. He came over and spoke to us, and after a short chat said, "Did you hear about Dr. Warr?" When I told him no, he told us that Dr. Warr was in the Fort

Sanders Hospital at Knoxville with lobar pneumonia and was not expected to live.

We were dreadfully sorry to hear of Dr. Warr's illness, for we considered him one of the finest gentlemen we knew and one of the best friends we had. In addition, we knew that the thought of returning to Memphis must be forgotten. The next day in Memphis' *Commercial Appeal* there was a story of Dr. Warr's death — another great disappointment for me. I had not only lost a good friend, but had again been thwarted in my hope to return to the practice of medicine.

My work was mostly administrative and I never did consider myself a good administrator. I wanted to do what I had been trained to do. The T.V.A. work was interesting but I still was not using what I had learned in medical school. I continued doing the best I could, although I was somewhat despondent at times because I was beginning to think of myself as a failure.

Life at Sheffield, however, was not altogether unpleasant. We joined the Baptist Church and began to take an active part in the work there. Jess and I were both made Sunday School teachers. One Sunday when our pastor was away, I was asked to fill the pulpit for both the morning and evening services. I gave talks based on sermons I had heard Dr. Fred Brown of Knoxville preach.

We had been members of the Sheffield Church for only a few weeks when we realized there was a terrific split in the church membership. The Pastor had discharged all the deacons, and appointed a Board of Deacons composed only of his friends. This action created a major disturbance.

Jess and I managed to stay out of the argument, and on the following Sunday we drove across the river and joined the First Baptist Church of Florence, Alabama. We found a warm church with a grand old gentleman (Dr. Motley) for a pastor and some mighty fine people as members. I was again put on the Board of Deacons and also was asked to take a class of men and teach. Jess was similarly put to work, and our boys liked the new church. We felt blessed at making such a good change.

I also joined the Sheffield Rotary Club. The club had a luncheon every week, and I learned to know most of the prominent

men in Sheffield. If I was out of town on the day the Sheffield Club
met, I would "make up," as was required of Rotarians, wherever I
was. I often would make up in Florence. This way I became
acquainted with the leading citizens of Florence also. I found many
good friends among Rotarians in both towns.

We enjoyed the fishing, sailing on Wilson Lake, and playing
golf at the Florence or the Tuscumbia golf courses. We were also
invited to numerous social events on both sides of the Tennessee
River as it separated Florence and Sheffield.

Dr. Bishop, who was Director of the Health and Safety
Department of the T.V.A., seemed to get some pleasure out of
reorganizing the Department. In 1937 his reorganization resulted
in my being transferred to Chattanooga where I was to be given
responsibility for the medical program of the whole area. Consequently we moved on January 1, 1938, to Crestview Drive in
Chattanooga. The health and safety central offices were in that
city's old post office.

XIV

Silver Years

In the late summer of 1938, Dr. E. L. Bishop, who had been Commissioner of Health of the State of Tennessee, knew that the State Health Department had funds for sending men (or women) to Johns Hopkins University School of Public Health and Hygiene. He told me that he would like to send me. I thought it might be worthwhile, for it could shift my interests away from clinical medicine and into public health work. Arrangements were made for Dr. R. B. Watson and me to go to Johns Hopkins for this session beginning in the fall of 1938. The state was to pay us $200 a month. I had accumulated about sixty days of annual leave so that my T.V.A. salary would continue for at least sixty working days, which would amount to twelve weeks. Jess and I felt we could manage without difficulty with this income. Moreover, my salary had been increased to $5,000 a year. So we decided that I would go to Johns Hopkins University.

In October, 1938, we put our furniture in storage, packed our car with all we thought we might need, and headed for Baltimore. We spent the first night out with Blanche in Bristol. Next morning we drove to Atkins, Virginia, where we met Dr. Bob Watson and his wife, Elena, who had spent the night with her mother there. We traveled together up through Virginia to Winchester and across the Potomac at Harper's Ferry, then eastward through Frederick, Maryland. This route was taken to avoid going through Washington. Dr. Watson had arranged for us to stop over in Pikeville until we could find suitable living quarters in Baltimore, and we were anxious to complete our 400 mile trip before dark.

We arrived in Pikeville, which is a suburb of Baltimore, at about 6:00 p.m. and went directly to the home of Mrs. Hendricks

211

with whom we were to stay. This home was a large, old house that at one time must have been quite a show place. Only Mrs. Hendricks and her husband lived in it so there was plenty of room for all of us. Mr. Hendricks had fallen on hard times and since the Depression began had been without employment. Mrs. Hendricks proved to be a delightful person and a fine hostess. She also was the first cousin of Wallace Warfield Simpson who had just married King Edward of Great Britain, precipitating the abdication crisis.

The day after our arrival we went into Baltimore where we met a young lady who was a real estate agent. After looking over several houses we found one which was ideal for us. It was a furnished two story house on Tilbury Way. It had three bedrooms and two bathrooms. The lady who owned the house had a son who was going to the University of Virginia, and she wanted to be with him during the nine months he would be in school. She said she would rather rent it to us than to people interested in horse racing at Pimlico, which was only a few blocks away. She also would be ready to move back into her home about the same time we would be ready to give it up.

I was a student again, only this time I was attenting the Johns Hopkins School of Public Health and Hygiene. It is internationally noted for its excellence and for the competency of its faculty. The student body was composed of students from all over the world. It was the school to which the Rockefeller Foundation sent foreign students. In my class there were Japanese, Chinese, Thais, Mexicans, Czechoslovakians, a Turk, and a student from Finland. The American students came from many parts of the United States. The students organized a "Ubiquiteers Club" to which, to my surprise, I was elected president. This "Club" was merely an organization of our class, and functioned only when some matter came up on which a decision of the whole class was desirable.

I enjoyed the fellowship of the foreign students and found many friends among the American students. The Turk, Dr. Idil, proved to be the champion chess player of the group. I was never able to beat him at the game. I found the Thai, Dr. Yararat, and the Czech, Dr. Prosek, also to be excellent chess players. We had two hours off at noon, and during that period the recreation room became the scene for many contests. The favorites were cribbage, bridge, chess and poker. There was much opportunity for visiting with fellow students.

Beyond this fulfilling social interaction, the subjects we studied were all of importance in the field of Public Health: Bacteriology, Immunology, Biostatistics, Epidemiology, Industrial Hygiene, Chemistry of Nutrition, Sanitary Engineering, Parasitology, Public Health Administration. All these subjects were taught by men and women who not only were dedicated masters of their subject, but also were excellent teachers. I had no trouble in getting down to the business of being a school boy again, although for the course in Biostatistics I had to make a quick review of algebra and trigonometry.

We made frequent "field trips," in Industrial Hygiene and visited some of the major industrial plants in Baltimore. We saw the Bethlehem Steel Corporation, the Western Electric plant, a copper refining plant, a glass company where bottles were made, a large plant which made alcohol for commercial use, and a plant where bathtubs and plumbing equipment were made. At all these plants the health hazards and the methods used to protect the employees were fully discussed.

We also made field trips in the Sanitary Engineering course. We visited the Sewage Disposal plants, a garbage incinerator plant, as well as the water supply of Baltimore at Loch Raven and its treatment plant. We also visited laboratories which continually tested the quality of the water.

In addition, I asked for the privilege of working two afternoons a week in the out-patient department of the Johns Hopkins Hospital. This experience was most interesting, and I enjoyed every minute of it. Five medical students were assigned to me, and I found myself instructing in clinical medicine again.

We enjoyed living in Baltimore and found its people to be very hospitable. To us it was a big old Southern city. The boys went to the Roland Park Grammar School and Fred, who had grown to be twelve years old, joined the Boy Scouts. They had no problem finding congenial playmates in our neighborhood.

We also enjoyed living with Bob and Elena Watson. Bob and I would put money in the "kitty" once a week, and from this all our groceries were bought and other household expenses paid. Our rent was only $100 a month and was equally divided between us. Bob and I took turns driving to school and would leave a car for the girls to use when shopping.

We were able to take drives over to Gettysburg, Annapolis, and other interesting places around Baltimore. We made several weekend trips to Washington, D.C., and saw a major historic site each time. We visited Mount Vernon, the National Cemetery at Arlington, the Smithsonian Institute, the Museum of Natural History, the Capitol, the Library of Congress, the F.B.I. building, and other interesting sites. By the end of the year we had seen nearly everything of interest in Washington. When school was out in the spring, I did not stay for graduation exercises, but had my diploma (Master of Public Health) mailed to me.

We were lucky that Dr. Langston, my associate in the T.V.A., was moving out of a house in Chattanooga which fit our needs perfectly. We therefore had a place when we arrived in Chattanooga.

On our return home we drove down to Annapolis where we crossed the Chesapeake Bay by ferry, then continued over to the Eastern shore of Maryland. We drove on into Delaware, and then south all the way to Cape Charles, Virginia. We then caught a ferry for the 15 miles trip across the Chesapeake, to old Fortress Monroe. This trip was about 15 miles. We had an excellent lunch on board the ferry which the boys and I enjoyed very much. Jess, however, because of the swells causing the boat to rock, got slightly seasick and ate very little.

We landed at the old fort and then drove through Hampton to historic Williamsburg, Virginia. We found a "Tourist Home" there where we put up for the night. Motels had still not come into being at that time. Tourist Homes were usually residences with several bedrooms which were made available to tourists by the couple living in them. In many of them meals also were available.

We toured Williamsburg that evening until dark. Next day we drove to Roanoke, Virginia, and then on to Bristol, where we spent the night with Blanche. The following day we left for Chattanooga where we moved into a comfortable house on Harcourt Drive, on the eastern slope of Missionary Ridge, near the McCallie Tunnel.

We got our furniture from the storage company and quickly began to live normally once again.

Our stay in Chattanooga was not unpleasant. We had numerous friends and liked the city. We began attending the First Baptist Church once again. With encouragement from us, Fred and Edgar accepted Christ publicly and were baptized there.

Our friends were mostly fellow T.V.A. employees. I joined the Hamilton County Medical Society and soon found many friends among the doctors there. I also read a paper before the society and made several talks on health subjects before several civic groups. I even gave a lecture on tuberculosis over the radio.

Dr. Bishop then decided to reorganize the Health and Safety Department of the T.V.A. This time the Tennessee Valley was divided into two sections. I was made "Master of the West," which included all the T.V.A. Health and Safety Department activities from the Guntersville Dam to the Ohio River. Dr. M. F. Langston was made "Master of the East" with his territory encompassing the eastern half of the T.V.A.

This reorganization meant that I was to be moved back to Sheffield, Alabama. This time I was not so reluctant to go, although I longed for the time when I could get into work that would permit me to buy a home and live in it permanently. My salary was barely equal to my living expenses, and I had been unable to save any money.

We moved in the summer of 1940. This time we lived in house No. 103 in Village One. Our house was on the "handle" of the "Bell." We found most of our old friends still there and we were soon back into the activities we had enjoyed previously. I again became a member of the Sheffield Rotary Club and we rejoined the First Baptist Church of Florence. I also was put back on the Board of Deacons, and was again asked to teach the men's Sunday School class. My work was very much the same as on my previous stay, but I had a greater responsibility for all the functions of the department.

Dr. Frank Roberts, Professor of Public Health of the University of Tennessee College of Medicine, knowing that I had training in industrial hygiene, asked Dr. Bishop if I might be allowed to visit Memphis periodically and give lectures to the medical students

on the subject. This request was granted so that I went to Memphis
every quarter to give lectures on industrial hygiene.

In October of 1943 on one of my trips to Memphis for the
industrial hygiene lectures, Dr. "Joe" Hamilton invited me to
attend prayer meeting with him. I was glad to accept his invitation.
I enjoyed visiting with him and Ruby, and I looked forward to
meeting my many friends I had made at the First Baptist Church. I
saw Dr. R. L. Sanders there. "Fred," he said, "I want to talk to you
after the service."

His remark set my mind in motion, wondering what he wanted
to talk to me about, to the extent that I had difficulty giving
attention to the prayer meeting service. Was he about to suggest
that I return to Memphis as his associate? The most interesting
phase of the T.V.A. work was fast drawing to a close. The greater
construction projects were being completed, and large groups of
employees with their families in construction villages were gradually being eliminated, medical needs were therefore diminishing. I
had long since decided that clinical medicine was much more
attractive to me than preventive medicine, or Public Health. I had
given up hopes of returning to East Tennessee.

After the prayer meeting was over, Dr. Sanders came to me
and said, "Fred, how would you like to come over and help my
brother Carl? You know the war is on and many doctors have left
Memphis for military service. Carl is having more work than he can
handle, and he would like to have you join him." He added, "You
know us and we know you, so there is no investigation to be done on
the part of either of us." I felt my prayers had been answered. "Dr.
Sanders," I said, "I don't know of anything that would please me
more."

I gave my lectures the following day, and at about five o'clock
that afternoon I went to the Sanders Clinic to talk to Dr. Carl, as Dr.
R. L. had suggested. Carl had me wait until he had seen his last
patient for the day, and then with his daughter Margaret, we went
to the Chisca Hotel for dinner. We discussed my joining him and
arrived at most generous terms. It was agreed I would later become
a partner in the group. I agreed to join them on January 1, 1944.
He took me back to my hotel, where I immediately called Jess and
gave her the good news.

After the Polyclinic had broken up, Dr. R. L. and Carl Sanders had opened offices in the Baptist Hospital annex, forming what they called the "Sanders Clinic." They each had a young man to assist them, but these assistants were only temporary employees. Their work had increased to such an extent that it was necessary to enlarge the group with another internist and another surgeon. Dr. R. M. Pool, a surgeon, was taken into the firm at the same time. Because the war was still going on, and because so many doctors had gone to the military forces, younger doctors were not available to join the group.

When I got home I notified Dr. Bishop, my superior in the T.V.A., that I was planning to leave. He said I was making a mistake. "You are leaving security for insecurity," he said, emphasizing the retirement plan of the T.V.A. His arguments could not make me change my mind. I had at last been given the opportunity to do the work I had hoped to do since I began the study of medicine. The two months before the move dragged along slowly.

Finishing my work with the T.V.A., I made arrangements to go to Memphis on January 15th. Fred and Edgar were in school at Columbia Military Academy and Jess would remain in Sheffield until we found a house in Memphis. I took our Dodge Sedan, filling it with my clothes and other necessities, and left for Memphis. There I went to the home of "Dr. Carl" (Sanders) and started to work at the Sanders Clinic at once. I began seeing patients from the start. Dr. Carl was very generous in referring as many patients to me as he could. I also made hospital "rounds" on all the patients we had in the hospital, and did my best to relieve Dr. Carl of as much work as possible.

I was a little rusty at the beginning and burned some "midnight oil" while reading up on latest drugs, laboratory procedures, and clinical methods. The nurses were kind to me and were a great help. I never studied harder in Medical School than when I again began to practice medicine. As the days and weeks passed I increasingly enjoyed doing what I had always wanted to do, and gradually gained confidence in myself.

Soon after coming to Memphis I called some realtors and asked to be shown a house which I could buy. I was shown several houses and was beginning to get discouraged. The houses were old, in bad locations, poorly arranged or in bad repair. I wanted one that I knew Jess would like. Then one day I received a phone call from a realtor I had not consulted. He said, "Dr. Strain, I'm Bill Kenworthy. I heard you are looking for a house. I believe I have the very house you are looking for." I told him I would like to see it.

Since he was on gasoline rationing, and I, being a doctor, was not, he asked me to take him out to see the house. We drove farther and farther out Poplar Avenue all the way to Goodlett Street. I began to think that to live this far out would be inadvisable. We turned south on Goodlett to Grandview Avenue, and finally less than a block east on this street, we found the very house I wanted. It had a large lot which would allow plenty of gardening space for Jess, and the arrangements of the house inside and out were very pleasing. Furthermore, the price, $14,000, seemed reasonable. I told Bill I thought I would take it, but I wanted Jess to see it. I called her and she came over the next morning on the train. I took her out to the house and she was delighted.

My problem then was paying for it. On moving to Memphis my total assets amounted to only $2,000 plus my T.V.A. pay which would continue for about two months for unused annual leave. My friend, Mr. Frank Maxwell, was manager of the Crosstown Branch of the First National Bank. I took the matter to him. I needed $4,000 down payment on the house, and he gave me a loan, accepting my insurance policies as security and Dr. R. L. Sanders as my co-signer. After I made further arrangements for paying for the house and checked on the title, the house was mine. I took time off from work and went to Sheffield to get Jess and make the move. We moved into our home on March 1, 1944. What a pleasure it was to have Jess with me again, and what a joy it was to realize that after twenty years of married life we at last had a home of our own! There was no prospect of our having to move again. When Fred and Edgar came home from Columbia Military Academy for Easter, they let it be known that they, too, were happy we were in our own home.

My work became more interesting and satisfying as time went on. I was seeing more patients who came to the clinic asking to see me, and I soon had a sizeable practice. I enjoyed seeing these

"My work became more interesting and satisfying as time went on."

patients and felt keenly my responsibility to each one of them; I did
all that I could to diagnose the causes of their symptoms and to give
them the best possible care. I was at last doing what I wanted to
do—practicing medicine like a real doctor!

From the time I began work at the Polyclinic, I was convinced
that group practice was much better than "solo practice." Group
practice offers the advantage of viewpoints available from other
specialists on a problem. Too, in group practice it is easier to keep
up with advances and problems of other specialities than it is in solo
practice.

As they did in the Polyclinic, Drs. R. L. and Carl promoted
constant study of medical journals and frequent reviewing of
experiences in our practice. For this purpose we had a staff
meeting every Friday night.

Much of the clinical teaching of medical students was done by
volunteer teachers. Because the war had taken so many doctors

from Memphis, the school was having problems obtaining teachers. When Dr. Conley Sanford, Professor of Medicine, asked me to help, I became active in teaching. The school year was divided into three quarters, with twelve quarters being required for graduation. I started out teaching Therapeutics and, after a few quarters, was asked to teach Internal Medicine. These activities resulted in my having to do much studying. It was fortunate for me, however, for I soon thoroughly reviewed Cecil's *Practice of Medicine* and, as a result, became a better doctor.

The war was finally over and many young doctors returned to Memphis. Dr. John Hughes and others organized a group which was called the Memphis Academy of Internal Medicine. I attended the called meeting of internists when the organization, made up of specialists who confined their work to Internal Medicine, was formed. There was considerable discussion as to whether those who were not Associates or Fellows of the American College of Physicians, or had not passed the examination of the American Board of Internal Medicine, should be admitted as members. These restrictions would prohibit our joining the society; therefore one or two other doctors and I left the meeting so that our presence would not affect the debate. It was finally decided, I was told the next day, that those doctors who limited their work to Internal Medicine would be admitted at the beginning. I joined the organization but decided to take the board examination and become a Fellow in the American College of Physicians.

I discussed the matter with Dr. Carl. He said it was foolish for me to take the examination because he knew I could not pass it. He told me that Dr. Scott of Cleveland, Ohio, who was on the Board, felt that no one more than forty years of age should be permitted to take the examination because very few over that age ever passed it. I wasn't discouraged. I said I would try. If I didn't pass it I would get along just as well. I did, however, dislike the thought that I was inferior to so many of my colleagues who were "Certified by the Board." I therefore applied for permission to take the examination and had my name presented to the College of Physicians for membership as an associate. Both were granted. I could become a "Fellow" in the American College of Medicine only if I passed the American Board examination.

Continuing my work in the clinic and my teaching at the medical college, I studied harder than ever. In November of 1947 I was accepted as a student in a two week post-graduate course in internal medicine to be given at the University of Wisconsin Medical School at Madison, Wisconsin. This was one of the many post-graduate courses sponsored by the American College of Physicians in various parts of the country every year. This course lasted from November 3rd to the 14th and, as an intensive study of the whole field of internal medicine, was ideal. The faculty was made up of men and women who were thoroughly grounded in their subjects and who were excellent teachers. This course brought me up-to-date on medicine and was just what I needed. I returned to Memphis much more confident in my ability to give my patients good medical care.

In April of 1948 I went to San Francisco to the yearly meeting of the American College of Physicians where I heard papers on various subjects and learned of many new developments in the field of medicine. With this background — teaching, attending the postgraduate course in Madison and the meeting of the American College of Physicians, along with much studying — I felt ready to take the Board examination. This examination was to be in two parts, written and practical. The written part was to be held in Nashville in October and the practical in New York the following April.

In October twelve of us went to Nashville from Memphis to take the examination. Of this number, we learned a few weeks later, only four of us passed. I was delighted to be included in that number. I was the oldest in the group; most of the others were relatively recent graduates who had just recently had good hospital training. In April of 1949 I went to New York to take the second part of the examination, the so-called "practical." I was assigned to examine two patients on the charity ward of Bellevue Hospital. I was allowed thirty minutes for each case, after which I was called before two physicians for intensive questioning. One of the physicians was Dr. Schnabel of Philadelphia, a dour old gentleman who asked a question and, without a change of expression to indicate whether my answer was right or wrong, asked another. The other physician who quizzed me was the same Dr. Scott of Cleveland who had reportedly said that nearly all doctors over 40 failed the examination. They both asked me questions, not only about the patients I had examined, but about anything else they thought of. Dr. Scott proved to be a very likeable gentleman, for when I answered correctly he said so; when I was wrong, he not only told me my answer was incorrect but gave me the correct answer as well. I was proud that I answered few of his questions incorrectly. I returned to Memphis feeling that I had passed the examination. When we received the results, I learned that, of the four who had passed the first part in Nashville, only three of us had passed the "practical" in New York. I was one of them! I was beginning to lose some of my inferiority complex. I was one of three who passed out of twelve who took the exam. The following fall I was elected president of the Memphis Academy of Internal Medicine, just three years after there had been some question as to whether I should be allowed to become a member.

In April of 1950, in Boston, I was made a Fellow of the American College of Physicians. Having achieved these two goals—a Diplomate of the Board of Internal Medicine and a Fellowship in the American College of Medicine—gave me a feeling of satisfaction that nothing else ever could. The country boy from Limestone had reached the goal for which he had long been striving.

XV

Doctor Strain

My life as a "qualified Internist" in Memphis was a satisfying one. I had a good practice and I enjoyed my association with my patients, most of whom were like personal friends. I had a good rapport with my fellow physicians as evidenced by the frequency with which I was elected to offices or positions in medical organizations.

In addition to being elected president of the Memphis Academy of Internal Medicine, in the years that followed I was honored by being elected or appointed to the following positions: President of the Department of Medicine of the Baptist Hospital (two times), President of the Memphis Heart Association, President of the Memphis and Shelby County Medical Society (700 plus members), Vice President of the Tennessee State Medical Association, President of the Staff of the Baptist Hospital, Chairman of the Nominating Committee for each of the above mentioned organizations, Member of the House of Delegates (the organization that is concerned with business and policies) of the State Medical Association for a number of years, Member of the House of Delegates of the Memphis and Shelby County Medical Society several years, and I served on many committees. I taught regularly in the Medical School, and became Clinical Professor of Medicine until my retirement. I also taught a Sunday School Class of adult men, and served on the Board of Deacons at the First Baptist Church. I found the colloquy to be stimulating at meetings of the American College of Medicine in St. Louis, Chicago, Atlantic City, New York, Philadelphia, Boston, New Orleans, Louisville and Milwaukee, and at other medical conventions in surrounding towns and cities. My income with the Sanders Clinic was such that I was able to pay for

"I believe I succeeded because I tried to live
according to the teaching of the Bible."

my home within seven years; to educate both of my sons, Fred in
Medicine and Edgar in Chemistry, and to live comfortably.

I felt that I had achieved a degree of success which I had once
only hoped for. In doing so I had forfeited only frivolity. I have
always been serious minded, and from the beginning I thought the
business of preparing myself for the future should have priority
over the ephemeral.

I believe I succeeded because I tried to live according to the
teaching of the Bible. The twelfth chapter of Paul's letter to the
Romans was an excellent guideline for me. I believe that those who
can follow this advice are much happier! And the admonition Paul
gives in Philippians 4:8 is worth heeding.

Maybe it was largely luck that resulted in one opportunity after
another coming just at the right time, and that I had a dear wife
who gave me nothing but help and cooperation through all the

years we have been together. For these blessings I can only thank the good Lord.

I might mention that I never had a job for which I applied. I was offered jobs by those who knew me, or was recommended for work by my friends. I thank God for all He has done for me. On a more tangible note, I believe that practicing medicine as long as I did enabled me to see life in the raw. Patients present themselves to the doctor nearly always without an attempt to be other than their natural selves. They confide the most intimate thoughts, fears, feelings and experiences. They make the doctor their confessor, their counselor, their advisor and most intimate friend. A preacher came to me with problems he could not discuss with anyone else. He told me that since he had no pastor he wanted me to act in that capacity for him.

I never betrayed a trust. A school teacher whose husband had been in military service in Europe eight months feared she might be pregnant. A mother of an eighteen year old son found he was a homosexual. A doctor's widow feared she might have a venereal disease. A Baptist preacher realized he was an alcoholic. A college graduate who was teaching school realized her high school drop-out, truck driver husband of only six months, had nothing in common with her. All these and many more came for counsel.

I enjoyed making house calls. On a house call a doctor can learn much about a patient he could never learn otherwise. There is no formality there. The character of the home, its furnishings, the way it is kept, its location, and the relationship of members of the family to one another tells more than the dress and demeanor of the patient in the doctor's office ever could. The doctor can better understand the problems a patient might have in taking care of the illness from which he or she is suffering.

The doctor is involved in many of the tragic and sorrowful experiences of his patients. He or she sees their reaction to crippling illness, to impending death, or the loss of a loved one. The wide variation in the type of reaction to these situations is noted. Rachel, our maid, said calmly when told she had a inoperable malignancy, "Well, I knew I'd have to die someday, and I might as well die of that as anything." A dear, elderly, retired school teacher, suffering from a terminal cancer of the lung, would tell me

when I called on her in the hospital, "Doctor, you don't need to
spend your time coming to see me so often. You know there is
nothing you can do for me. Spend your time taking care of the
patients whom you can relieve or cure."

The practice of medicine, dealing with all kinds of people, is
not without earthy, humorous experiences. I recall leaving one
hospital room where the situation was tragic enough to bring tears
and then going into another patient's room and finding a comical
situation. I went in to see Mr. Murphy, a farmer from Arkansas.
His grown daughter and his wife were with him.

"Good morning, Mr. Murphy, how are you today?" I asked.

"Feeling good, Doc."

"Did you sleep well last night?"

"Yes, sir."

"Did you have a good breakfast?"

"Yep."

"Have your bowels moved this morning?"

"Yep. Have yours?"

A negro patient complained of frequent urination. "Does it
burn?" I asked. "I don't know, doc. I ain't never set fire to none of
it."

I asked a lady if she had any indigestion. She said, "Yes, but my
doctor at home said it was due to a high tail hernia." Of course I
knew she meant a hiatal hernia. A farmer's wife from Arkansas
once told me, "I taken some of that Hadacol; hit hope pap."

A dear old preacher friend came in for an examination one
cold winter day. I asked him what his trouble seemed to be. He said,
"I think I have had too many candles on my birthday cake" (He was
ninety years old.) I asked him to take his things off so I could
examine his heart. He complied, taking off his overcoat, then his
coat, then a sleeveless sweater, a vest, and a shirt. As he started to
take off his undershirt, he turned to me and said, "I am like the
prodigal son, I am about to come to myself!"

Regardless of the patient's station in life, I tried to treat them
all alike. The doctor who came to me for advice and merely opened
his shirt and asked me to listen to his heart was told, "Doctor, you
are the patient. I'm the doctor. Take off your clothes so I can

examine you." I never saw the doctor who wasn't pleased to have a complete examination.

I have learned that wherever you go, you can find lovely, likable people, if you look for them. It makes no difference whether they are Northerners, Southerners, Westerners, or Easterners. And the same is true for nationality and race. The way to find good friends, when moving to a new location, is to go to church. That is where the best people are; and to have friends, one must be friendly.

Life for Jess and me after returning to Memphis, except for some of the events I have described, was little different from that of most any family. I therefore thought it unnecessary to include a detailed account of it here. Perhaps it would be just as well to end the story by simply saying, "And they lived happily ever after."

INDEX

Acuff, Dr. Herbert, 192, 195
Albany, N.Y. 156
Al G. Field Minstrel, 150
American College of Physicians, 221–223
American Journal of Medicine Science, 164
American Social Hygiene Association, 205
Annapolis, Md., 214
Armistice Day 1918, 113–114
Archives of Internal Medicine, 164
Arnold, Pauline, 29
Ataway, Va., 78–79
Appalachian Exposition of October, 1910, 32, 34–36

Ballard, Rose, 125
Baltimore, Md., 212–213
Barksdale, Dr. Jack, 182
Battery, the, 156
Beale Street, 40
Beard, Dr., 65
BeCraft, Winnifred, 76, 135
Belle Plain, Kan. 55, 109, 111
Biddle, Charles, 21, 63, 195
Biddle, Mrs. Nellie, 23
Bilbo, Theodore, 186–187
Biloxie, Miss. 189–190
Bishop, Dr. E. L. 198, 210–211
Boone, Dr. A. U., 160
Boswell, Dr. Henry, 175–186
Bristol, Tenn., 15, 134–135, 168–169, 171, 192, 211.
Brooks, Dr. Herbert, 113
Bryan, William Jennings, 52
Bulls Gap, Tenn., 57, 70, 82, 99

Caltagirone, Dr. J. V., 156
Campbell, Nannie, 58
Campbell, Charlie, 58
Campbell, Dr. Willis, 132–133

Calvert School of Baltimore, The, 185
Camp John Sevier, N. C.
Canton, Miss. 177
Carty, Joe, 63
Cape Charles, Va., 214
Charlotte, N.C. 100
Chattanooga, Tenn. 73, 210, 214
Chicago, Ill., 151–152
Cincinnati, Oh., 174; and Hamilton County Tuberculosis Hospital, 175
Civilian Conservation Corps, 197, 205
Cleveland, Oh., 204
Cleveland, Tenn., 39–40
Columbus, Miss., 178
Commerce, Ok., 94
Conner, Gov. Mike, 187
Crockett, Va., 77

Dakin's Solution, 125
Davis, E. M., Soap Manufact. Co., 61
Decker, Charlie, 5
Decker, Dick, 4
Decker, Theodore, 4
Denton, Tx. 189
Depression, The Great, 192
DeShea, Dr. L. J., 120, 128
Dunham, Dr. Kennon, 174
Durrett, Dr. J. J., 149

Eddy, Mary Baker, *Science and Health with the Key to the Scriptures*, 121
Edgewater Gulf Hotel, 189
Elizabeth College at Roanoke, 75–76
Embreeville, Tenn., 3–4
Erwin, Tenn., 3

Ferrell, Rev. Lewis, 178
Franklin, Tenn., 89
Fortress Monoroe, Va., 214

Ford Motor Co., 200
Francis, Dr. E.E., 115, 117, 166

Gaby, Lucy, 29
Galt, Edith (wife of Woodrow Wilson) 74
Good, Russell, 30
Gravellene Bayou, 190
Greene, Henry, 38
Greene, Joab, 55
Greenville, Tenn., 171
Greenwood, Miss. 194
Guthrie, Ok.

Hall, James, 102
Hamilton, Dr. J. F., 148, 150, 158, 176,
    189
Hancock County, Tenn., 38
Harbert, Jason, 72
Hardy, Ark. 121, 128
Harris, Dr. Cummings, 158
Hart, John, 73, 89
Hattiesburg, Miss., 181
Henry, J. P., 163-164
Hoge, Josephine, 46
Horner's Syndrome, 182
Holston Conference, 16
Hoskins, Dean J. A., 70-71, 190
Hudson River, 156
Hughes, Dr. John, 220
Hyman, Dr. O. W., 103

Insulin Treatments, 146

Jackson, Miss., 177, 188, 191, 193-194
Jaynes, Charlie, 12
Jaynes, Herbert, 59
Jockey Creek, 12
Jockey, Tenn. 10
Johns Hopkins University, 211; and Johns
    Hopkins University School of Public
    Health and Hygiene, 211
Johnson, Paul, 73
Journal of the Tennessee Medical Association,
    163
Johnson City, Tenn., 9-10, 32, 154, 192
Johnson, Samuel, Rassalas, 17
Joplin, Mo., 95-96
Journal of the National Tuberculosis Associa-
    tion, 164
Judd, Fred, 92-93
Judd, Lloyd, 97, 106

Kansas City, Mo., 57
Kansas State Psychiatric Hospital, 92
Kamp Kia Kima, 121, 123, 127, 131

Klepper, Johnny, 27
Knoxville, Tenn., 32-34, 58, 63, 84, 87-89,
    102, 104-105, 107, 119-120, 170,
    194-200; and Chilhowee Park, 34; and
    Economy Drugstore, 63; and Empire
    Marble Works, labor at, 58-61; and
    First Baptist Church of Knoxville,
    196; and Goode's Restaurant, 119; and
    Knox County Medical Society, 196;
    and Knoxville Journal, 89; and Knoxville
    Sentinel, 20-21; and the Knoxville
    Sevierville and Eastern Railroad, 69;
    and Newcomers Department Store,
    68; and the Southern School of Phar-
    macy, 64; and Thompson's Restaur-
    ant, 69; the University of Tennessee at
    Knoxville, 66, 68, 70, 89-92, 170
Kolmer Wassermann Tests, 145
Konnarock, Va., 83, 87
Kraus, Dr. William, 148

Langston, Dr. M. F., 214-215
Levy, Dr. Louis, 114
Limestone, Tenn., 6, 7, 10, 14, 15, 20, 21,
    32, 36-37, 39, 58, 87, 171, 197, 222;
    and Limestone Creek, 11-12, 22, 30;
    and Limestone High School, 24, 46;
    and Lone Oak Inn, 39
Longview Texas, 189
Lead and Zinc Mining in Ok., 97-98

Magee, Miss., 185-186, 191
Marion, Va., 78, 82, 87
Mayflower Hotel, Wash. D.C., 165
Mayo Clinic, 163
Marshall, Texas, 188
Maxwell, Oklahoma, 97
McKinley, President William, 10
McMinnville, Tenn., 168-170; and Sed-
    berry Hotel, 168-169
Medical fraternities, 106
Memphis, Tenn., 40-41, 102-103, 106,
    112, 120, 123-128, 135, 137, 142-143,
    145-146, 149-151, 154-155, 159,
    161-167, 175, 192-194, 215-217, 219,
    221-223; and Baptist Hospital, 105,
    117-118, 124, 128-129, 167, 217, 223;
    and Black Cat Cafe, 40; and Brodnax
    Jewelry Store, 106; and Central Bap-
    tist Church, 159; and Central High
    School, 206; and Chisca Hotel, 40;
    and Claridge Hotel, 207; and Falls
    Building, 125; and First National
    Bank, 218; and First Baptist Church,
    160, 176, 223; and Gartly-Ramsy

Hospital, 131; and Gayoso Hotel, 124, 148; and Home of the Incurables, 126; and J. T. Hinton and Son Funeral Parlor, 131; and Hodge's Athletic Field, 206; and King Cotton Hotel, 189; and Lyric Theatre, 150; and Madison Heights Methodist Church, 147–149; and Memphis Academy of Internal Medicine, 220; and Memphis Chickasaws professional baseball team, 105; and Memphis General Hospital, 120, 128, 137, 139, 143, 146, 148–149; and Memphis Health Department, 146, 148; and Memphis Hospital Medical College, 116; and Memphis and Shelby Co. Medical Society, 165, 207; and *Memphis Commercial Appeal* 41, 148, 152; and Memphis Municipal Airport, 193; and Orpheum Theatre, 105; and Pipkin Building, 123; and Russwood Park, 105; and "Roof Garden, The" 125, 129; and Sanders Clinic, 216–217; and St. Joseph's Hospital, 115, 130–131; Technical High-School, 207; Tuberculosis Society of Shelby Co., 151; and Uneeda Biscuit Co. 159.
Miami, Ok., 93–94, 98, 106–107, 109–110
Mims, Bill, 106
Mississippi Medical Assn., 191
Mississippi State Sanatorium, 175, 177–182, 186
Mississippi River, 40, 41; and flood of 1937, 206
Morristown, Tennessee, 38
Murfreesboro, 141

Nashville, Tenn., 200
National Institute of Health, 166
National Tuberculosis Association, 165
Neshoba River, 98
New York Central Railroad, 151
New York City, 156, 204; and Columbia University, 156; and Flowers Hospital, 158; and Grand Central Station, 156; and Harlem, 156; and Harlem General Hospital, 156
Ninnescah River, 109
Norris Dam, 197
Nolichucky River, 3, 30
Norris, Tenn. 199

Oakville Sanatorium, 150; see Mississippi State Sanatorium, 175, 177–182, 186

Oakville Memorial Tuberculosis Hospital, 149
Oklahoma City, 189
O.K. Storage Company
Ottoway County, Ok., 94

Paulk, George, 92
Payne, Mayor Rowlett, 149
Penn, Jarrell, 135
Philadelphia General Hospital, 137
Pitcher, Ok., 94, 109
Pneumothorax, 182
Polyclinic, 161, 163–164, 180, 192–193
Ponca City, Ok., 109
Pool, Dr. R. M. 117
Presidential Election of 1900, 7
Priestly, Virginia, 72
Public Works Adm. 197

Queen and Crescent Railway, 57

Radio Station W.K.N., 141
Radio Station W.M.C. 141
Randolph Macon College, 84
Remine, Aunt Lena, 58
Remine, Maynard, 39-40
Remine, Grandpa, 53
Remine, Schuyler, 58, 87
Remine, Walter, 195
Riley, James Whitcomb, "When the Hearse Trots Back"
Roanoke College, 76
Roanoke, Va., 214
Roark, Eldon, xi–xiii
Roberts, Dr. Frank, 215
Rockefeller Foundation, 212
Rockefeller Institute, 156
Rudner, Dr. Henry, 161
Roosevelt, Theodore, 34–35

Sanatorium, Miss., 176–177, 198
Sanford, Dr. Conley, 220
Saunders, Dr. Carl, 163, 172, 216
Saunders, Dr. R. L. 163, 216
Sanders, Graydon, 68
Saranac Lake, N.Y. 152, 154
Savannah, Tenn., 72
Scottsboro, Al., 73
Sheffield, Al., 199, 200, 209, 217; and Sheffield Rotary Club, 209–210; and Sheffield Hotel, 200, 204
Shreveport, La., 188
Sluder Technique, 114
Smith, Dr. Billy, 153–154, 165
Smith, Paul, 73

Smokey Mountains, 197
Smythe County, Va., 78, 87
Snell, Henry, 73
Southern Medical Association, 205
Southwestern Publishing Company of
    Nashville, 73
Stonecifer, Dr. Ab., 82
Stonecifer, Kate, 82, 87
Stromquist, Walter, 197
Springfield, Mo., 99
Spring River, 121
Sugar Grove, Va. 78, 80–82

Taft, President William Howard, 52
Tate Springs, Tenn., 171
Taylor, Gov. A.A., 4
Taylor, Alf, Jr., 6
Taylor, Blaine, 6
Taylor, Bob, 6
Taylor, Dave, 6
Telford, Tenn. 9, 31
Tennessee Central Railroad, 57
Tennessee College in Murfreesboro, 125
Tennessee River, 33–34, 168
Tennessee Valley Authority, 197–198,
    200–208, 216–217; and Appalachia
    Dam, 204; and Chatuga Dam, 204;
    and Chickamauga Widows Bar, 204;
    and Fontana Dam, 204; and Gun-
    tersville Dam, 202; and Hiawassee
    Dam, 204; and Kentucky Dam, 202–
    204; and Loudon Dam, 204; and
    Notely Dam, 204; and Pickwick Dam,
    202, 204; and Watts Bar Dam, 204;
    and Wheeler Dam, 202; and Wilson
    Dam, 199–201
Thompson, Jess, 134, 139, 145
Toledo, Ohio, 152

Toombs, Dr. Percy, 167
Topeka, Ks., 91
Treece, Ks. 109
Trudeau School of Tuberculosis, 151, 153,
    174
Tuberculosis, Military, 162
Tularemia, 162–163, 166
Tupelo Miss. Tornado of 1936, 205–206

Underwood, Dr. Felix, 194
University of Tennessee, see Knoxville,
    Tenn.
University of Tennessee College of Medi-
    cine at Memphis, 93, 99, 116, 139–
    140, 164, 215

Vanderbilt Medical School, 140
Vicksburg, Miss. 177, 178

Wahpeton Inn, 128
Walker, Dr. Emmett, 177
Warfield Simpson, Wallace, 212
Warr, Dr. O. S., 163, 173, 208
Watson, Dr. R. B. (Bob), 200, 203, 211
Webb City, Mo. 95
Wellington, Kansas, 41, 52, 53, 99, 110,
    189 and Sumner County High School,
    46, 49, 110; and Wellington Daily News
Whitesburg, Tenn., 39
Whitehead, Bill, 93, 104
White Top Mountain, Va., 84–85
Wichita Eagle, The
Williamsburg, Va., 214
Wilton, Alabama, 176
Wittenborg, Dr. A. H., 103–104, 108
Wytheville, Va., 73, 75, 87, 99–100, 135

Yeager, Bruce, 14